# Ayodhya Ram Temple and Hindu Renaissance

# Ayodhya Ram Temple
# and
# Hindu Renaissance

**Dr. Kapil Khanna**

Corporate Office:
**EMPTY CANVAS PUBLISHERS** TM
4435-36/7, 1st Floor
Ansari Road, Daryaganj
New Delhi-110002
Email: emptycanvaspublishers@gmail.com

Registered Office:
**EMPTY CANVAS PUBLISHERS** TM
AP-119C, Pitam Pura
New Delhi-110034 (India)
www.emptycanvaspublishers.com

Edition : 2022

ISBN: 978-81-949219-7-4

# Ayodhya Ram Temple and Hindu Renaissance

Author: Dr. Kapil Khanna

Author takes full ownership of the literal content of the book and is solely responsible for ensuring that his work doesn't hurt religious and political sentiments of people.

Published by:
EMPTY CANVAS PUBLISHERS TM
New Delhi-110034 (India)



Processed And Printed in India

# Preface

On August 5, 2020, as Prime Minister Narendra Modi will lay the first foundation brick for the Ram temple in Ayodhya, India will look forward to a fresh start. A new beginning beyond the protracted, communally charged Ram Janmabhoomi-Babri Masjid dispute. An issue which had somewhat constricted the country's socio-political discourse for about four decades. However, away from politics, the legal battle over the piece of land in Ayodhya where the Babri Masjid once stood, will surely go down in history as one of the longest ones of our country.

A five-judge bench of the Supreme Court in India has unanimously held that the possession of the most-contested piece of land in Indian political history—the 2.77 acres where the Babri Masjid Mosque once stood—should in fact be exclusively given to the Hindu claimants of the case. At the same time, the Court invoked its special power to do 'complete justice' under Article 142 to restitute the damage caused by 'egregiously illegal' idol installation (1949) and Masjid demolition (1992). Hence, it ordered the government to allot an alternate plot of 5 acres to the Sunni Muslim Waqf Board at a 'prominent place' in Ayodhya for the construction of a new mosque.

The Ram Mandir will be etched in the sands of time as a symbol of Hindu awakening and restoration of pride of a community that has always believed in 'live and let live'.

The nineteenth century witnessed a remarkable and largely unexpected renaissance in Hindu thought, Yoga, Veda and Vedanta that brought back to life and placed in the modern context, the world's oldest spiritual heritage. An ancient religion that seemed on the verge of extinction was suddenly awake and able to express and assert itself on the stage of the modern world, providing a new view of humanity, culture and religion that could enrich all cultures and countries.

The Hindu renaissance naturally became strongly aligned with the Indian independence movement as India was a Hindu majority country. However, the Indian independence movement proved over time to be both a boon and a curse to the Hindu renaissance, expanding it in some areas but contracting it in others.

Hindu Dharma has already undergone a remarkable renaissance in the modern age. Less than two hundred years ago Hinduism seemed to be on the verge of complete collapse. It was caught in inertia and under siege by the missionary and colonial forces that had been ruling India for centuries. Yet at that extremity it didn't collapse but renewed itself, going back to its ancient roots to provide for new and expansive growths.

This is a reference book. All the matter is just compiled and edited in nature, taken from the various sources which are in public domain.

The book is a must-read for leaders of public opinion, parliamentarians, jurists, media stalwarts, professionals, administrators, and the young generation. For, what is at stake is India's future.

—*Editor*

# Contents

CHAPTER 1

# Ram Mandir

The Ram Mandir will be etched in the sands of time as a symbol of Hindu awakening and restoration of pride of a community that has always believed in 'live and let live'.

Societal collapse, also known as the civilizational collapse is the fall of a complex human society. Possible causes of a societal collapse include natural catastrophe, war, pestilence, and depopulation. A collapsed society may revert to a more primitive state, be absorbed into a stronger society, or completely disappear. Disintegration may be relatively abrupt, like the Maya civilization, or gradual, as in the case of the fall of the Western Roman Empire. Examples of such societal collapses are— the Anatolian Hittite Empire, the Mycenaean civilization, the Manchus of Manchuria, the Mesoamerican Mayas, the Angkors in Cambodia, the Han and Tang dynasties in China, the Mughal empire, infamously called the "gunpowder empire, the Mali empire and of course, the Phoenician empire which centuries back ruled the Mediterranean, from Cyprus to the Iberian peninsula, before disintegrating into oblivion.

In one of his speeches, Sadguru Jaggi Vasudev said, "In the past we were divided into at least 200 different states; we had 200 political entities; yet we were recognised as one nation. We eat differently; we dress differently; we speak different languages, yet we remain one. What holds us as one nation is the spiritual thread." Well, truer words could not have been said. Clearly, it was the spiritual strength that kept India intact as a nation, and Hindus as a living civilisation.

The ancient Greek, Roman and Egyptian civilisations are long dead. You find them on the pages of history books. Not so with the Indian, the Hindu civilisation, which has not only survived but is thriving. What can the Hindu civilisation contribute to the world we are living in and, more importantly, to the world-thought? Sadhguru explained, "Non-imposition of any belief system, and to encourage 'seeking.' It does not matter what the scriptures say. It does not matter what the leaders say. Each person, every individual must seek."

Yes, Hindu Thought, Hindu Mind, Hindu Philosophy does not depend upon any dogma or doctrine. Religious rituals are acknowledged and appreciated, but the "Hindu Mind" also recognises that spirituality is not built upon the platform of such rituals. There is not a single ritual that is enforced upon all Hindus. None. There is no uniformity. This freedom of thought, freedom to express one's thoughts and beliefs, and to act according to one's belief, is the survival-secret of the Hindu civilisation, as also its contribution to the world, according to noted spiritual activist, Anand Krishna.

The significance of the Ramayan and Shri Ram, in sustaining and strengthening the Hindu faith, in the face of innumerable onslaughts is, therefore, something that can never be undermined, as it is the binding glue that has shrugged off every form of religious expansionism by supposedly liberal, western forces. The spiritual fervour with which Hindus worship Shri Ram and imbibe his ethos is evident in many respects, especially so with regard to Prabhu Ram's adherence to dharma, said the renowned Kidambi Narayanan, in a discourse. Lord Ram, the prince who later became the king of Ayodhya, after a 14-year long exile in the Dandaka forest, promised his father Dasarath, that he would go to the forest and not stake his claim to the throne. Despite his sibling Bharat's insistence, Shri Ram explained to Bharat that the dharma sastras said that only a father had the right to decide what to do with his property.

That being the case, how could Ram interfere in Dasarath's right to decide who should be the next king of Ayodhya? Moreover, Dasarath was the king, and how could a king's order be disobeyed? Dasarath had also instructed and taught his children and in this sense, he had been an Acharya to them.

And one could not disobey one's Acharya. The reason for Dasarath's decisions may have been motivated by his wife, Kaikeyi, but Ram would still do as instructed by his king and his father, said Shri Ram to Bharat.

Obeying one's parent was far superior to performing yagyas, explained Prabhu Ram, to Bharat. Shri Ram's words on dharma, the need for obedience to one's parents, the need for following the law of the land and the importance of adherence to the Acharya's orders, are all reflected beautifully by Bhagwan Ram in his advice to Bharat, on what constitutes dharma, when Bharat tries to dissuade Ram from leaving Ayodhya, to serve his 14-year-long "Vanwaas".

But here was Dasarath, who not only snatched away Ram's right to govern the land but also banished him to the forest. And yet Shri Ram never violated dharmic principles. He not only preached dharma but also adhered to it. The values that Prabhu Ram espoused—gentleness, righteousness, selflessness, dutifulness, commitment to a larger cause, courage, valour, nobility and above all, the desire and ability to follow the path of dharma in the face of tremendous personal hardships, are symbolic of everything that Sanatan dharma stands for. Every year, the Ramlila culminates into Deepavali, a day that marks the return of Shri Ram to Ayodhya after his exile— his just rule was unparalleled and is still remembered as an epitome of what exemplary public service is all about.

The Ram Janmabhoomi, is, therefore, symbolic of the civilisational struggle faced by scores of Hindus, for almost 500 years. The tireless efforts and sacrifice of millions of Kar Sevaks including those who lost their lives at the stampede at Sarayu bridge, the tragic death of the brave Kothari brothers, the 16 Kar Sevaks who were gunned down on the orders of Samajwadi Party's Mulayam Singh Yadav, a fearless Kalyan Singh who supported the Kar Sevaks and refused to be intimidated by political pressure, the iconic "Rath Yatra" of L.K.Advani and "Ekta Yatra" of Murli Manohar Joshi, the selfless toil and grit of Vishwa Hindu Parishad (VHP's) Ashok Singhal who is no more, the feisty Uma Bharti, the admirable resoluteness of nonagenarian lawyer, K.Parasaran and Digvijay Nath of Goraknath Mutt, the indefatigable commitment and undying passion of the Rashtriya Swayamsevak Sangh (RSS), the vision of Balasaheb Deoras, the rock solid determination of RSS Sarsangchalak, Mohan Madhukar Bhagwat, the dedication of Uttar Pradesh Chief Minister, Yogi Adityanath, the devotion of Nrityagopaldas Maharaj and Champat Rai of the Ram Janma Bhoomi Tirtha Kshetra Trust and ofcourse, the boundless energy, pride and unflinching faith of millions of Hindus and BJP karyakartas, became part of a socio-cultural renaissance on August 5, 2020.And yes, no one should ever forget that it is Karmayogi, Prime Minister, Narendra Modi, under whose astute leadership, the BJP finally kept its tryst with Shri Ram Lalla, by restoring Hindu pride.

Modi is unapologetic, assertive without going overboard, proud of his Hindu roots and yet endearingly and effortlessly secular. It comes naturally to him because Hinduism is the only secular religion in the world.

Unfortunately, the word secularism became a much-abused one over the last many years, thanks to the rabid brand of pseudo-secularism practised by Congress leaders in the last few decades, with an intent to divide vote banks on religious grounds. Right from Nehru, to Indira Gandhi to Sonia and now, Rahul Gandhi, the Congress has always dismissed Hinduism, as a subaltern. Indira Gandhi buried the excavation reports of archaeologist, B.B.Lal, who found proof of temple remains under the Babri Masjid and stopped the excavation work mid-way. Later, K.K.Muhammed, former Regional Director, North, Archaeological Survey of India (ASI), too found remains of a temple, under the masjid structure.

Sanatana-dharma is the oldest religion in the world. Many historians claim it is pre-historic and absolute in nature. While the term Hindu or Hindu dharma is a term given by Persians only a few centuries ago, to mean the people living beside the river Sindhu, Hinduism is in effect, nothing but another name for Sanatan dharma. Unlike other religions, Hinduism has no one founder but is instead a fusion of various beliefs. Around 1500 B.C., the Indo-Aryan people migrated to the Indus Valley, and their language and culture blended with that of the indigenous people living in the region.

After the influence of European, especially British, due to the colonization of Indus Valley civilization, Hindu religion came to be called Hinduism. But the actual name of the religion is Sanatana Dharma, where Sanatana means eternal and Dharma means duty. Sanatana Dharma means eternal duty.

The Babri mosque, built after ravaging and destroying a temple that existed there, marking Bhagwan Ram's birthplace, therefore became a rallying point for Hindus and rightfully so. Those who allege that celebration of the construction of the "Ram Mandir" at Ram Janmabhoomi in Ayodhya by Hindus, is only a means of giving voice to Hindu fanaticism, have got it completely wrong. There is no such thing as Hindu fanatics or Hindu radicals. Radicalised Islam, according to many, is a reality, as its very core is reported, based on the flawed concept of superiority of Allah over all other gods. Radical Islam in many ways says historians, thinkers theologists and philosophers, is both territorial and expansionist in nature. It believes in dogmatic singularity, whereas Hinduism is based on pluralism and oneness, with the magical ability to absorb diversity in myriad forms, without losing its uniqueness.

Going back in history, Babur, was the founder of the Mughal Empire and first Emperor of the Mughal dynasty in the Indian subcontinent. He was a descendant of bloodthirsty warlords and plunderers like Timur and Genghis Khan, through his father and mother respectively. The date of construction of the Babri Masjid is uncertain. The inscriptions on the Babri Masjid premises found in the 20th-century state that the mosque was built in 935 AH (1528–29) by Mir Baqi, in accordance with the wishes of Babur. Posterity and millions of Hindus worldwide will never ever forget, how an almost 500-year-old wrong was finally rectified on August 5, 2020, by the Modi government, by giving back to Shri Ram, what always belonged to him—his birthplace.

The powerful interplay of religion and politics is not new. Be it Lokmanya Tilak, who started the Ganapati festival as a rallying force against British rule, M.K. Gandhi, who used religious symbolism during the freedom struggle, Swami Karpatri Maharaj of the Ram Rajya Parishad in independent India, rehabilitation of Syrian Christians by Hindu kings in Kerala, religion and politics have fed off each other. While the State and religion are separate and rightfully so, in reality, it is difficult to alienate the two. Even at a global level, political Islam and rule of the Sharia, drive policy-making of many Islamic nations, like say Turkey, for instance.

Those who accuse the BJP and the Modi government of political Hindutva, are the very hypocrites and turncoats, who have no hesitation in endorsing the politics of the Vatican, which in the contemporary world, plays an important if an ambivalent role in international affairs. On February 25, 1971, in Moscow, Archbishop Agostino Casaroli, head of the Vatican's Bureau of Public Affairs, affixed the signatures of papal representatives to the ratification of the international treaty, limiting the proliferation of nuclear weapons. The participation of papal representatives in this international agreement raises a number of queries in the political order, not the least of which is the fundamental problem regarding the nature of the papacy as sovereignty. No other religious institution in the modern world functions as body of the church and also as a political organization that exchanges diplomatic representatives and yet, claims total recognition as an independent member of the community of nations!

The French Revolution of 1789-90 was not merely an uprising against the monarchy of Louis XVI, driven by agrarian distress. It was primarily a mass protest that began with attacks on Church corruption and the wealth of the higher clergy, an action which even many devout Christians could identify with. Even today, the anti-clericalism and de-Christianisation of large sections of the French population during the revolution is a grim reminder of how the Gallican or Catholic Church of that era, held a dominant role in pre-revolutionary French politics.

Political Hindutva, in comparison, follows the BJP's template of "justice for all and appeasement of none".The BJP's brand of Hinduism has ample restraint, is not hesitant to discard outdated practices and is progressive. It is not shy to take pride in India's Vedia rituals, the knowledge of the Upanishads or the immortal teachings of the Bhagwad Gita and the Manusmriti, with revisions in rituals &customs, in sync with changing times and the changing socio-legal framework of contemporary society.

Political Hinduism of the BJP is neither coercive nor intimidating. It is not majoritarian—equally, it is not afraid to call the bluff of pseudo seculars, who, over the decades, have disparaged all things Hindu under the garb of regressive appeasement which they tried passing off, as secularism. Those who mock at Pavanputra Hanuman, as a "monkey god", or say Prabhu Ram was only a mythological figure, is that very lot which never ever questioned supernatural miracles "performed" by Mother Teresa when she was alive.

For Christians, "Easter", marks the resurrection of Jesus from the tomb. "Ascension", which is celebrated forty days after Easter, commemorating the ascension of Christ to heaven, has no historical record but is a matter of faith. However, Hindus have never disrespected the faith, superstitions or rituals of other religions. Hinduism, a polytheistic religion (unlike Islam), with over three hundred and thirty million gods and goddesses, has survived, thrived and flourished, despite repression and oppression, because of its inherently invincible features. Bhagwan Ram, the 7th avatar of Lord Vishnu is its main deity and stands for "Aastha, Ahimsa and Balidaan", as told by Prime Minister Narendra Modi, in his outstanding address at the Ram Janmabhoomi, while laying the foundation for the construction of a "Bhavya Ram Mandir", on August 5, 2020. The universal appeal of Maryada Purushottam, Shri Ram, is evident from manifold sources. Dasaratha Jataka is the earliest known version of what later came to be known as the Ramayan.

Some glimpses are also found in Michael Madhusudan Dutta's Meghnad Badh Kavya – written in 1861 and based on an episode of Valmiki's Ramayan. The famous retelling of Valmiki's Ramayan in Bengali is called Krittivasi Ramayan (Shri Ram Panchali) by Krittibas Ojha (15th century). A 6th century manuscript of the Ramayan has also been found at the Asiatic Society Library in Kolkata. There are many versions of Ramayan in many Indian languages, including Kamba Ramayan (12th century) by the Tamils. Many Indian religious traditions – Buddhist, Sikh and Jain – have their own adaptations. There are also Cambodian, Indonesian, Thai, Lao, Burmese, Filipino and Malaysian versions of this epic.

Valmiki's Ramayan – located between 5th BCE and 1 BCE by scholars – consisting of 24000 Sanskrit shlokas or verses, may not be the first text to introduce Rama. But it is considered as the "original" Ramayan – one of two great epics of Indian literature, and also of world literature. The other great epic – arguably the greatest, is Vyasa's Mahabharata: longer than Homer's Iliad, the Odyssey and Virgil's Aeneid all put together, says the erudite Devdan Chaudhuri, in a painstakingly detailed essay on Lord Ram and the Ramayan.

Moving away from the Ramayan, what Sadguru Jaggi says, best explains the eternal and formidable nature of Hinduism. He says, "The invaders were not successful, as there has been no one single Hindu church". According to him, the end of all spiritual experiences was 'liberation' – moksha. Moksha, or liberation, can also mean "freedom to think, freedom to express, freedom to act, while respecting others' freedom to do the same." Yes, moksha is not an afterlife experience alone. Moksha must be and can be, attained while living in this world, amidst the maddening crowd, and in the marketplace. Moksha is living free while at the same time respecting, honouring others' freedom. Moksha is not freedom from life. Death is not moksha. Death does not guarantee moksha. Moksha is living freely, as free women and free men. It is this spirit, the spirit to "strive for liberation" in Sadhguru Jaggi Vasudev's words, that has kept India intact as a nation, "in spite of numerous attacks by the external forces, and the invaders. For more than thousands of years they tried. Elsewhere they succeeded, but not here in India." Well, history supports the guru.

Coming back to the politics of Hinduism and Hindutva, no devout Hindu should ever forget how the Congress marginalised the Hindu movement, for decades together, with brazen impunity. On December 22, 1949, Uttar Pradesh Chief Minister Govind Vallabh Pant, at the behest of the then Prime Minister Jawaharlal Nehru, ordered to expel the Hindus from the temple of Ram Lalla.

But Faizabad District Collector K.K Nair refused to implement the order, pointing out that the real stakeholders were performing Pooja there and the move would lead to riots and bloodshed. Nair was soon thereafter suspended from service.

Like her father Nehru, Indira Gandhi also scuttled the rights of Hindus by inserting the word "Secular", via the 42nd Amendment to the Indian Constitution in 1976.For many years post that amendment, Hindus in India were pushed around and discriminated against, in their own country, under the garb of secularism. Who can forget or forgive the Congress party for calling Prabhu Ram a fictional character in the affidavit submitted in the Supreme Court in the Ram Setu case in 2007?

Those like AIMIM chief Asaduddin Owaisi, who accuse the BJP's Ram Janmabhoomi movement as an assertion of Hindu majoritarianism and Hindu colonisation, would do well to know that despite a brute majority, Prime Minister Narendra Modi chose to follow the path of dharma, by choosing to leave the verdict on Ram Mandir, to India's apex court. His faith in the law of the land eventually held millions of Hindus in good stead. The political Hinduism of BJP is progressive, modern, humane and secular, with respect for the richness of diversity that India represents. Equally, the BJP has never shied away from its religious and cultural roots and rightfully so. Why should the Hindus in a country of 1.37 billion people feel apologetic about legitimately celebrating who they are? Well, the proud Hindus in Modi's India no longer do. Clearly, the Ram Mandir will be etched in the sands of time as a symbol of Hindu awakening and restoration of pride of a community, that has always believed in "Live and let live".

Timeline of Ram Mandir, at the Ram Janmabhoomi in Ayodhya—

1528: Babri Masjid built by Mir Baqi, commander of Mughal emperor Babur.

1885: Mahant Raghubir Das files plea in Faizabad district court seeking permission to build a canopy outside the disputed Ram Janmabhoomi-Babri Masjid structure. Court rejects plea.

1949: Idols of Ram Lalla placed under a central dome outside the disputed structure.

1950: Gopal Simla Visharad files suit in Faizabad district court for rights to worship the idols of Ram Lalla.

1950: Paramahansa Ramachandra Das files suit for continuation of worship and keeping the idols.

1959: Nirmohi Akhara files suit seeking possession of the site.

1981: UP Sunni Central Waqf Board files suit for possession of the site.

Feb 1, 1986: Local court orders the government to open the site for Hindu worshippers.

Aug 14, 1989: Allahabad HC ordered maintenance of status quo in respect of the disputed structure.

Dec 6, 1992: Ram Janmabhoomi-Babri Masjid structure demolished.

Apr 3, 1993: 'Acquisition of Certain Area at Ayodhya Act' passed for acquisition of land by Centre in the disputed area.1993: Various writ petitions, including one by Ismail Faruqui, filed at Allahabad HC challenging various aspects of the Act. - Supreme Court exercising its jurisdiction under Article

139A transferred the writ petitions, which were pending in the High Court.

Oct 24, 1994: SC says in the historic Ismail Faruqui case that a mosque was not integral to Islam.

Apr, 2002: HC begins hearing on determining who owns the disputed site.

Mar 13, 2003: SC says, in the Aslam alias Bhure case, no religious activity of any nature be allowed at the acquired land.

Mar 14: SC says interim order passed should be operative till disposal of the civil suits in Allahabad HC to maintain communal harmony.

Sep 30, 2010: HC, in a 2:1 majority, rules three-way division of disputed area between Sunni Waqf Board, the Nirmohi Akhara and Ram Lalla.

May 9, 2011: SC stays HC verdict on Ayodhya land dispute.

Feb 26, 2016: Subramanian Swamy files plea in SC seeking construction of Ram Temple at the disputed site.

Mar 21, 2017: CJI J.S Khehar suggests out-of-court settlement among rival parties.

Aug 7: SC constitutes three-judge bench to hear pleas challenging the 1994 verdict of the Allahabad HC.

Aug 8: UP Shia Central Waqf Board tells SC mosque could be built in a Muslim-dominated area at a reasonable distance from the disputed site.

Sep 11: SC directs Chief Justice of the Allahabad HC to nominate two additional district judges within ten days as observers to deal with the upkeep of the disputed site.

Nov 20: UP Shia Central Waqf Board tells SC temple can be built in Ayodhya and mosque in Lucknow.

Dec 1: Thirty-two civil rights activists file plea challenging the 2010 verdict of the Allahabad HC. - Feb 8, 2018: SC starts hearing civil appeals.

Mar 14: SC rejects all interim pleas, including Swamy's, seeking to intervene as parties in the case.

Apr 6: Rajeev Dhavan files plea in SC to refer the issue of reconsideration of the observations in its 1994 judgement to a larger bench.

Jul 6: UP government tells SC some Muslim groups were trying to delay the hearing by seeking reconsideration of an observation in the 1994 verdict.

Jul 20: SC reserves verdict.

Sep 27: SC declines to refer the case to a five-judge Constitution bench. Case to be heard by a newly constituted three-judge bench on October 29.

Oct 29: SC fixes the case for the first week of January next year before an appropriate bench, which will decide the schedule of hearing.

Nov 12: SC declines early hearing of petitions in the case requested by Akhil Bharat Hindu Mahasabha.

Nov 22: SC dismisses PIL seeking direction to organisations and public at large to "behave" and not air their views that can spoil the atmosphere till it decides the Ram Janmabhoomi-Babri Masjid title dispute case.

Dec 24: SC to take up petitions on the Ram Janmabhoomi-Babri Masjid title dispute case for hearing on January 4.

Jan 4: SC says an appropriate bench constituted by it will pass an order on January 10 for fixing the date of hearing in the title case.

Jan 8: SC sets up a five-judge Constitution Bench to hear the case headed by Chief Justice Ranjan Gogoi and comprising Justices S A Bobde, N V Ramana, U U Lalit and D Y Chandrachud.

Jan 10: SC reschedules the hearing for January 29 before a new bench after Justice U U recused himself.

March 2019: The Supreme Court appoints a mediation panel headed by Judge (retd) FMI Kallifulla for an out-of-court settlement on March 8.

August 2019: The mediation panel fails to reach an amicable settlement. The Supreme Court begins hearing on August 6.

Oct 2019: After hearing the case on a day-to-day basis for 40 days, the court reserves its order on October 15.

October 16: After a marathon 40-day daily hearing, the SC concludes hearing in the case. It says that a verdict will be delivered by CJI Gogoi before his retirement on November 17, 2019.

November 8: The Supreme Court lists Ayodhya title suit judgment for November 9.

November 9, 2019: In a unanimous verdict, the Supreme Court Bench led by Chief Justice Ranjan Gogoi, orders that the disputed land in Ayodhya should be given to Ram Janmabhoomi Nyas for construction of a temple, and the Muslim side should be compensated with five acres of land at a prominent place in Ayodhya for a mosque. The court also orders the central government to formulate a scheme within three months to implement the order

December 12: The Supreme Court dismisses review petitions challenging the November 9 verdict in the Ayodhya title dispute. "Applications for listing of review petitions in open Court are dismissed. We have carefully gone through the review petitions and the connected papers filed therewith. We do not find any ground, whatsoever, to entertain the same. The review petitions are, accordingly, dismissed, " says the five-judge bench headed by Chief Justice S.A. Bobde.

August 3, 2020: As the countdown for the grand ceremony of 'Bhoomi Pujan' for the construction of the Ram temple began, Ayodhya District Magistrate, Anuj Kumar Jha hands over the five-acre land to the Sunni Waqf Board at Dhannipur village in Faizabad, as mandated by the Supreme Court in lieu of the Babri mosque.

August 4: The 'Ramarcha' puja begins in Ayodhya, a day ahead of the 'bhumi puja'. The entire Ram Janmabhoomi area is decorated with saffron marigolds. All invitees to the August

5 foundation stone-laying function for the new Ram temple in Ayodhya in Uttar Pradesh will have to carry a mandatory coronavirus-negative certificate. Every guest who is invited for the 'bhumi pujan' ceremony, will be gifted a silver coin as 'prasad'.According to sources, over 1.25 lakh laddoos, called 'Raghupati laddoos' will be distributed to guests, residents of Ayodhya and others on August 5.A total of 175 people have been invited to the Sri Ram Temple Trust for bhumi pujan, including about 135 saints who will come from different parts of the country. There is a code on every invitation card, which is designed for security.

August 5, 2020: Beginning his speech with the slogan of "Jai Siya Ram, " Prime Minister Narendra Modi, undoubtedly, post-independent India's most powerful and popular leader ever, calls the "sthapna" or foundation-stone laying event of the Ram Mandir, a historic occasion. "I am grateful to witness history being made. Crores of Indians cannot believe that this day has come. The entire country is in the spell of Lord Ram, " Modi says, after he lays down a 40 kg silver brick, to mark the foundation ceremony of Ram Temple in Ayodhya, heralding a new dawn in the Hindu regeneration, that has truly come of age.

## RAM RAJYA RATH YATRA: RETURNING TO RAM FOR 2019

When Parliament was debating issues like farmers' distress and growing unemployment, a RSS-affiliated outfit was busy organizing a 60,000 km-long road trip to revive the Ram Janmabhoomi issue. Unlike its previous version in which the chariot had Ayodhya as its destination, this time the journey was to start from Ayodhya in Uttar Pradesh to reach Rameshwaram in Kanyakumari, the southernmost point in mainland India.

The yatra, named Ram Rajya Rath Yatra, was flagged off on February 14 and has already crossed the most important pilgrimage centres of UP including Varanasi and Allahabad.

The journey will last 41 days and cover six states including Karnataka, that would face keenly contested polls in April-May. Other states which are to be covered include Madhya Pradesh, Maharashtra, Kerala and Tamil Nadu.

Most political observers were under the impression that the issue of the Ram Temple had outlived its political utility. Many were inclined to believe that the BJP-RSS combine will not use the issue again as it might not yield any significant dividends.

However, proving them wrong, the combine had started raising the issue the moment it came to power. It has been attempting to combine other issues such as gau-raksha or cow protection, love jihad and triple talaq to the core issue of construction of Ram temple at the disputed site of the demolished Babri mosque. The target, obviously, was the minority Muslim community.

The current yatra has also enlarged its canvas, demanding that the Ramayana be included in school syllabus across the country, that Thursday be declared a weekly holiday and also declaration of a World Hindu Day. So, the RSS has this time expanded the temple agenda to include other Hindutva-centric agendas. The destination of Rameshwaram has been chosen to stress the demand of recognition of the Ram Setu.

Though other long-term agendas have been added to it, the core agenda still remains the same. The yatra is being conducted at a time when the Supreme Court is preparing for a final hearing of the contentious Ram Janmabhoomi case from March 14. When all the political parties and religious organizations have said that they would accept the court verdict, what is the need of organizing a yatra on the issue?

The court is yet to give a verdict and the organizer — the Vishwa Hindu Parishad — is asserting that a grand Ram temple will be erected at Ayodhya before Ram Navami next year. The rath or chariot has been modelled as per the design of the proposed temple. The yatra also began from

Karsevakpuram, the venue where the artefacts of the proposed temple are being created. The place was established during the Ram Mandir agitation of 1990 under the leadership of veteran BJP leader LK Advani.

We can see how pressure is being built upon the judiciary. Spiritual Guru Shri Shri Ravishankar has initiated a dialogue between Hindus and Muslims with some chosen religious leaders. The dialogue is aimed at finding an out-of-court settlement.

Noted legal expert and vice-chancellor of National Law University Faizan Mustafa has rightly pointed out that such an effort is unconstitutional and it undermines the constitution. He has also pointed that Ravishankar has been found guilty of violating environment laws by the National Green Tribunal and evading depositing the penalty he has been asked for. The fresh build up around the Ram temple issue is obviously being made keeping in view the 2019 General Election.

We have seen how during the Gujarat assembly polls this issue was also invoked. The RSS is determined to go ahead with the agenda of building a Ram temple at Ayodhya.

But unlike its response in the past, the Muslim community is taking it with some indifference. "They have withdrawn themselves. This has happened after demolition of the Babri mosque," says eminent journalist Kuldip Nayar. He says that the event has left a dark spot on the secular credentials of the country. He blames the Congress government led by PV Narsimha Rao for the demolition, saying that had Rao not turned a blind eye the mosque would not have been demolished.

Will RSS allow the creation of a Ram temple to pass as an event without turmoil? This is unlikely because the whole purpose will be defeated if some violent incident doesn't take place. RSS-affiliated outfits will try their best to polarize people on religious grounds. In any case, this has to be done at the time of polls to make gains in terms of votes. So, the mobilization has been done well in advance. Whether they are able to polarize the people will only be seen at the time the yatra enters Karnataka and Kerala. Karnataka is ready for polls and the atmosphere is already charged. Kerala has already been witnessing violent clashes between RSS and CPM workers.

Expressing fear of violence, the CPI(M) said in a statement: "Politburo of CPI(M) expresses its deep concern at the grave implications of the 'Ram Rajya Rath Yatra' flagged off at Ayodhya in Uttar Pradesh. This rally was flagged off by the RSS-affiliated VHP General Secretary in the presence of Faizabad BJP MP, Ayodhya's BJP Mayor and other BJP leaders".

The party has rightly expressed its concern over the fact that the route of the yatra proceeds through BJP-ruled states of Madhya Pradesh and Maharashtra, spending nearly a fortnight in Karnataka where Assembly elections are due, then proceeding via Kerala to reach Rameswaram in Tamil Nadu.

"This yatra has an incendiary potential to sharpen communal polarization in order to strengthen the communal Hindutva vote bank for the RSS-BJP. There are grave implications of possibilities for stoking communal tensions, violence and mayhem," the party has said.

The cleverly planned yatra has avoided to rope in big leaders. No big BJP stalwart has so far attended the yatra. UP Chief Minister Yogi Adityanath was supposed to flag off the yatra, but he didn't turn up.

Only a few months back, he had chosen Ayodhya to launch the campaign for the state's local polls. This distance is possibly being maintained to make it appear as a non-political initiative. Maybe, the organizers are trying to make the ruling BJP governments at the Centre and the states free from the blame of abetting communal tension.

Changing the slogan of Ram temple to Ram Rajya has its own meaning. This seems to be a claver manipulation on the part of RSS and the BJP.

The Hindutva forces have long been trying to legitimize their ideology. They have been trying to appropriate the legacy of the freedom struggle and leaders like Sardar Patel are being portrayed as supporters of Hindutva. They are now trying to appropriate Gandhi's slogan of Ram Rajya. This may be an attempt to get rid of the Hindu Rashtra slogan which is clearly communal.

The word 'Ram Rajya' was used by Mahatma Gandhi to symbolize an ideal rule. By adopting it, the RSS is trying to bring some respectability to concept of Hindu Rashtra. Whatever may be the political outcome of this yatra, it is clear that it will further marginalize the minority community. The attempt is not limited to the agenda of building a Ram temple at Ayodhya, it is aimed at establishing Hindu symbols in the country's public life. This will undermine the constitution.

## PM MODI ENDS 29-YEAR AYODHYA 'EXILE' WITH BHOOMI PUJAN

Prime Minister Narendra Modi says Lord Ram belongs to all, centuries' long wait is finally over, and the temple will be 'an instrument to unite the country'.

Prime Minister Narendra Modi returned to Ayodhya on Wednesday after 29 years to fulfil his promise and perform the "bhoomi pujan" of the proposed Ram Mandir. Clad in a golden dhoti-kurta, PM Modi addressed the gathering after the foundation stone-laying ceremony of the grand temple, saying it would be the modern symbol of our traditions and "an instrument to unite the country".

"A grand temple will now be built for our Ramlala who had been staying in a tent. Today Ram Janmabhoomi breaks free of the cycle of breaking and getting built again, that had been going on for centuries," said PM Modi as he shared the dais with RSS chief Mohan Bhagwat, Ram Janmabhoomi Trust chairperson Mahant Nritya Gopal Das Maharaj, Uttar Pradesh Governor Anandiben Patel and Chief Minister Yogi Adityanath.

As chants of "Jai Siya Ram and "Bharat Mata ki Jai" reverberated in the air, PM Modi added, "It'll become a symbol of our devotion, our national sentiment. This temple will also symbolise the power of collective resolution of crores of people. It will keep inspiring the future generations... Despite efforts to eradicate existence of Lord Ram, he still lives in our heart and is basis of our culture. Ram is everywhere, Ram belongs to all."

The ceremony, which was held 10 months after the historic verdict of the Supreme Court, was certainly curtailed due to the ongoing Covid-19 pandemic, but it marked the pinnacle of the BJP's decades-long movement that brought it to the political centre-stage. 5 August also marks one-year anniversary of the abrogation of Article 370 which was the other ideological core to the BJP.

CM Yogi Adityanath, at the event, said it was PM Modi's "foresight and wisdom" that paved the way for peaceful resolution of the Ram Mandir issue.

"Our country believes in 'Vasudev Kutubhkam' i.e. World is One Family. We believe in taking everyone along. Today is a new beginning of a new India," said RSS Chief Mohan Bhagwat, mentioning how the RSS and other like-minded organisations worked over 30 years to fulfil the dream.

PM Modi, along with CM Adityanath, first visited the Hanuman Garhi temple to offer prayers and was presented a silver "mukut" and a stole by the head priest. Then he went to the Ram Janmabhoomi and performed "sashtangpranam" to Ramlala and before taking part in further ceremonies, he also planted a Parijat sapling, which is considered a divine plant.

"The way Dalits, OBCs, tribals, every section of the society supported Gandhiji during the freedom struggle, this pious work of building Ram temple has started with the cooperation of people from all over the country... There is no aspect of life where our Ram does not inspire us. There is no such feeling of India in which Lord Ram is not seen. Ram is in the faith of India, Ram is in the ideals of India. Ram is in the divinity and philosophy of India," PM Modi added.

The soil for the "bhoomi pujan" was brought in from more than 1,500 places and holy water was collected from 2,000 places. Bricks engraved with "Jai Shri Ram" were also used in the puja which began with the head priest chanting Sanskrit "shlokas". For the "bhoomi pujan", a 40-kg brick made of pure silver was also used.

Ayodhya turned into a fortress on Wednesday as roads were lined with festoons and flags of every shade of saffron which also fluttered from rooftops. Road-facing houses were coated with bright yellow as hoardings welcomed the Prime Minister.

Mahraj Jairam, the deputy mahant of Shri Ram ashram, said: "It is a very emotional moment for us as our forefathers had fought for the mandir and now we will see it being built before our eyes. Lord Ram has come back to the city at his own home and it is a moment of great joy and pride for us."

## AYODHYA VERDICT: INDIAN TOP COURT GIVES DISPUTED SITE TO HINDUS

India's Supreme Court has awarded Hindus control of a disputed religious site in the town of Ayodhya for the construction of a temple, in a landmark verdict announced amid heightened security across the country. Muslims will be given five acres of land at an alternative site in Ayodhya, in northern Uttar Pradesh state, the top court ruled on Saturday.

***Hindu devotees celebrate after the Supreme Court's verdict***

## *Keep Reading*

Timeline: Babri mosque-Ram temple caseIndian town anxiously awaits landmark Babri mosque-temple verdictThe BJP's rise to political eminence lies in an old temple town

In a unanimous decision over the site claimed by both Hindus and Muslims, the five-judge bench asked the government to set up a trust that will construct a temple for Hindu deity Ram.

"The judgement is not satisfactory but we respect it. We will have discussions and then decide further course of action," Zafaryab Jilani, Sunni Waqf Board lawyer, was quoted as saying by NDTV news channel.

Faizan Mustafa, vice-chancellor of NALSAR University of Law, Hyderabad, termed the verdict "controversial".

"The judges tried their best to have a kind of a balance but ultimately it's the mystery of the faith over rule of law, because they [judges] said that we can't be doing anything about the Hindu belief and if they believe that Ram was born here ... we have to accept it," he said.

"Belief is good for the purposes of religion, but can it become a basis to resolve property disputes?"

Al Jazeera's Anchal Vohra, reporting from New Delhi, said a board of trustees [appointed by the government] would be formed in three months to essentially decide how to go about the construction of the temple.

She added the alternative site for Muslims would be decided by the central government or the state government.

"Muslim intellectuals had already offered this when the mediations took place early this year as a possible solution to have broader peace between the two communities," Vohra said.

Prime Minister Narendra Modi hailed the verdict, saying it had "amicably" ended the decades-old dispute.

"The halls of justice have amicably concluded a matter going on for decades. Every side, every point of view was given adequate time and opportunity to express differing points of view. This verdict will further increase people's faith in judicial processes," Modi tweeted.

Hardliners among India's majority Hindus, including supporters of Modi's Hindu-nationalist Bharatiya Janata Party (BJP), believe that Lord Ram, the warrior god, was born at the site where the Babri mosque existed. They say that the first Mughal emperor Babur built Babri Mosque on top of a temple at the site.

Muslims said they prayed at the mosque for generations until 1949, when Hindu activists placed idols of Ram.

The 460-year-old mosque was demolished in 1992 by Hindu mobs triggering nationwide religious violence that left about 2,000 people dead, most of them Muslims.

Muslim-majority Pakistan, India's rival neighbour, responded to the decision on Saturday.

"This decision has shredded the veneer of so-called secularism of India by making clear that minorities in India are no longer safe; they have to fear for their beliefs and for their places of worship," the foreign office in Islamabad said in a statement.

"The Indian government should ensure the protection of Muslims, their lives, rights and properties and avoid being yet again a silent spectator of Muslims becoming the victims of Hindu extremists and zealots.

"The international community, the United Nations and other human rights organisations in particular should play their role by restraining India from its pursuit of an extremist ideology."

## Hindus welcome verdict

The streets of Ayodhya wore a deserted look with very few businesses operating.

At some places, people were seen raising slogans of Jai Shree Ram (Hail Lord Ram) and congratulating each other.

Most Hindus celebrated the court's decision while Muslims hoped that Ayodhya would remain peaceful. In 1992, dozens of Ayodhya Muslims were killed in the wake of violence. "The Hindus of India have for so long wanted a temple at the place where Ram was born," Rajesh Kumar said.

Pappu Singh, of the neighbouring state of Bihar, said the verdict was a victory for the entire nation.

"I have been waiting for this moment for several years. Finally, the courts have heard my plea and this nothing less than a miracle.

"With this verdict, the court has given a new life to Ram. The court has ensured that both the parties got something.

Muslims in the Hindu holy town, however, expressed disappointment at the verdict.

"The court has not specified where it would give the land for the mosque. If the court would have specified it, Muslims would have been pleased," said Mohammed Shibu Khan from the Syed Bada area of Ayodhya.

"However, I am happy that this has come to an end as the people of Ayodhya are tired of frequent shutdowns throughout the year."

In the Muslim-majority area of Jamia Nagar in the capital New Delhi, people said they did not get justice.

"[That] the Hindu mob which demolished Babri Masjid went unpunished only proves India's incompetence as a democracy," Nabiya Khan, a student, told Al Jazeera.

"December 6, 1992 and November 9, 2019, will be remembered as days of death of secularism in India."

Mohammad Mussa, 58, of Zakir Nagar, said the mosque on the site belonged to Muslims.

"Whatever the judgement is, we should accept it because we live in an India run by the right-wing BJP which thinks this country belongs to Hindus only. Muslims should stay calm and not react to anything because there are forces who want bloodshed in the country."

## *Appeals for calm*

The Supreme Court on Saturday said a structure existed under the Babri Mosque, which was not built on vacant land.

A 2010 lower court ruling had divided the disputed 2.77 acres (1.12 hectares) into three equal parts, with two-thirds going to the Hindu community and one-third to Muslims. That order was challenged by both sides.

The five-judge bench, headed by the Chief Justice Ranjan Gogoi, opted to hand over the site to one of the Hindu groups that had staked a claim to it.

I have been waiting for this moment for several years. Finally, the courts have heard my plea and this nothing less than a miracle.

After Saturday's verdict, Modi called for calm and police went on alert, with thousands of extra personnel deployed and schools closed in and around Ayodhya, the centre of the bitter dispute, and elsewhere.

In some towns, internet services were also suspended to stop the spread of rumours.

Muslim organisations have appealed for calm to prevent communal flare-ups.

The BJP has campaigned for years for a temple to be built at Ayodhya, and a verdict clearing the way for that is a major victory for 69-year-old Modi, just months into his second term.

The verdict, it is hoped, will put an end to an angry and at times arcane legal wrangle that British colonial rulers and even the Dalai Lama tried to mediate.

# CHAPTER 2 Ram Janmabhoomi

Ram Janmabhoomi is the name given to the site that is hypothesized to be the birthplace of Rama, believed to be the seventh avatar of the Hindu deity Vishnu. The Ramayana states that the location of Rama's birthplace is on the banks of the Sarayu river in a city called "Ayodhya". A section of Hindus claim that the exact site of Rama's birthplace is where the Babri Masjid once stood in the present-day Ayodhya, Uttar Pradesh. According to this theory, the Mughals demolished a Hindu shrine that marked the spot, and constructed a mosque in its place. People opposed to this theory state that such claims arose only in the 18th century, and that there is no evidence for the spot being the birthplace of Rama.

The political, historical and socio-religious debate over the history and location of the Babri Mosque, and whether a previous temple was demolished or modified to create it, is known as the Ayodhya dispute. In 1992, the demolition of the Babri Masjid by Hindu nationalists triggered widespread Hindu-Muslim violence. Several other sites, including places in other parts of India, Afghanistan, and Nepal, have been proposed as birthplaces of Rama.

## Babri Masjid site

The *Ramayana*, a Hindu epic whose earliest portions date back to 1st millennium BCE, states that the capital of Rama was Ayodhya. According to the local Hindu belief, the site of the now-demolished Babri Mosque in Ayodhya is the exact birthplace of Rama. The Babri mosque is believed to have been constructed during 1528-29 by a certain 'Mir Baqi' (possibly Baqi Tashqandi), who was a commander of the Mughal emperor Babur (r. 1526–1530). However, the historical evidence for these beliefs is scant.

In 1611, an English traveller William Finch visited Ayodhya and recorded the "ruins of the Ranichand [Ramachand] castle and houses". He made no mention of a mosque. In 1634, Thomas Herbert described a "pretty old castle of Ranichand [Ramachand]" which he described as an antique monument that was "especially memorable".

However, by 1672, the appearance of a mosque at the site can be inferred because Lal Das's *Awadh-Vilasa* describes the location of birthplace without mentioning a temple or "castle". In 1717, the Moghul Rajput noble Jai Singh II purchased land surrounding the site and his documents show a mosque. The Jesuit missionary Joseph Tiefenthaler, who visited the site between 1766-1771, wrote that either Aurangazeb (r. 1658–1707) or Babur had demolished the Ramkot fortress, including the house that was considered as the birthplace of Rama by Hindus. He further stated that a mosque was constructed in its place, but the Hindus continued to offer prayers at a mud platform that marked the birthplace of Rama. In 1810, Francis Buchanan visited the site, and stated that the structure destroyed was a temple dedicated to Rama, not a house. Many subsequent sources state that the mosque was constructed after demolishing a temple.

Police officer and writer Kishore Kunal states that all the claimed inscriptions on the Babri mosque were fake. They were affixed sometime around 1813 (almost 285 years after the supposed construction of the mosque in 1528 AD), and repeatedly replaced.

Before the 1940s, the Babri Masjid was called *Masjid-i-Janmasthan* ("mosque of the birthplace"), including in the official documents such as revenue records. Shykh Muhammad Azamat Ali Kakorawi Nami (1811–1893) wrote: "the Babari mosque was built up in 923(?) A.H. under the patronage of Sayyid Musa Ashiqan in the Janmasthan temple in Faizabad-Avadh, which was a great place of (worship) and capital of Rama's father"

H.R. Neville, the editor of the *Faizabad District Gazetteer* (1870), wrote that the Janmasthan temple "was destroyed by Babur and replaced by a mosque." He also wrote "The Janmasthan was in Ramkot and marked the birthplace of Rama. In 1528 A.D. Babur came to Ayodhya and halted here for a week. He destroyed the ancient temple and on its site built a mosque, still known as Babur's mosque. The materials of the old structure [i.e., the temple] were largely employed, and many of the columns were in good preservation."

## Opposition to the claim

A section of historians, such as R. S. Sharma, state that such claims of Babri Masjid site being the birthplace of Rama sprang up only after the 18th century.

Sharma states that Ayodhya emerged as a place of Hindu pilgrimage only in medieval times, since ancient texts do not mention it as a pilgrim centre. For example, chapter 85 of the Vishnu Smriti lists 52 places of pilgrimage, which do not include Ayodhya. Sharma also notes that Tulsidas, who wrote the Ramcharitmanas in 1574 at Ayodhya, does not mention it as a place of pilgrimage.

Many critics also claim that the present-day Ayodhya was originally a Buddhist site, based on its identification with Saketa described in Buddhist texts. According to historian Romila Thapar, ignoring the Hindu mythological accounts, the first historic mention of the city dates back to the 7th century, when the Chinese pilgrim Xuanzang described it as a Buddhist site.

## Proposed Ram Janmabhoomi temple

In 1853, a group of armed Hindu ascetics belonging to the Nirmohi Akhara occupied the Babri Masjid site, and claimed ownership of the structure. Subsequently, the civil administration stepped in, and in 1855, divided the mosque premises into two parts: one for Hindus, and the other for Muslims.

In 1883, the Hindus launched an effort to construct a temple on the platform. When the administration denied them the permission to do this, they took the matter to court. In 1885, the Hindu Sub Judge Pandit Hari Kishan Singh dismissed the lawsuit. Subsequently, the higher courts also dismissed the lawsuit in 1886, in favour of status quo. In December 1949, some Hindus placed idols of Rama and Sita in the mosque, and claimed that they had miraculously appeared there. As thousands of Hindu devotees started visiting the place, the Government declared the mosque a disputed area and locked its gates. Subsequently, multiple lawsuits from Hindus, asking for permission to convert the site into a place of worship.

In the 1980s, the Vishwa Hindu Parishad (VHP) and other Hindu nationalist groups and political parties launched a campaign to construct the Ram Janmabhoomi Mandir ("Rama birthplace temple") at the site. The Rajiv Gandhi government allowed Hindus to access the site for prayers. On 6 December 1992, Hindu nationalists demolished the mosque, resulting in communal riots leading to over 2,000 deaths.

In 2003, the Archaeological Survey of India (ASI) conducted excavations of the site on court orders. The ASI report indicated the presence of a 10th-century north Indian style temple under the mosque. Muslim groups and the historians supporting them disputed these findings, and dismissed them as politically motivated. The Allahabad High Court, however, upheld the ASI's findings. The excavations by the ASI were heavily used as evidence by the court that the predating structure was a massive Hindu religious building.

In 2009, the Bharatiya Janata Party (BJP) released its election manifesto, repeating its promise to construct a temple to Rama at the site.

In 2010, the Allahabad High Court ruled that the 2.77 acres (1.12 ha) of disputed land be divided into 3 parts, with $^{1}D_{3}$ going to the Ram Lalla or Infant Lord Rama represented by the Hindu Maha Sabha for the construction of the Ram temple, $^{1}D_{3}$ going to the Muslim Sunni Waqf Board and the remaining $^{1}D_{3}$ going to a Hindu religious denomination Nirmohi Akhara.

The five judges Supreme Court bench heard the title dispute cases from August to October 2019. On 9 November 2019, the Supreme Court ordered the land to be handed over to a trust to build the Hindu temple. It also ordered to the government to give alternate 5 acre land to Sunni Waqf Board to build the mosque.

## Other places

Those who believe that Rama was a historic figure, place his birth before 1000 BCE. However, the archaeological excavations at Ayodhya have not revealed any settlement before that date. Consequently, a number of other places have been suggested as the birthplace of Rama.

In November 1990, the newly appointed Prime Minister Chandra Shekhar made an attempt to resolve the Ayodhya dispute amicably. Towards this objective, he asked Hindu and Muslim groups to exchange evidence on their claims over Ayodhya. The panel representing the Muslim organization Babri Masjid Action Committee (BMAC) included R. S. Sharma, D. N. Jha, M. Athar Ali and Suraj Bhan.

The evidence presented by them included scholarly articles discussing alternative theories about the birthplace of Rama. These sources mentioned 8 different possible birthplaces, including a site other than Babri Masjid in Ayodhya, Nepal and Afghanistan. One author - M. V. Ratnam - claimed that Rama was Ramses II, a pharaoh of ancient Egypt.

In his 1992 book *Ancient geography of Ayodhya*, historian Shyam Narain Pande argued that Rama was born around present-day Herat in Afghanistan. In 1997, Pande presented his theory in the paper "*Historical Rama distinguished from God Rama*" at the 58th session of the Indian History Congress in Bangalore. In 2000, Rajesh Kochhar similarly traced the birthplace of Rama to Afghanistan, in his book *The Vedic People: Their History and Geography*. According to him, the Harriud river of Afghanistan is the original "Sarayu", and Ayodhya was located on its banks.

In 1998, archaeologist Krishna Rao put forward his hypothesis about Banawali being Rama's birthplace. Banawali is an Indus-Sarasvati civilization archaeological site located in the Haryana state of India. Rao identified Rama with the Sumerian king Rim-Sin I and his rival Ravana with the Babylonian king Hammurabi. He claimed to have deciphered Indus seals found along the Sarasvati rivers, and found the words "Rama Sena" (Rim-Sin) and "Ravani dama" on those seals. He rejected Ayodhya as the birthplace of Rama, on the grounds that Ayodhya and other Ramayana sites excavated by B. B. Lal do not show evidence of settlements before 1000 BCE. He also claimed that the writers of the later epics and the Puranas got confused because the ancient Indo Aryans applied their ancient place names to the new place names as they migrated eastwards.

## THE CONFLICT OF HISTORY

According to the Hindus, the land on which the Babri mosque was built in 1528 is the 'Ram Janmabhoomi' (birthplace of the god-king Rama). But, Mir Baqi, one of Mughal king Babur's generals, is said to have destroyed a pre-existing temple of Rama and built a mosque called Babri Masjid (Babur's mosque) at the site. Both the communities have worshiped at the "mosque-temple", Muslims inside the mosque and Hindus outside it. However, in 1885 a petition was filed by the the head of the Nirmohi Akhara asking for permission to offer prayers to Ram Lalla inside what was known as the Babri Masjid.

The permission was not given but in 1886, district Judge of Faizabad court FEA Chamier gave his verdict and said, "It is most unfortunate that a masjid should have been built on land specially held sacred by the Hindus, but as that event occurred 356 years ago, it is too late now to remedy the grievance." It was in 1950 that a local resident Gopal Singh Visharad filed a complaint in the civil courts requesting permission to offer prayers in the mosque where the idols were installed.

## Court's verdict

The Allahabad High Court ruled the disputed land in Ayodhya will be divided into three parts. The 2.77 acres land will be divided between Hindus, Muslims and the Nirmohi Akhara. A bench of Justices Aftab Alam and R.M. Lodha stayed the September 30, 2010 judgment of the Lucknow Bench of the High Court after admitting a batch of appeals from both Hindu and Muslim organisations. The bench considered the verdict by the Allahabad High Court as 'strange' as no party prayed for it. The Bench said the status quo at the disputed site would remain as directed by the 1994 Constitution Bench and the order passed on March 13-14, 2002.

## Recent developments

Earlier this year Vishwa Hindu Parishad (VHP) announced a nationwide drive to collect stones for construction of the Ram temple in Ayodhya. Recently, two trucks of stones arrived in the city and the president of Ram Janam Bhumi Nyas, Mahant Nritya Gopal Das told PTI there was a "signal" from the Modi government to build the temple "now".

This assertion of the VHP might face opposition from the state government as Principal Secretary (Home) Devashish Panda had said that the Uttar Pradesh government would not allow arrival of stones in Ayodhya for Ram Mandir. "Since the matter is sub judice, the government will not allow starting of any new tradition regarding Ayodhya issue," he had said.

# ARCHAEOLOGICAL EVIDENCES OF RAM JANMABHOOMI

The significance of archaeological evidence in the context of Ramjanmabhoomi-Babri Masjid controversy, is being keenly stressed by both the contending parties - VHP and BMCC. Being one of the few having the first hand experience of both as a historian and a field archaeologist for many decades, I would like to point out the inadequacy of archaeology as the only or even a dominant source for the reconstruction of ancient

Indian history. Our knowledge about our past will be very poor if we ignore archaeology and it will be still poorer if we depend on archaeology alone as our most important source. While archaeology is a young and growing science in India, other sources such as epigraphy, numismatics and literary evidences have for much longer time been analysed and collated to build a framework of ancient Indian history, and therefore, archaeology as a tool is useful for confirmatory evidence mainly.

Archaeology, as a positive science gives us information about material life of periods as unfolded by different stratas exposed from it that what it has not exposed, never existed. Momentous archaeological discoveries are like Archimedies 'Eureka' i.e. chance discoveries, and the same chance goddess may bestow luck to other archaeologists disclosing from within the womb of the mother earth such knowledge missed by previous, may be well-versed, archaeologists. So it is always safe and wise to qualify the results of archaeological discoveries as 'to-date' or 'so far.' This self-evident, but often ignores, virtue of caution can be demonstrated. When we were excavating Chirand, luxurient chalcolithic ceramic culture eas noticed on the earliest exposed level in many trenches down to the virgin soil. But in one of the trenches was discovered evidence of an earlier neolithic culture, a pleasant surprise to the excavator who was almost going to close the excavation, then underway for many years. What a loss to knowledge it would have been! Again if R.D. Bannerji and Marshal had been excavating "Mohenjadaro" today under the present-day financial constraints and expensive archaeological technique of vertical digging, it was very likely that they would have stopped the digging after laying bare the so-called coolie quarters with elements of "Harappan" pottery & building activities; but then we would have missed the massive Harappan architecture and its special monuments for which the civilisation is most famous.

The point is that in view of lack of extensive horizontal excavations of all stratas of a site, its full history is not possible to be grasped. Moreover, in the context of getting archaeological proof of our pre-historic past & personalities one should ask the question what sort of evidence will prove the historicity or non-historicity of the Epic or Vedic characters. As no evidence of writing before Asoka (leaving out the Harappan script) has been available so far, no contemporary written material for the time of "Rama" or Krishna" should be expected. The cultural sequence exposed in the various stratas could give only relative chronology but no absolute chronology. Even when "C 14" (carbon-14 archaeological test) dates would give some approximate bracket in absolute dates to the excavated cultures, as there is no certainty or unanimity about the exact period of time when "Rama" or "Krishna" flourished, how far one would be right in assigning one or the other set of "dated cultures" unearthed in trenches as the culture of the time of Rama or Krishna.

This would be arguing from the unknown to the unknown, particularly when we are not sure whether cultures depicted in the "Ramayana" or the "Mahabharata" works which were definitely much later composed than the time of the heroses, must have contained elements of culture, more of their authors' times then of their pre-historic heroes. Thus the inadequacy of archaeological evidence and literary works as well for the period of Rama or Krishnaparticularly, material culture-architecture should be self-evident. In view of no evidence of use of stone as building material before "Ashoka" or of burnt brick before "Buddha" is available, the literary references to the luxurous buildings described in Epics and the "Puranas" will never be confirmed by archaeology. Wood-construction must have perished under the bowels of earth down the millennia. The difficulty of reconciling the literary evidence and the archaeological evidence "to date" is thus obvious. The easiest way chosen by many is to reject wholesale the testimony of the ancient literature the Epics and the Puranas for the period before the time of the Buddha. But this selective rejection is not beyond reproach. The same scholars who reject the Puranic dynastic lists before the Buddhist period, have used the same

Puranas for the political and dynastic history of the Buddhist period. But, it is hardly fair then, giving allowances for emendation, glosses, imagination to reject the entire pre-Buddha dynastic list as sheer figment of imagination, particularly when some kings, priests and peoples mentiones in the Vedic literature are mentioned in the Epics and the Puranas.

Now, according to Pargiter's reconstruction of the Dynastic synchronisms of the Puranas, Rama-Dasarathi is about 30 generations or so, earlier than Krishna of the Mahabharata. But, according to archaeological evidence to date Ayodhya, the traditional homecity of Rama is not earlier 8th century B.C., while in Hastinapur and other Mahabharata sites, PGW culture equated with the Mahabharata pottery by Mr. B.B. Lal is dated between 110-800 B.C., & the Mahabharata war was fought according to Lal in 836 B.C., according to Pargiter in 950 B.C. So, Rama who was not the founder of Ayodhya must have come much after 800 B.C., and should be nearer Buddha than Krishna; especially when many archaeologists place PGW later than Lal has put it. But, the excavator of Dwarka and the pioneer of marine archaeology, Mr. S.R. Rao has found evidence of the submerged city of Dwarka of Krishna, which he would place not later than 1500 B.C. Dwarka was later than Hastinapur which was founded by Kuru, while the former was founded by Krishna himself.

All this discussion just points to the insufficiency of the available archaeological date and lack of consensus among archaeologists about the period of the Epic-Puranic heroes. Would it therefore be wise today to fix the chronology, and even relative chronology of Rama and Krishna with any degree of certainty. More extensive diggings may shed some more light on the vexed problem. It would be sheer bravado, therefore on this evidence to deny the historicity of Rama and Krishna so richly portrayed in ancient historical traditional accounts. Even the archaeological excavations do not confirm the history of Ayodhya in the past, post NBP or Post-Maurya period.

The Sunga, Kuhana and Gupta stratas have been rather bare, but epigraphy, coins and literature speak of flourishing Ayodhya in these and earlier periods. Archaeology has not revealed anything of the prakars, pratolis, devapatha referred to by Patanjali in the Mahabhashya. Neither we have found in the excavation evidence of Buddha's and Adinathas' association with Ayodhya. Should we reject Buddhist and Jain evidence as imaginary as the Epic? We should particularly remember that the Jaina tradition of line of Tirthankars is consistent and quite reasonably reliable. 1st, 2nd, Ikshavaku dynasty of Ayodhya, which this certainly antedated 8th century B.C. Dhanadeva's inscription, the coins of Mitra-kings of Ayodhya, and the fortification of Ayodhya, its capital city-architecture of the time of Gupta Kings, Vikramaditya & Baladitya of the 5th-6th century A.D., are all unknown to archaeology of Ayodhya. Would we be justified to reject the epigraphic, numismatic and literary evidence?

And where are the Samgharamas described by Hsuan Tsang and associated with Vasubandhu and Asanga? It is not only the "Epic Ayodhya" but even "Gupta Ayodhya" that is uncorroborated from archaeology. But, both traditions and other historical sources vouchsafe for an active and living Ayodhya-Mahatamaya appended to the Skanda-purana should be dated not later than 9th century A.D. It refers to "Sir Ram Janmabhoomi" and other sacred places. According to Vikramankadeva charita, Bilhana came to Ayodhya on pilgrimage. Therefore, to think of Ayodhya as an important place for Hindus only from the 14th century onwards is all hogwash. Sculptural representations of Ramayana scenes in temples have been found in different parts of India from the 3rd century onwards. Sri Krishnadeva has drawn our attention to senes from Ramayana sculptured at the Ikshavaku art centre of Nagarjunikonda in Andhra pradesh dated in the 3rd Century A.D. The sculptured stucco panels at Aphasad in Bihar, depicting as many as eight scenes from the Ramayana were introduced to the scholarly world by the present author, and they are dated in the 7th century A.D. The depiction of redemption of Ahalya by Rama is vividly depicted in the Gupta temple at Deogadh dated in 6th Century A.D. Similar scene depicted on a terracotta and belonging to the Gupta period has been found at Sravasti. In a stone niche from Nachna (4th-5th Century A.D.) earlier than Deogadh example, Surpanekha's episode has been beautifully engraved. Numerous Ramayana scenes on Angkorvat (Vishnu temple) in Cambodia are testimony to the spread of Ramayana fame in the S.E Asia. Ramayanic scenes at Ellora (8th century) are well-known. Sculptures representing Ramayana scenes are found in Karnatak.

The scene depicting Meghanada dragging Hanuman to Ravana's court was first noticed as Nachna (M.P.) and is found at the Varahi temple at Chaurasi (dt. Puri, Orissa) of the 10th Century A.D. From the Chinese sources it has been shown that the Ramayana was a well-known and popular story in the time of Vasubandu. The public recitation of the Ramayana is referred to the manuscript of kalpanamanditika of the 2nd century A.D. found in Central Asia. The Paumacarita of Vimalasuri dated in the 1st Century A.D. is a recast of the Ramayana story. The Khotanese and the Tibetan version of the Ramayana further prove the antiquity and widespread of the Epic story.

A distinguished scholar (B. N. Puri) held that on the basis of available evidence the Ramayana was known in Central Asia from the 2nd century A.D. may be still earlier, as Asvaghosha who wrote Buddha charita was indebted to Valmiki and is said to have lived in Ayodhya. The recitation of the Ramayana is referred to in a Kambuja inscription of the 6th century A.D. Recitation of only secret texts is reasonable. The above very bried summary of Rama in art and literature from the 1st century A.D. down to the 12th Century A.D., makes it clear that Rama was held in great reverence not only in almost all parts of India, but also in South-East Asia, and Central Asia. The worship or deification of Rama is also as ancient. Even if we exclude the evidence of the Balakanda and the Uttarkanda or the Ramayana showing Rama to be an incarnation of Vishnu, believed to be no part of the original Ramayana of Valmiki, they are certainly not as late as Ramanand or Kabir. But Kalidasa in the Raghuvansa (4th-5th Century A.D.) refers to Rama as a divine figure.

However, while archaeology has so far failed to prove or disprove the hoary antiquity of Ayodhya going back to 2nd millennium B.C., or that of the historicity of Rama, it has certainly clearly indicated that the Babri Maszid stands on the ruins of a pre-Islamic structure of the 10th-11th centuries. That brick-pillar bases placed at uniform distances going into section of the excavated trenches are extending into the Babri Maszid complex cannot be doubted. About a dozen pillars used in the mosque are standing testimony to the fact that parts of a damaged Hindu structure have been appropriated in the construction of the mosque. It is now contended by some leading motivated historians that the structure was a Buddhist one, may be one of which Husan Tsang refered to in his account of Ayodhya.

But, the distinguished historians failed to mention rather may be as a deliberate move to spread disinformation that the Chinese pilgrim has mentioned no less than 10 'deva' temples, which would be Brahmanical only. What is wrong to ascribe one of these Brahmanical templese lying ruined under the Maszid? And should we forgive the Muslims for destroying the Buddhist structure? One is reminded of Goldsmiths' famous schoolteacher who went on arguing though vanquished still. However, the most crucial point in the archaeological evidence has been missed. The structure belongs to the 10th-11th centuries A.D. So it was constructed more than a couple of hundred years after the Chinese pilgrim. The chances of the structure being Buddhist are dim. We all know that as a result of Shankaracharya's digvijaya and other causes Buddhism suffered mortal injuries and soon disappeared from the land of its birth. We know that under the patronage of the Buddhist Pala kings, it survived in Bihar and Bengal only. One would like to know if Buddhist monuments of substantial dimensions were erected in the 10th century and later, east of Banaras. It is, therefore, a valid point to hold that Babri Maszid stands on the destroyed Hindu temple of the Pratihara or sahadavala times, who were all Hindus by faith. We are not aware of any ruling dynasty of 9th-10th centuries in this part of the country claiming to be Buddhist by faith, and it is well established that Buddhism largely flourished on royal munificance. Unfortunately, the details of the so-called Salabhanjika figure found in the Babri Maszid have not been given. But, granting the presence of the motif, it is hardly fair to rule the ruined structure, whose parts were appropriated in the Maszid, on this ground alone as Buddhist. It has been well-argued and documents elsewhere that in the post-Gupta periodthe motif was adapted by Hindu sculptors & salabhanjika model was modified to represent Lakshmi, Ganga and Yamuna.

In the Harshacarita Lakshmi has been compared to a salabhanjikaadorning the arm of a great hero like a victory-stand. From the same book it has been inferred that columns engraved with salabhanjika motifs were found in royal apartments. The word salabhanjika occurs in Aryasaptasat of Goverdhanacharya, a court poet of Lakshamanaursena (12th century A.D.) a Hindu by faith. The Allahabad Museum houses many salabhausika figures in dancing poses under mango tree. They are representatives of Jamsat-art. So the motif was not exclusively Buddhist in the post-Gupta period. It is really strange that while the obvious conclusion is that the structure was Hindu, the obduracy to ignore Hindu religion and art has made a particular brand of historians to look for a very unlikely explanation instead of the obvious one.

There should be no valid reason, now to hold that the structure over which the Babri Maszid stands was not Hindu in character. Then who destroyed the temple? It is possible that Mahmud Ghazni or more probably Muhammad Ghori plundered Ayodhya as well, but as traditions persist that the maszid was built in the time of Babar, and it is natural to hold that the temple was destroyed in his time as well. Since the time of the prophet Muhammed, the Muslim conquerors or invaders have been destroying un-Islamic structure and idols from China to Spain including Arabia, Iran and India. And Babar could very well emulate the persistent tradition. Meer Baqi's inscription in the mosque clearly states that it was built at the command of Babar in 1528. And if not Babar, Mohmud Ghazni or Muhammad Ghori. How does it weaken the Hindu standpoint? Unfortunately, the pages containing the events between April 2 and 18 September have been long lost irretrievably. Babar believed in and led jihad against Hindu rivals, and he did smash jain idols and mutilated many jain temples in 1925 such as in Urwah Valley near Gwalior as is admitted in his autobiography. In 1927 after his victory over Ranasanga in jihad against non-muslims, Babar took the title of Ghazi, as he himself claims in Babarnama. Before the battle, on the eve of his jihad against the Rana, he broke his drinking cups into pieces in a manner, in which if Allah wills, the idols of the idolators will be smashed." So where remains the case that Babar, a tolerant ruler, could not destroy the Hindu temple at Ayodhya. He certainly demolished many Hindu temples at Chanderi when he occupied it and Babar was in for a jihad covering a dar-ul-hab into dar-ul-Islam. There is a persistent evidence coming from Muslim sources since 1858 that the controversial site was known as Janmabhumi site on the basis of earlier medieval sources certainly not on British detail.

In our opinion the Hindus were never reconciled to the loss of this sacred place and it may be due to opposition that the mosque was not completed - it is without minarets and a pond for ablution (wazu) of namazis in the mosque by the faiithful doen the centuries. In was probably in recognition of the strength of the Hindu opposition (in vast majority in the city) and in deference to his policy of toleration that according to local tradition Akbar is said to have built the Chabutara on which Hindu idols were installed for worship and the adjacent spot known as Sita-ki-Rasoi was called Sitapak. The Muslim rulers dared not destroy the sacred site of architecture. But Hindu sense of grief and loss continued and often violent clashes over the issue of Ram Chabutara or the Janmabhoomi continued in the time of the great Mughals like Jehangir and Aurangzeb, and of the nawabs which must have caused consideratable loss of life. Long before the British occupied Ayodhya, the European traveller Tieffenthaler who visited the place in 1767, wrote about the Hindu worship being reguylarly conducted in the Maszid and mentions the tradition of the Janmabhoomi temple having been destroyed to make way for the existing mosque. It is sheer blindfoldness to assert that the dispute was concocted by the British for divide and rule. One cannot expect the great muslim divine and scholar Maulana Abdul Hai to be writing under British inspiration. He categorically writes that the Babri Maszid was constructed by Babar on the site of birth place of Sri Ramchandraji.

So there should be no doubt in any reasonable unprejudiced mind that the Babri maszid was built after destroying a Hindu temple. It is sheer obduracy to argue that Mir Baqi got the Hindu pillars from a few kilometers away to instal in the mosque. Why was he so much in love with the pillars? It is obvious that he used the pillars which he found after destruction of the temple on the site and a similar evidence has been found in Kutubminar complex. And it is beyond dispute that for hundreds of years if not thousands, the Hindus have believed this site to be the birth place of their divine Lord Rama. You cannot whisk away such long held pious belief of millions with even tons of weighty polemics. Who could dare dispute that the hair in Hazratbal mosque in Srinagar does belong to the Prophet Muhammad?

It is absolutely desirable for the Muslim community in the interest of peace and goodwill of the vast majority of their co-nationals to respect the aroused sentiments of the Hindus to agree to relocate the mosque and co-operate with the Hindus in construction of Rama's temple on the site. Mosques have been and are being relocated on much minor grounds even in muslim countries. And particularly when the mosque has not been in constant use by the namazis for decades. I have been a regular visitor of Ayodhya since 1926, and I have seen the continuous worship of 'Rama's idols on the "chabutara" and except for the some Muslims at prayer in the mosque compound. As has been said above, the mosque without facilities for essential ablution (wazu) for namaz was never very popular with namazis. And the Hindu worship and also struggle for the repossession of the site continued unabated. As early as in 1936-37, a bill was introduced in the legislature council of U.P. to transfer the site to the Hindus. Sri G.B. Pant, the Chief Minister tried to assuage the roused feelings of both the communities, and it is said that the bill was withdrawn on the unwritten understanding that no namaz was performed; the caretaker and his family could be the only namazis. And in 1949, the idols were discovered and installed in the garbhagriha, and till 1986, the continuous worship of Sri Ramalala has been on in the maszid with no entry of muslims there. The Hindu devotees received parshads, had darshan of the deity through iron-grilled window, protected by police. Since 1987, the Hindus have been worshipping the deities installed in the mosque without any hindrance. So the Babri Maszid does represent the humiliating experience of the Hindus and the militancy of Islam, and the Hindus throughout centuries have not accepted the fait accompli. This is not that much true of Mathura or Dwarka sites. The maszid on the otherhand has never been a very prominent and popular place of worship for the Muslims who congregated in Faizabad with splendid mosques. The maszid has not been in use since 1936. In view of all this, is it too much for the Hindus now to build a temple on the site which is traditionally the most pious site for the Hindus, after carefully and piously relocating the mosque at some distance from the site! The muslims may be assured that if they show the necessary grace, wisdom and sense of realism, no aggressive mass Hindu movement against other mosques could be again built up. Should not the Babari Maszid Co-ordination Committee, and the VHP and BJP think on such a course of action to assure communal amity and peace, the bedrock on which the stability and prosperity of the nation depends.

## FROM MYTHOLOGY TO POLITICS

A decision either way is likely to exacerbate communal tensions in a land riven by deep divisions. What, then, is the history of the Ayodhya case? How can a dispute over the title to a small plot of land in small-town India shake the very foundations of the republic? The supreme court is being asked to restore to India's Hindu majority the possession of land on which a mosque stood for over 400 years prior to Dec. 06, 1992. If the court agrees, it is likely to be seen as having succumbed to majoritarian instincts bedeviling governance in the Indian subcontinent.

On the other hand, a rejection of the Hindu claim might appear to perpetuate a medieval-period Muslim injustice, wherein Mir Baqi, a general of the first Mughal emperor, Babar, allegedly built a mosque after destroying a temple commemorating the birthplace of Hindu god Ram.

A decision either way is likely to exacerbate communal tensions in a land riven by deep divisions. Whether there really existed a temple before the mosque was built is at the core of the controversy. A further question is if a wanton destruction 400 years ago can be avenged politically, or rectified through any legal process that would be constitutional, in a nation governed by the rule of law.

The most important political question, however, is: What kind of a republic is India? Is it to be a secular republic, treating all faiths equally? Or is it to be one where its majority Hindu faith is to be predominant in all public actions?

### A brief retelling

A scanning of the facts set out in the legal briefs of both sides reveals that in 1857, the chief priest of the nearby Hanumangarhi temple took over the eastern part of the mosque courtyard. This is where the "Ram Chabutra"—a platform on the area alleged to be Ram's birthplace—was built. Later that year, Maulvi Muhammad Asghar, the muezzin of the Babri Masjid, petitioned the local magistrate, complaining of a forcible takeover of the courtyard.

In 1885, mahant Raghubar Das filed a suit praying for a legal title to the land and for permission to construct a temple on the *chabutra*. He claimed to be the *mahant* (priest) of the *janmasthan* (birthplace) of Ram. Significantly, no claim that a temple ever stood at the spot where the mosque was built, was made at that stage. The suit was dismissed in 1886.

Shortly after India's independence in 1947, idols of Ram appeared inside the mosque in 1949. On Jan. 16, 1950, a civil suit was filed by Gopal Singh Visharad (a member of the Hindu Mahasabha), asking for worship without obstruction and a perpetual injunction against the removal of the idols. A court ordered that the idols could not be removed. It also directed that the *puja* (worship) not be interfered with. The state of Uttar Pradesh filed an appeal against the injunction on April 24, 1950. In 1959, the Nirmohi Akhara, a monastic sect of Hindus, filed a suit praying that the entire mosque be handed over to it. Then, in 1961, came a suit claiming right over the mosque filed by the Sunni Central Waqf Board—the umbrella organisation of Sunni Muslim religious endowments. Besides the legal disputes, the period between 1951 and 1986 passed without any major incident.

## Deadly balancing act

In 1985, prime minister Rajiv Gandhi had given in to Muslim fundamentalists in the Shah Bano affair. A supreme court judgment favouring of divorced Muslim women was overturned by parliamentary legislation. Gandhi's opting to appease the Muslim orthodoxy left the Hindu mainstream uneasy. The latter was a constituency the Sangh Parivar was trying to consolidate. A few months later, the prime minister tried to restore the balance by giving the Hindus something, too.

An application to the Munsif (local magistrate) for the opening of the gates of the mosque had been filed by one Umesh Chandra Pandey in 1985 at the district headquarters in Faizabad. This was only five years after the Bharatiya Janata Party (BJP), the political wing of the Sangh Parivar, had been floated. Interestingly, Pandey was not a party to the case at all.

Former president Pranab Mukherjee writes that the opening of the Ram Janmabhoomi temple in Ayodhya was an "error of judgment."

An application to advance the hearing on Pandey's plea was dismissed by the Munsif's court. An appeal was filed before the district judge, who ordered that the locks on the Ramjanmabhoomi-Babri Masjid in Ayodhya be removed and left the question of law and order to be handled by the district magistrate and the state government of the day. The state government, in turn, received its instructions from the centre. The district magistrate and superintendent of police personally appeared before the Faizabad district court and stated that removing the lock from the main gate of the disputed structure would not create any law and order problem.

Until 1985, a priest had been permitted to perform *puja* once a year for the idols installed there in 1949. Now, all Hindus were seemingly given access to what the majority considered the birthplace of Lord Rama. In his memoirs, former president Pranab Mukherjee writes that the opening of the Ram Janmabhoomi temple in Ayodhya was an "error of judgment."

## Trail of blood

On Sept. 12, 1990, Lal Krishna Advani, the then president of the BJP announced a *rath yatra* (chariot procession) from the ancient temple of Somnath in Gujarat to Ayodhya. He sought to build a grand temple at the site of the mosque. Led by Advani, the procession's logistics were handled by the party's then youthful general secretary Narendra Modi, today India's prime minister. Speeches accusing the union government of "appeasing the Muslim minority" and "denying Hindus of their legitimate" rights were made. Thousands of *kar sevaks* (people who volunteer their services for a religious cause) descended on Ayodhya. A pitched battle with the police and paramilitary forces ensued. At least 20 *kar sevaks* died. Their deaths were used to stoke religious tensions in Uttar Pradesh. Numerous riots followed.

In the 1991 election, the BJP had doubled its vote share to almost a quarter of the total votes cast, made inroads into southern India, and formed governments in four states in the north. Meanwhile, its sister organisations laid the groundwork towards the final assault on the Babri Masjid. In 1992, the Vishwa Hindu Parishad, another right-wing Hindu nationalist organisation, announced that Dec. 06 had been chosen as the day for the work on the temple to commence. The temple would be built by *kar sevaks* from all over the country. Thousands poured in.

That morning, *kar sevaks* assembled to listen to fiery speeches from BJP leaders, including Advani, Murali Manohar Joshi, and Uma Bharati. The first attack on the mosque was mounted around noon, with *kar sevaks* climbing onto the domes of the mosque. Outnumbered by the mob, the local police fled. By 5PM, the mosque had been reduced to rubble. A makeshift temple with the idol of Ram was installed at the spot. To this day, the unfinished temple, with an idol under a makeshift roof, stands.

It was thought that an act of such vandalism in a democracy bound by the rule of law would not be condoned. The current attorney general for India, KK Venugopal, then appearing as a senior advocate for the state of Uttar Pradesh on that day at an emergency sitting of the supreme court, submitted: "My head hangs in shame."

The Kalyan Singh government in Uttar Pradesh was subsequently dismissed and president's rule was imposed. The deed had, however, been done. Soon after the demolition, the union government promulgated a law to acquire the disputed areas. This was challenged in the supreme court.

At the same time, a presidential reference—a constitutional provision under which the president of India can request the supreme court to provide its advice on certain matters—was also made. Among other questions, the reference queried the court: "Whether a Hindu temple or any Hindu religious structure existed prior to the construction of the Ram Janma Bhumi-Babri Masjid (including the premises of the inner and outer courtyards of such structure) in the area on which the structure stood?"

## The slow turning of gears

In its 1994 judgment in Ismail Farooqui's case, the supreme court by a majority of 3:2 upheld the validity of the law providing for the state's acquisition of land in the Ram Janma Bhoomi-Babri Masjid Complex. The presidential reference was, however, returned unanswered by the court, which declined to answer it for various reasons.

Justice SP Bharucha noted, "Ayodhya is a storm that will pass. The dignity and honour of the supreme court cannot be compromised because of it." In the supreme court's ruling of 1994, the civil suits (from the 1950s and 1960s) based on title were revived and sent back to the Allahabad high court for adjudication, with directions that the status quo as of Jan. 07, 1993, be maintained. This meant that the makeshift temple erected on the disputed site after Dec. 06, 1992, would remain.

In September 2010, the Allahabad high court delivered its verdict in the Ayodhya title suit. The bench declared that there would be a three-way division of the land between the Sunni Waqf Board, the Nirmohi Akhara, and the guardian of the deity "Ram Lalla."

As expected, the verdict didn't satisfy either party, and appeals were filed before the supreme court. In 2011, the supreme court clarified its status quo orders, stating that in "the 67.703 acres of acquired land located in various plots detailed in the Schedule to Acquisition or Central Area at Ayodhya Act, 1993, which is vested in the Central Government, no religious activity of any kind by anyone either symbolic or actual including *bhumi puja* or *shila puja*, shall be permitted or allowed to take place."

## Final act

In 2014, Modi was sworn in as prime minister. Amongst members of the ruling dispensation, the demolition of the Babri Masjid is seen more as an assertion of the legitimate rights of Hindus, rather than as an instance of the total breakdown of the rule of law. The building of a grand temple in Ayodhya at the very spot that the mosque once stood is now seen as only a matter of time by supporters of the ruling dispensation.

The case in the supreme court is seen as an unnecessary impediment to be overcome by a judicial verdict or by a parliamentary law. If there is seen to be no definite movement towards the construction of the temple, it would be taken as a breach of political faith on the part of the Hindu nationalist BJP. In March 2017, BJP member of parliament Subramanian Swamy (who was not originally a party to the Ayodhya dispute) intervened in the appeals pending before the supreme court, and asked for an early hearing. The application for the opening of the gates of the mosque (that ultimately led to the events of 1992) was also made by a stranger to the proceedings.

Swamy's original plea for an early hearing was rejected by the court. However, in July 2017, the court agreed to list the appeals for hearing. After various administrative delays, the matter came to be listed on Dec. 5, 2017, a day before the 25th anniversary of the demolition.

**All told, a final judicial verdict either way will not result in a solution.**

The bench hearing the appeals is headed by chief justice Misra. He is to retire in October 2018 and would have to adjudicate the appeals before retirement. Should the judgment indeed be delivered before October 2018, it would come only months before the 2019 general election. Whichever way the court decides, the judgment will introduce an emotive religious issue that is likely to be used by the ruling party and the opposition to gloss over issues related to governance and the economy.

If the title is vested in the Hindu side, it may well be seen as another instance of an organ of state succumbing to majoritarianism. If the title is vested in the Muslim side, it is unlikely that the mosque can be rebuilt without major repercussions on the ground.

All told, a final judicial verdict either way will not result in a solution, but is more likely to exacerbate existing fissures in a multicultural society. And what is more likely to suffer is the reliance upon and adherence to the rule of law. This then is the Shavian preface to the request for a deferment of the case beyond May 2019. The request having seemingly been refused, the stage is set for the final act. India's moment of self-recognition awaits.

## AYODHYA MAHATMYA

The frame story of this paraphrase is presented as a conversation between Siva and Parvati. Siva proclaims the *Ayodhya Mahatmya* and Parvati acts as an interlocutor, wanting to know the significance of particular places in the city.9 The text begins by providing a broad outline of Ayodhya, detailing its mythic origins and establishing its dimensions.10 The 1875 AM says that it was built on Rama's *sudarshanchakra* (chariot), while other recensions say that Visvakarma built the city. In the text Ayodhya resembles the eternal city of the gods but what is specific is that the celestial city is linked to forts, palaces, city halls and lakes that are found in the actual town. The AM provides an outline of the holy *kshetra* (field) around the town. The traditional dimensions of the town are 12 *yojanas* (1 *yojana*=7 km) in length and 3 *yojanas* in width. The rivers

Saryu and Tamasa form the northern and southern borders of the holy places in the city. Most pilgrimages described lie within these borders, although this paraphrase describes some holy places to the south of the Tamasa as well. The average distance between the two rivers is about 20 kilometres. The city is said to have the form of a fish of which the head lies in a ford of the Saryu river, called Gopratara and the tail at an unspecified part in the east.

As we know it now, Ayodhya is located on a curve of the Saryu River, which girdles the town on three sides. The eastern and western boundaries are made up of marshes, with the latter spreading to neighbouring Faizabad. The middle of the town known as Kot Ramchandar or Ramkot, is dotted with innumerable temples and *maths* (monasteries). The southwestern side of Ramkot, named Kubertila, is strewn with bricks and stones, most of them from the demolished Babri mosque. The 1875 edition describes Ramkot as a fort ringed by gates and protected by Hanuman, Sugriva and Angad, Nala and Nila, and Sokhain. Just beyond the fort, at its eastern, western and northern boundaries, splendorous palaces are described, made up of gem encrusted stones and diamonds.

In the centre of Kubertila is the *janmasthan*, which is also the site of the demolished Babri mosque. The most conspicuous fact relating to the pilgrimage around the *janmasthan* is that a description of this principal holy place is found in all the recensions of the AM, and yet the pilgrimage is not mentioned in any of the classical sources. 'Such a silence is all the more surprising in view of the fact that archaeological evidence indicates the existence of a temple at this *tirtha* [pilgrimage] in the eleventh century' (Bakker, Vol. II: 143). The AM connects the *janmasthan* with an elaborate description of *Ramnavmi* (celebrated as the birthday of Rama) and provides the spatial dimensions within which the birth occurred. This area stretches more than 500 *dhanus* (910 metres) westwards of the dwelling of a sage called Lomasa, 1008 *dhanus* (1835 metres) eastwards of a monastery occupied by the Ramanandi sect, called

Vighnesvara and 100 *dhanus* (182 metres) from Buddhist ruins called Unmatta, in an unspecified direction. In the middle of this area the royal palace called *janmasthan* is situated. A monastery called Ramgulela is believed to represent Lomasa. Janaki's kitchen, the text says, is northwest of the *janmasthan*, and 40 yards to the north of *janmasthan* is the house of Kaikeyi (the mother of Rama's brother, Bharata). 60 yards to the south of this house is the dwelling of Sumitra, mother of Rama's younger brothers, Satrughana and Lakshmana. Southeast of the *janmasthan* is the *sitakup*, also known as the *Jnanakup*. The sages, Brihaspati, Vasishta and Vamadeva drink its waters.

After the demolition of the mosque in Kubertila, a makeshift temple, apparently marking the exact place of the birth of Rama, was erected in the central dome. The temple is enclosed by railings and is guarded by a number of security personnel. No Muslims are allowed to enter the precincts and Hindus may come only as far as the fence in front of the entrance gate. The temple itself is located on a small altar, near which groups of Hindus engage in continuous prayer and*kirtana* (hymn). During my visit to Ayodhya in 2008, a pamphlet (in English) distributed among pilgrims read:

Shri Ramjanmabhumi of Ayodhya is a very sacred place. Anticipating Hindu-Muslim friction, the Govt. has declared it a disputed place and has taken possession over it. Regular case is being conducted in the civil and criminal court. Since December 27, 1949 day and night Akhand Kirtan [unlimited chanting or hymn] is being performed with a determination that it will continue so long as Ramjanmabhumi is not freed. It is the sacred duty of the entire Hindu Community to finance this holy cause donations (sic) and thus earn immense PUNYA [virtue and grace].

The deities can be seen through iron railings and offerings can be made through their bars. On special occasions groups of Hindus, eleven to a unit, are allowed to proceed beyond the railing to worship Rama and his brothers' deities.

The *ghats* (bathing places), the most important of which is known as Svargadvara (lit. gate to paradise), are situated along the Saryu and lie about 700 meters to the north of Ramkot. Gopratara, about 8 kilometres to the west of Ramkot, is the site of a second major bathing place. The 1875 AM says that Svargadvara, known also as Negeshvara and Muktidvara (gate of deliverance) is at 318 yards to the east of the thousand-streamed Lakshmana *kund* (pond or lake). 'All men, Hindus and Muslims, who die here go to the place of Vishnu,' and that 'Ramachandra in the form of Bharata, Satrughan, Lakshmana and his own, greet them there.' Svargadvara is made up of seven *ghats*: Chandrahari, Guptahari, Chakrahari, Vishnuhari, Dharmahari, Bilvahari and Punyahari. These baths are said to extend over a distance of 636 dhanus (1157 metres) to the east of Sahasradhara. Effectively, this includes the entire northern and north-eastern side of Ayodhya along the riverbed as far as another bathing place known as the Janakitirtha. A ruined mosque, dating to the time of Aurangzeb called Treta-ke-Thakur, is located 250 metres east of Chandrahari. Various temples lie along these ghats—the Saryumandir and the Nagesvaranathmandir are the important ones. The more recent ones are called Caturbhuji ka Mandir and Vidhiji ka Mandir, both occupied by the Ramanandi sect. Associated with these bathing places are water bodies, mainly ponds or lakes. This AM names more than 50 water bodies, most of which are associated with pilgrimages during specific months of the lunar calendar.

The linking of water bodies to places of pilgrimage establishes correspondence between the order of the world and that of ordinary action; more appropriately, ordinary time is integrated as part of an eternal order. This integration is instituted in the calendar. I follow Ricœur (1988: 105–09) in suggesting that the calendar marks a time of fabulation in three different ways. First, the calendar establishes a founding event—the creation of the city on Rama's chariot. This creation initiates a new era, determining the axial moment in reference to which every other event is dated. Thus the topography of Ayodhya is described after its institution as *janmabhumi*. The axial moment gives to the calendar a form of time that is external to physical and lived time and it is this that expresses the specificity of fabulation. It cosmologizes lived time and humanizes cosmic time and in this way the time of the fable is re-inscribed into the time of the world.

Second, by referring to the founding event we see how time flows in two directions—from the past towards the present, and from the present toward the past. This flow establishes a closed loop and fixes the architecture of the city. This fixing, then, allows for the AM to be used as a map so that terrestrial spaces and water bodies are oriented in terms of cardinal directions and in relation to each other. It is this fixity that allowed for the AM to be used as a map for the coronation of the English King. This orientation makes time spatial.

Finally, we find a set of units of measurement that designate and establish the dimension of the city. But these designations are more than spatial. We find constant intervals between the day, the week and the month marked by the recurrence of cosmic phenomena and miracles. In the calendar this establishes a division between the light and dark half of the month, and the month itself is an interval between the conjunction of the waxing and waning moon.

Through the calendar, the link between Rama and Ayodhya becomes a means of ordering the city. Each pilgrimage, each oblation offered establishes a present marked by the infinite repetition of virtue. In the process, this present adjudicates the practice of affirming the birthplace and the land of birth of the Rama deity. The importance of these virtues is that they invigorate and make whole the worshipper in the city and it is in this way that the calendar itself becomes an ethical doctrine. Against the postulate of a beginning and an end, the calendar establishes a present. When the birthplace and the land of birth enter adjudication, we find explicit references to the Rama deity and the birthplace as jural beings. In the process, the Babri Mosque circulates in articles of law and loses its specificity as an architectural entity. It becomes a revenant. For this reason, if law accounts for the finitude of the Ayodhya dispute, then the placing of the Rama deity at the heart of its decisions is not without its problems. It is to this problematic placing that I now turn.

## The revenant in the High Court

In tracing the revenant and its disruptive presence I consider two modes of judicial accounting. In the first part I read the accounts of witnesses called to testify in the High Court, specifically as they describe the demolished Babri mosque and the family of terms within which it is enveloped. The second section details how the three judges, in their separate findings, made a case for the jural deity and named this mosque. In testimony we get a kind of messianic time that is activated through pilgrimages and ritual observances, but a time that almost always looks sideways at the absent mosque, while the decisions of the three justices show how the demolition is worked upon and made habitable in law. In the process, rather than indicating the demands of this or that litigant, these decisions act like a speech prosthetic, by which inanimate objects (such as the deity and the mosque) become voluble. While the deity is enmeshed within an eternal present, the demolished mosque dislocates. The decisions orient themselves to this doubling by pointing to a vertiginous simultaneity of time. The mosque haunts this eternal present. Gordon (1997) thinks of haunting as signifying a social figure, which is then mined for its poetic potential. Rather than consider the mosque as a unit of signification I follow its career not simply for the poetic potential that it allows, but because its demolition and subsequent appearance as a ghostly figure puts into crisis the future of the Rama temple itself.

Before I present the testimonies I will outline how they are framed within the 'gist of the findings' of the three judges.

Justice SU Khan: The 'disputed structure' was constructed as a mosque by and under orders of the Mughal emperor Babur and no temple was demolished in its construction. But the mosque was constructed over the 'ruins of temples,' which were lying in 'utter ruins' for a very long time (2010 ADJ I: 115).

Justice SC Agarwal: It is declared that the area covered by the 'central dome of the three-domed structure, *i.e.*, the disputed structure being the deity of Bhagwan Ram Janamsthan and place of birth of Lord Rama as per faith and belief of Hindus, shall not be obstructed or interfered in any manner by the defendants' (2010 ADJ III: 2871).

Justice Dharamveer Sharma: The 'disputed structure is the birthplace of Lord Rama. The place of birth is a juristic person and a deity. The disputed building was constructed by Babur, the year is not certain, but it was built against the tenets of Islam [...]. The disputed structure was built on the site of an old structure after demolition of the same. Thus, the structure could not have the character of a mosque.' (2010 ADJ III: 3453)

What is clear is that the 'disputed structure' or three-domed structure (never the Babri mosque) was associated with ruins, with obstruction and interference and with demolition. We will see later how these terms, in alliance with proper nouns, come to circulate in the judicial account.

Testimony 1: Mahant Ram Vilas Das Vedanti, (in his affidavit of 2005 he says he is 51 years old. He was cross-examined by Tarunjeet Verma representing the Nirmohi Akhara, and by Zafaryab Jilani representing the Sunni Waqf Board). Ram Vilas, at the time of his deposition claimed to be the priest of a temple and had been living in Ayodhya since 1968. He holds a doctorate in grammar from the Varanasi Sanskrit College.

Prior to the demolition of the disputed structure at the Sriram Janambhumi premises, the main gate for entry was in the east, which was called the Hanumatdwar [...]. On entry to the disputed structure a platform towards the south was called Ramchabutra, where the idols of Lord Rama, Laxman, Sita, etc. were present and were worshipped regularly by Hindu devotees. Below the Ramchabutra was the 'cave temple.' [What follows is an elaborate architectural description of the birthplace, ringed as it is, by a series of proper names of Hindu deities and places mentioned in the *Ayodhya Mahatmya* of 1875].

Testimony 2: Raja Ram Pandey, 87 years old (affidavit of 2003), cross-examined by Zafaryab Jilani representing the Sunni Waqf Board.

Raja Ram Pandey was a resident of Kaushalya Ghat in Village Ramkot, the site of the demolished mosque. He had been living in Ayodhya since 1930.

In March 1934 a Hindu-Muslim riot occurred when many Muslims were killed and a large number of graveyards were damaged, but no part of the Sriram Janmabhumi temple or its dome was damaged. The outer wall was damaged slightly. The Muslims were terror-stricken and they stopped going towards the temple. I was 19–20 at that time.

What follows in this testimony is the same elaborate description of the architecture of the birthplace, of the deity and the form of worship.

Testimony 3: Narendra Bahadur Singh, 72 years (affidavit of 2004, cross-examined by the same lawyer as in Testimony 2).

I gained maturity at the age of about 11 years [...]. The structure collapsed on 6 December 1992 and thereafter my visits to the temple were reduced.

As with the other accounts, this one is rich in details on the geography of the birthplace, the place of deities and the various pilgrimages that occur around the year.

If Hindu accounts were meticulous in their evocation of the birthplace, Muslim testimonies focused on the status of the mosque.

Testimony 4: Maulana Atiq Ahmad, 47 years (affidavit of May 2010. Cross-examined by the advocates of the Nirmohi Akhara and by the Next Friends of the Deity).

Nowhere in Islam does the style of mosque construction find specific mention. The name 'masjid' is given to a piece of land that is gifted for offering Namaz. Even if this building has no domes or minarets, it will be called a masjid. Even if there is a graveyard in the vicinity of the mosque, that does not change its character. You killed our people, you destroyed our graves. But the mosque remains. A mosque once constructed will always be a mosque [...]. If the followers of other religions start practicing their religious faith in a mosque, then also the status of the mosque does not change.

Other Muslim testifiers echo much the same sentiments.

In which way does the decision of individual judges intersect with such testimony? In considering the expectations of the litigants, the High Court judges actualize legal operations by consolidating existing norms, projecting their effects into the future and attempting to produce expectations based on re-installed or altered norms.

Let me briefly indicate the direction of how I think the name is being used in the pair Rama-Ayodhya. In the judicial decision, the name delivers the expectations of the litigants. In eliding the historical facticity of the mosque, the judicial decision also conveys that what is there differs from what is or was present before 6 December 1992. The names of Rama and Ayodhya are present in and of themselves. What becomes present after the demolition contracts into what is accessible as worship, as deity and birthplace. But the mosque returns and splits this access into what was present before 1992 and what is really there. The disputed structure complex, in its alliance with the destroyed cemetery, becomes a metonym for Rama and Ayodhya, ensuring that this place-name will forever be incomplete. This is because the Babri Mosque haunts the deity and its birthplace in appropriately spectral ways, an absence that sits side-by-side with an assumed presence, a stubborn response to the sacredness of Rama and Ayodhya.

For this reason, too, in Ayodhya Hindu worship is not without its doubts. With reference to the 'Rama temple' there is a kind of precautionary formula used in prayer. When I visited Ayodhya in 2008 I was advised to use expressions like, 'whether you want to be called Rama or Lakshmana, or Gopal, hear my voice,' and 'if this is the name by which you would like to be called.' Underlying this call to the name are the following sorts of questions. Do you need to know the name of the deity you're praying to? If you get the name of the deity wrong, what happens to your prayer and your oblations? Who gets to decide whether the name works? (You, or the deity, or neither?) The name and birthplace of the deity are, as I have tried to show, not only a declarative (by which you move from the name to the city and vice-versa), whose invocation in law establishes an institutional fact, but also a mode of censorship by a specific community of Hindu devotees. The avowal of the name of the deity here must rest on a disavowal of the Babri Masjid. In other words, these questions sense the frisson of a spectral presence circulating uncertainly in articles of law but without material presence. It is not inconceivable that the Rama temple, if it is constructed on an officially controlled landscape, will not quite shake the presence of ghosts from disturbed graves and a demolished mosque.

The Deity and the Janmasthan: The names, Rama and Ayodhya and the Babri mosque, as they occur in the 2010 judgment, have a variable and flexible character. This is understandable since they are linked to a cluster of other names, made up of single or multiple rights and virtues. We have seen that these rights and virtues that make up Rama and Ayodhya come in thick bundles and in large clusters. In the case of the Babri mosque the cluster of other names within which it is located is hollowed out. Instead there is something like an ontological vacancy built into this name. But before I develop this argument further let me briefly delimit the relationship of Rama to Ayodhya. Put more elaborately, how is the juristic personality of the deity framed within the backdrop of the demolition of the Mosque, and how do we find a place for gods in the adjudication around the dispute?

An obvious dimension of the name Rama is its relationship to property as Ayodhya. If the proper name denotes a person, in a common-sense way one assumes that person and property (being a thing) are mutually exclusive. The 2010 judgment, we will see below, qualifies this distinction, by showing that the legal rights and duties that make someone count as person and something count as property are shifting and variable. The name Rama bears the features of property, particularly *janmabhumi* and *janmasthan*, as much as it is exalted as a virtuous god-king. This doubling—of property and virtue—is found in the Allahabad High Court decision, but also in the lease deed executed between the Uttar Pradesh state government and the Shri Ram Janmabhumi Trust in 1992. Earlier in 1989, the Uttar Pradesh state government had acquired the land around the Babri Mosque and the plan was to build a grand temple dedicated to Rama. The Trust was established in 1989 to oversee the construction of a grand temple.

The object of the Trust was to establish a religious theme park over state acquired land, approximately 56 acres that surrounded the mosque and various Hindu temples. The lease mentions that the object of the park was to, 'create experience of the cultural aspects emerging from the great epic Ramayana [...]. The park should be integrated with the overall development of that Ayodhya mentioned in the great Mahatmyas.' A state appointed surveyor mapped, scheduled and delineated the red-boundary plot of land over which the park would be built. It would be called the Ramkatha Park, reflecting ostensibly the relation between the Kingdom of Rama and the present. The lease announced the precise birthplace of Rama, known as the *janmasthan*, and Ayodhya the *janmabhumi*. It would also function as the object of nationalist-religious pedagogy where inhabitants of the complex, dressed in Vedic period costume, arranged guided tours for school children. What was, thus, set in motion was a process of landscape interpretation, with the mosque as an ever-present eyesore.

The lease deed, in the process, turned topography into a set enmeshed in scriptural signs that had to be read instead of being simply viewed. These signs imagined the park as a site of national regeneration and a pastoral landscape, an edited panorama, where the mosque could exist only between the visual registers of danger, Vedic authenticity and political invisibility.

In 1989 a suit was filed by three plaintiffs: Sri Ramalala Virajman, the Asthan Rama Janmabhumi, Ayodhya (O.O.S. No. 5 of 1989) and a Vaishnava Hindu who argued that the Rama deity, installed in the central dome of the mosque, and the place of birth were juiristic persons. It also declared that the entire premises of Sri Rama Janmabhumi at Ayodhya belonged to the plaintiff deities and asked for a perpetual injunction against the defendants (the Sunni Waqf Board, the Nirmohi Akhara, Gopal Singh Visharad and 24 others), prohibiting them from interfering with or raising objections to the construction of the new temple building at Sri Rama Janmabhumi, Ayodhya.

The Allahabad High Court attempted to resolve the above suit by arguing that both the *janmasthan* and Rama Lala (Child Rama), surreptitiously installed in the central dome of the Babri Mosque in 1949, were jural persons. In so doing the judges located the subject of legal rights and duties on a threshold where judicial decision was marked by a continuous emergence from a sacral past into the future. This opening into the future can be elaborated through three basic issues posed by the High Court. The first issue (Justice Khan) considered whether the deity was a perpetual minor and if so, whether this minor was subject to the Limitation Act of 1963. The second matter (Justice Agarwal) dealt with the form of divinity and belief, specifically *swayambhu* (self-revealed image) and *pran pratistha* (infusion of breath into the deity). The third concern (Justice Sharma) was the link between the deity and the image.

As far as the status of the deity as a perpetual minor was concerned, Justice Khan considered whether the minor was entitled to the benefit of the Limitation Act of 1963. This Act raises the following question: if a person entitled to institute a suit or make an application for the execution of a decree is reckoned a 'minor, or insane or an idiot' (ADJ I: 80), can this person institute the same suit or execute an application, after the disability has ceased? Analogically, the deity, in the position of a minor, was unable to make an application itself or institute a suit, since it suffered from the same infirmities. The Justice, however, argued that the minor status of the deity was confined only to the purpose of filing a suit—in all other instances the deity was not a perpetual minor. Furthermore, as a minor it could never be freed from this disability. This meant that if the deity were a perpetual minor, then the limitation would never come to an end. In his order, Justice Khan declared 'that the portion below the central dome where at present the idol is kept in a makeshift temple will be allotted to Hindus in final decree,' thus pointing to the jural status of the Rama deity (ADJ I: 80).

Just as Justice Khan recognized the legal status of the deity, Justice Agarwal argued that both the deity and its place of birth were jural persons. Citing Ram Janki Deity Vs. State of Bihar, (1999 (5) SCC: 50), the Justice held that the birthplace was self-revealed (*swayambhu*), a product of infinite nature without beginning, and it was left to worshippers to simply discover its existence. Furthermore the *swayambhu* image did not require *pratistha* (consecration of breath); the act of worship gave the place the essential features of a temple. It was Justice Dharam Veer Sharma who provided the most elaborate explanation of the jural deity and birthplace.

To establish that the Babri Mosque was built after razing a Hindu temple, Justice Sharma decided to call on the assistance of 'archaeological science' (2010 ADJ III: 2927). Accordingly, the Archaeological Survey of India was directed by the Court in August 2002 to excavate the disputed site. The excavation, according to the Justice, revealed that the Ram *Chabutra* (platform), had 'five different structural phases in its construction' (2010 ADJ III: 2954). In its enlarged form it was '22 metres in east-west and about 14 metres in north-south orientation' (2010 ADJ III: 2954). The survey found evidence of a massive structure that could be dated from the tenth century onwards. The Justice proceeded to quote from various sources to establish that the structure was a Rama temple. Verses from the Rig Veda were put alongside expert testimony, including those drawn from the Ministry of Steel and Mines, epigraphy and histories of ancient India. In effect, the Babri Mosque had usurped the place of the Rama temple (2010 ADJ III: 2970).

Having concluded that the massive structure razed in the construction of the Babri Mosque was a Rama temple, Justice Sharma went to great lengths to prove that this structure belonged to the deity, by contending that the latter was a jural person. Furthermore, it was not only the deity that was a jural person, but the birthplace itself was a jural entity. More than the deity, the *janmasthan* was *swayambhu* (self-revealed) and did not require any form of consecration. The consequence of considering the *janmasthan* and the Rama deity as jural persons meant that the two could not be alienated from each other though it was only in the 'ideal sense that the idol is the owner of endowed properties' (2010 ADJ: 3409) and could have no beneficial interest in the endowment. The attempt nevertheless was to make a case for Hindu forms of worship and to link these forms to Ayodhya incarnated as the name of Rama. The Justice was categorical in his assertion that 'the religious right of Hindus to worship Ram Lala at the *janmasthan* became concretized before the Constitution came into being and the same requires to be protected,' and that no plea could be entertained to prohibit this practise (2010 ADJ III: 3439). Furthermore Ayodhya itself was marked out through *parikrama* (circumambulation). Circumambulation of the Rama deity was of three types—40 *kose*, 14 *kose* and 5 *kose* (1 *kose* is approximately two miles). In the process, the movement from *janmasthan* (birthplace) to *janmabhumi* (land of birth) was secured.

What place did the Mosque have in this complex of names and territory? The final section of this paper addresses the absent Mosque. Referring to one of the original suits filed by the Sunni Central Waqf Board against various Hindu defendants and the state of Uttar Pradesh, Justice Khan asked whether the demolished building was a mosque, its date of construction, the exact plot of land on which it stood, its ownership till 1949, when its owners were dispossessed, and finally whether the Hindu devotees of Rama had 'perfected right of prayers at the site by adverse possession' (2010 ADJ I: 58). In effect, the issue that concerned this Justice was one that related to property ownership. In his findings he observed that the 'disputed structure' was constructed as a mosque under direct orders from the Mughal emperor Babur and that no temple was demolished in its construction. Yet, he observed, before 1855 the Ram *Chabutra* and Sita's kitchen had come into existence inside the boundary wall of the mosque. This complex was called the *Chabutra* Masjid. In view of the above, both Hindu and Muslim parties and the Nirmohi Akhara were awarded joint possession of the entire premises (2010 ADJ I: 107–16). Thus, as property, in Justice Khan's estimation the Babri Mosque was linked to the disputed structure and to the*Chabutra* Masjid. What was absented from his order was that the mosque had also been a site of Islamic prayer. In his prelude he perhaps admitted to a sense of loss—'Here is a small piece of land (1500 square yards) where angels fear to tread. It is full of innumerable land mines. We are required to clear it [...]. We do not propose to rush in like fools lest we are blown. However, we have to take a risk [...]' (2010 ADJ I: 27).

If Justice Khan was succinct in his order, his colleague Justice Sudhir Agarwal, more than made up for his economy of words. Extending to almost 3000 pages, the judgment provides a detailed survey of various records, from beyond antiquity to the present, oral testimonies, the deposition of witnesses, a reading of public reports and the discovery of lost objects following archaeological excavations. Justice Khan's 'small piece of land,' was now fleshed out in greater detail. 'The disputed structure is divisible into three parts. (1) The main roofed structure, (2) the inner courtyard, and (3) outer courtyard [...]. On the outer courtyard there is a Chabutra which has been in possession of the Hindus' (2010 ADJ I: 128). The Babri Mosque, in this rendition was associated with the 'inner courtyard.' It was also called a 'three-arched structure,' with 'three broad but pointed arches on the façade. The *liwan* (sanctuary) that stood on a low plinth was composed of three square bays, roofed by three single broad and high domes' (2010 ADJ I: 128). Inscriptions in Persian and from the Quran marked the pillars of this 'three-arched structure.' And yet what was demolished was not a mosque, for the inner and outer courtyard belonged to the deity.

In answer to the claim of the Sunni Waqf Board that the inner courtyard was a mosque under the care of the waqf Board, Justice Agarwal argued that 'a deity is not damaged or comes to end due to destruction in any manner, since the spirit of Supreme Being continues to exist and it will not disappear, particularly when the deity is Swayambhu, *i.e.* self-created' (2010 ADJ III: 2847). The *janmabhumi* similarly was *swayambhu*. The courtyard, inner and outer, therefore had a dual character, being both deity and property. From here he argued that 'It is quite possible that the entire city may be held to be very pious and sacred on account of some occurrence of divinity or religious spirituality' (2010 ADJ III: 2848). In answer to the claim that the disputed structure was a mosque constructed in 1528 by Babur and that namaz had been offered continuously till 1949, he said that it could not be established that the mosque was built in 1528 and that prayers had been offered in the mosque since that year. At best, the Friday prayer was offered from 1860 till 16 December 1949 and that too intermittently (2010 ADJ III: 2855). While this structure had a *mutawalli* (keeper of the mosque), he found the absence of a muezzin surprising. The *mutawalli* had not been appointed following due procedure, the possession of waqf could not be claimed by him and by extension the (Muslim) worshipper could not claim possession of waqf property. Given that there was evidence of namaz being offered at the site, the Justice held that part of the disputed structure was indeed a mosque, but that 'there also existed a religious place of non-Islamic character before the construction of the disputed structure' (2010 ADJ III: 2860).

If the mosque was built on usurpation could it really be a mosque? Quoting from Quranic verses Justice Dharam Veer Sharma argued that the *waqif* (person holding the waqf) must be the owner of property, and there is nothing on record to suggest that the emperor Babur, a Hanafi Muslim, had acquired the title of the temple. Accordingly, he could not erect a mosque against the tenets of Islam (2010 ADJ III: 2971–75). For this reason, the claim of the plaintiffs that the mosque was dedicated to Allah was decided against them. And even if the 'building' had been used by members of the Muslim community for offering prayers since the time of its construction, a non-Muslim now adversely possessed it (2010 ADJ III: 2976). Effectively, the mosque had become a temple.

CHAPTER 3

# Hindutva Movement and Sangh Parivar

While the foundational core of Hindutva is inculcated in the RSS swayamsevaks (volunteers) through training that begins from childhood in its local shakhas (cells), the broad based work of spreading the ideology and its politics is undertaken through a network of organizations.

The RSS (or more commonly, the Sangh) has created and propagated organizations in every facet of socio-political life in India—from political parties to children's centers, trade unions and militias. These groups are together known as the Sangh Parivar or the Sangh Family of organizations. In recent years, the Sangh Parivar has also expanded its operations outside India and made significant efforts to reach the 'Hindu' diaspora, especially in the US, the UK and the Caribbean.

## Constituents of the Sangh Parivar

The spread of the Hindutva ideology in India is carried out at the grassroots level through an army of swayamsevaks deployed by the Sangh Parivar. The recruitment and ideological 'orientation' towards Hindutva is done on many levels and fronts: at the grade school level, or earlier, with Hinduised education, including such 'educational' activities as the holding of Ramayan and Mahabharat competitions for school children in tribal areas—largely with the goal of supplanting tribal culture and traditions; with the 'celebration' of Hindu festivals on a grand scale in areas with large non-Hindu populations; and simultaneously, with the distribution of anti-minority pamphlets and literature and the sporadic creation of anti-minority programs such as the grabbing of minority land or buildings or the promotion of riots and murder.

For these purposes, the Sangh has set up hundreds of smaller organizations all over the country, all supervised by volunteers from the Sangh and centrally coordinated, even though each claims to be independent of the Sangh.

While the RSS itself cannot currently accept monetary contributions for its activities from abroad, each of the Sangh-affiliated organizations has been designated a 'charity' and the Sangh actively solicits foreign funding for these organizations.

In other words, given that the RSS has no corporate form and ensures an ambiguity around its specific location and form, it would be quite correct to argue that this myriad of smaller organizations together is what precisely constitutes the RSS.

The most visible and active organizations of the Sangh Parivar are represented below in a necessarily incomplete organizational chart of the Parivar.

Each of these organizations has an equivalent "sister" organization in the US, which is shown in brackets in the chart below.

The central organizations of the Sangh Parivar are:

- its parliamentary wing, the *Bharatiya Janata Party* (BJP, Indian Peoples Party),
- its cultural/political mobilization wing, the *Vishwa Hindu Parishad* (VHP – World Hindu Council),
- its paramilitary wing, the *Bajrang Dal*, and
- its service wing, the *Seva Vibhag*.

Each of these has a US equivalent –

- the *Hindu Swayamsevak Sangh* (HSS) mirrors the RSS with the Friends of India Society (FISI) functioning as its public arm,
- the *Overseas Friends of the BJP* runs the affairs of the BJP in the US,
- the *Vishwa Hindu Parishad of America* does the same for the VHP, and
- the IDRF looks after the Seva Vibhag's activities in the US.

Further, Sewa International is the Seva Vibhag's coordination body for all international funds and service programs.

## FOUNDING OF THE SANGH

THE IDEA of establishing the Sangh became gradually crystal-lized in Doctorji's mind. It now only remained to translate that concept into actuality. Doctorji chose the sacred day of Vijaya Dashami, 1925, for the historic occasion)That day was, indeed, very auspicious for launching the work, since Vijaya Dashami traditionally symbolized the conquest of good over evil. Founding the Sangh was the first step in the future victo-rious march of the Hindu Nation – from the individual to collective life, from subservience to invincibility. About 15-20 young men gathered in Doctorji's house on that day. Chief among them were Bhauji Kawre, Anna Sohni, Vishwanathrao Kelkar, Balaji Huddar and,Bapurao Bhedi. Doctorji announced to the gathering : " We are inaugurating the Sangh today." He elicited the views of all of them in regard to the activities of the Sangh. "All of us must train ourselves physically, intellectually and in every way so as to be capable of achieving our cherished goal," he declared.

Founding of any institution is usually preceded by fixing up its name, constitution, office, fund collection, etc. There is also a lot of advance publicity. But strangely, there were no such preparations when the Sangh was started. The sole capital of the Sangh at the time of founding was Doctorji's own life of utter dedication and sterling character, his un-surpassed organizing ability and spirit of self-effacing service.

Activities relating to physical training were conducted by Doctorji's friend Anna Sohni, who was an adept at handling lathi, dagger, lance and such other conventional weapons. He was himself a well-built figure and his unique technique of coaching fascinated the youth. A special feature of his posture-training was the normal stance *siddha-sthiti* of the body, gracefully and perfectly balanced on the two feet. Even more impressive was the *yuddha-yoga,* an effective technique of defence. Training in drill, marching, etc., was imparted on Sundays by another friend of Doctorji, Martandrao Jog. On Thursdays and Sundays there were discourses on national affairs. These sessions later on came to be known as *Bouddhik Varga.* Doctorji and Vishwanathrao Kelkar lectured at these sessions. Among the younger leaders, Balaji Huddar, Dada Paramarth, Bhaiyaji Dani and others were encouraged by Doctorji to speak.

The Swayamsevaks thus began to assemble every day on the grounds of a primary school. As the number grew, that place proved insufficient. The Mohitewada ground, which was then in utter neglect, was cleared and the Shakha was started there. From 28th May of 1926, the daily*Shdreerik* (physical culture) programme was commenced as a regular routine. New commands*Sdvdhdn', Daksha', 'yiratna'* were first used there. But Doctorji was not blind to practical needs and exigencies. For the physical training he did not hesitate to employ the existing English vocabulary as well as methodology. He regarded the adoption of the British conventions in this field as *dpaddharma.* In more recent times, of course, Sangh has introduced Sanskrit expressions in place of the English ones.

The tradition of commencing the daily activities with salu-tation to the *Bhagawd Dhwaj* and concluding with the prayer was instituted with a view to deepening the intellectual and emotional content of the training)The prayer then consisted of a combination of a Marathi verse and a Hindi verse. The meaning of the first part of it was as follows :

Salutations to the Motherland where I am born.

Salutations to the Hindu Land where I have been brought up.

Salutations to the Land of Dharma for which may my body fall.

To Her, I salute again and again.

For the naming of the Sangh, Doctorji arranged a *baithak* in his house on 17th April 1926. Twentysix Swayamsevaks participated in the discussion. Several names were suggested, and there was elaborate discussion about each. After the pro-cess of elimination, three names remained in the tally :

(1) Rashtriya Swayamsevak Sangh ;

(2) Jaripatakd Mandal ; and

(3) Bhdratoddharak Mandal.

The name adshtriya Swayam-sevak Sangh' was finally decided upon.

Referring to that discussion, Professor Sawalapurkar says: "Surely, Doctorji must have decided about the name of the Sangh after prolonged thought even before that *baithak.* But he gave the aspiring Swayamsevaks an opportunity to sug-gest names, so that the young enthusiasts could feel them-selves as part of the decision-making process.

A student who had just joined the college also suggested a name and spoke vehemently in support of it. Others too suggested their choices and spoke. Doctorji then suggested to me to expound the appropriateness of the name `Rashtriya Swayamsevak Sangh.' I spoke for about half an hour. Doctorji was very much pleased, and patted me on my back. Needless to say, was able to speak convincingly only because of the training that I had imbibed from Doctorji over a long period."

The name aashtriya Swayamsevak Sangh' was evolved by Doctorji after long and intense deliberation. Especially, the choice of the word 'Rashtriya' to denote the work of Hindu consolidation was intended to emphasize the fact that it is the Hindus who form the backbone of the nation in Bharat and that organization of Hindus is a task of supreme national importance.

One lamp lights up another. One inspired heart kindles another. This was how Doctorji touched the hearts of count-less Swayamsevaks and kindled in them the spark of idealism. While activities on the playground were many and varied, it was in Doctorji's house that the true character-moulding work was carried on.

Doctorji's rapport with the Swayam-sevaks was of the most intimate kind ; he evinced keen interest in the welfare of each Swayamsevak. His warmth and friendliness endeared him to every one of them, young or old. Through suggestive questions, he whetted their power of thinking, and goaded them into activity. All the Swayam-sevaks would meet once a month, and plan the programme for the ensuing month.

Doctorji desired that Swayamsevaks should, out of their own devotion to the cause, be able to act without waiting for instructions from others. Doctorji had several ways of instruct-ing the Swayamsevaks. He would ask, "Why did you take to learning lathi?"

"Suppose you learn lathi singly ?" "How many new persons can you contact and mobilize ?" Through such simple questions he would instil in them a sense of cor-porate thinking and working. When there were intelligent young men around, he asked questions such as "What is Swaraj ?"

"How many people are there who demand Swaraj, and how many are there who work for it ?" He would thus bring home to the young minds the need for more young people to actively join the movement for Swaraj. And again he would put some searching questions such as "Supposing on your way back home a policeman takes you to the station and confronts you with the question, 'You had gone to Dr. Hedgewar; what was the topic of discussion there ?' – what would you answer ?", "What makes you come to the Sangh?", and so on and gauge the Swayamsevak's sharpness of under-standing.

There is a report of a *baithak* held on 21st June 1926 recorded by Raghunathrao Bande who was the Nagpur Kciryavdha at that time. In that session Doctorji asked each Swayamsevak to state in writing his ideal, the ideal of the Sangh, and how he would organize the Sangh and its activities if he were made the Chdlak, i.e., chief.

The statements were to be handed over to Doctorji before 28th. This indicated the measure of Doctorji's concern that the Swayamsevaks should themselves think over and imbibe the Sangh ideal and pursue the Sangh activities with self-sustaining zeal and devotion.

In 1926, Doctorji initiated certain measures to instil the spirit of hard discipline in the Swayamsevaks. He requested Martandrao Jog who had retired from the army in 1920 to conduct the weekly parade of Swayamsevaks. Jog was the chief for the Congress Seva Dal also at that time ; but no party considerations existed for Doctorji.

Martandrao in a letter to Guruji later on wrote : "I am now totally one with the Sangh. It is the Sangh which has developed my personality. It was Doctorji's love which had carved out a place for me in Sangh." Doctorji also encouraged the setting up of cavalry units wherever it was possible.

Wearing of uniform during parades was made obligatory for the Swayamsevaks. Upasani, an army officer of Gwalior, used to visit Nagpur during holidays. Doctorji deputed a few Swayamsevaks to him for advanced training in physical fitness and discipline. Swayamsevak who took part in the first route march numbered 30. Stepping signals were given through the whistle on that day, and the need for the bugle was then keenly felt. And it was with great difficulty that money was raised for purchasing the first ever band instrument. The throb of joyous enthusiasm that coursed through the Swayamsevaks at the first sound of the bugle truly defies description !

A special training programme for selected Swayamsevaks was also begun in May 1927. The object of the programme was to equip the Swayamsevaks to enable them to carry on the Sangh activities on their own, wherever they might go. The programme was therefore called the Officers Training Camp-0. T. C. In the first camp of 1927, there were only 17 participants. There were physical culture sessions from 5 to 9 in the morning and again in the evening. The afternoon hours from 12-30 to

5 p m were spent in discussion, writing, etc. There were also swimming exercises. These intensive summer train-ing camps have continued to this day under the name of 'Sangha Shiksha Varga.' Every province now has its own separate camp.

Doctorji was keen on developing the various necessary qualities among the Swayamsevaks. He was very particular that the allotted job should be executed well and efficiently by every one of them. A worker should never try to shift his responsibility to another, nor should he beat his own drum when the work is finished. Doctorji would narrate an experi-ence of his own in this connection. Once, after a feast at Raja Lakshmanrao's palace, chewing lime was exhausted, with only *pan*going round. Lakshmanrao ordered his junior to bring lime. He in turn passed on the order to his junior. Thus the order for lime passed on from mouth to mouth, but no lime came. However, Doctorji, who was well acquainted with the household, quietly went inside and brought the lime. But the shouting for lime continued for quite some time even after that!

Doctorji had no dearth of interesting anecdotes to drive home his point. Here is one such. Once a king ordered that every one of his subjects pour before sunrise a cup of milk into a big pot in the temple. However, each one thought, "After all, every one else is pouring milk. What difference does it make if I pour a cup of water instead ? " As a result, every one poured his own quota of water. By sunrise the huge vessel was filled to the brim, with pure water and not a drop of milk !

Another weakening trait among the Hindus was the firmly rooted mentality – "I am alone, what can I do ?" Once an incident took place in Nagpur which was narrated by Doctorji to bring home the disastrous results of such an attitude.

Once, all of a sudden, a commotion started in a public meeting. A few persons stood up, some began to run and soon the rest also took to their heels helter-skelter. In that mad rush several were trampled, hundreds left their chappals and dhoties behind, and the entire audience number-ing thousands was speeding in all directions as if chased by some wild beast. The speakers and the president too did not lag behind; they too sped as fast as their legs could carry.

Later on, on enquiry it was found that it all started with a person in the middle of the meeting suddenly getting up as he felt something like a frog entering his dhoti. Persons sitting around him also got up, with one of them crying out 'snake, snake !' That was the signal for all others to join the running spree. Not one of them knew what had actually taken place : each said that because others were running he also started running ! Doctorji, who met the organizers the next day, asked them : "Let alone the audience, but why did *you* not try to control the situation ?" Each one of them replied, "What could I alone do ?" In fact, every one of the fleeing heroes was pleading the same reason – "What could I alone do ?"

The Sangh grew slowly but steadily with enrolment of young men one after another, in ever increasing numbers. Doctorji spent every single minute of his waking hours in building up the nascent organization.

Poverty continued to haunt Doctorji's household as before. It was not possible to run the household from his elder brother's meagre earnings. Because of his public activi-ties, Doctorji had an endless stream of visitors from morning right up to midnight. Hospitality, which could not be avoided, meant expense. In addition to it, Doctorji was a strict adhe-rent of *aparigraha;* no one dared to offer any financial help to him.

Raja Lakshmanrao Bhonsle, who was all admiration for Doctorji, once made a personal effort through his secretary Vasudeva Shastri Sangamkar to lessen Doctorji's financial strain. The effort failed. Nanasaheb Talatule of Sindi was a close friend of Doctorji, and Doctorji customarily spent a few days with him every year. He too sounded Doctorji a couple of times regarding financial assistance. But Doctorji remained cold. Once while in Sindi, Nanasaheb and Appaji Joshi broached the subject cautiously and told Doctorji, "Financial worry is chasing you like a shadow ; some arrangement must be made." Doctorji replied, "I shall ask for it when there is need. Help should not be felt like an obligation, and should not strain the mind. I have no objection to accepting help from people with whom I feel free, but right at present there is no need for it."

While Doctorji put his friends at ease, he continued to refuse help. Coming to know of the trying situation at Doctorji's house, Narayanrao Deshpande of Arvi and Appaji Joshi began secretly handing over fifty rupees every month to Doctorji's sister-in-law. But Doctorji soon scented it, and the practice had to be given up after two or three months.

About this time some friends of Doctorji started a company under the name of Ideal Insurance Company, and made Doctorji the chief of medical examination unit of the company. This brought a remuneration of four to five hundred rupees every year. The arrangement, which continued up to 1935-36, met Doctorji's domestic needs to some extent.

In the year 1926, for the *Ramanavami* festival, Doctorji took the Swayamsevaks, all in uniforms, to Ramtek. The Swayam-sevaks helped in organizing the huge concourse for the *darshan* of the deity, in arranging for adequate supply of water, etc. The presence of Swayamsevaks saved the pilgrims from the guiles of the Muslim moulvis, as well as from the exploitation of the *pandas*.

Though the ideal of Sangh as well as its actualization through the Shakha was conceived and worked out by Doctorji, he never regarded the Sangh as his personal creation. He always described it as a collective effort, saying, "*WE* have started the Sangh." But in order to ensure smooth opera-tion, it was unavoidable to have centralized planning and direction. For this reason, Doctorji was designated as the formal chief of the organization at a *baithak* held on 19th December 1926. The relevant resolution read : "In order to carry on the activities of the Sangh in a regular, smooth, and disciplined manner, it is essential that there should be one chief person at the helm.

For this reason, this meeting unanimously appoints Dr. Hedgewar as the chief organizer (Chalak)."

After strenuous efforts of a year and a half, the Sangh became firmly rooted in Nagpur and Wardha. Through it was shaped the technique for rejuvenating the collective social life of Hindus, which had virtually gone out of existence for the past several centuries. Wherever the Shakha was started, every evening the *Bhagawa Dhwaj* fluttered with the glow of the sacrificial fire. And full-throated chants offering every-thing at the altar of *Matribhoomi* and *Dharmabhoomi*were heard in unison from scores of hearts.

## JAI SHRI RAM: A SLOGAN THAT CHANGED POLITICAL CONTOURS OF INDIA

Jai Shri Ram literally means victory to Lord Ram, the prince of Ayodhya mentioned in various versions of Ramayana. This slogan is in the news for long. Jai Shri Ram slogan trends every other day on social media in India. In recent times, this religious slogan has hit the headlines for the wrong reasons. Raising this slogan is no longer considered religious, it is a political slogan to further the agenda of the Bharatiya Janata Party (BJP).

While the entire BJP and its ally Shiv Sena uses Jai Shri Ram slogan as a battle cry, their opponents, particularly West Bengal Chief Minister Mamata Banerjee has launched a massive campaign against it.

During Lok Sabha election, Mamata Banerjee was seen stopping her car to slam those shouting Jai Shri Ram. Her irritation with the slogan has taken an unusual turn where her opponents have started teasing her by shouting Jai Shri Ram if they see her at an event.

In May, days after Lok Sabha election results were announced, seven people were arrested in Bengal for shouting Jai Shri Ram as Mamata Banerjee's cavalcade passed through their area.

To counter the BJP's charge of Muslim appeasement, Mamata Banerjee flagged off Jagannath Puri rath yatra last week. She was greeted with chants of Jai Shri Ram from the crowd and a section of BJP supporters.

Nobel laureate Amartya Sen, too, has joined Mamata Banerjee in raising his voice against Jai Shri Ram slogan saying it is not part of Bengali culture.

All this has happened in the backdrop of cases of mob lynching in which victims belonging to Muslim community were forced to chant Jai Shri Ram by the perpetrators.

Tabrez Ansari, 24, was allegedly lynched in Jharkhand last month. He was accused of stealing a motorcycle in Seraikela Kharsawan district of the state.

Ansari was allegedly tied to a pole and beaten up with sticks by a mob that forced him to shout Jai Shri Ram after ascertaining that he was a Muslim.

This incident took place on June 17. Ansari died of his injuries on June 22. In a similar incident, a 16-year-old boy in Uttar Pradesh's Kanpur was beaten up after his assaulters found him wearing a skull cap and asked him to chant Jai Shri Ram which he refused to do at first.

## Where it all began

It is not yet clear when Jai Shri Ram entered the political space but it came to be identified with the BJP around the 1990-92 Ram temple movement, which was launched by the Vishwa Hindu Parishad (VHP) - an extended arm of the Rashtriya Swayamsevak Sangh (RSS) family. An active participant in the temple movement was BJP leader Lal Krishna Advani and his protege Narendra Modi.

But before the BJP made Jai Shri Ram slogan as its own, it was already in popular use in late 1980s courtesy the TV serial Ramayan produced by filmmaker Ramanand Sagar. The slogan, Jai Shri Ram was used in the TV serial as a battle cry by Hanuman and others in Lord Ram's expedition against

Ravaṅ, the king of Lanka who had abducted Sita, the wife of Ram.

The earlier popular slogan or chant was Sita-Ram and Siya-Ram, which were frequently used as words for greeting one another. The popularity to Sita-Ram is credited to a freedom fighter and peasant activist Baba Ramchandra, who had impressed Pandit Jawaharlal Nehru with his organisational skills.

In his autobiography, Nehru credits Baba Ramchandra for making an old cry of Sita-Ram "an almost warlike significance" and "a signal for emergencies as well as a bond between different villages".

After Ram Janmabhoomi movement of the VHP and parallel political campaign of the BJP, Sita-Ram gave way to Jai Shri Ram and became an essentially political slogan raised more during the time of elections.

## Now in Parliament, streets

Riding on the slogan of Jai Shri Ram, the BJP improved its tally in the Lok Sabha from two seats in 1984 to 85 in 1989, to 120 in 1991 and to single-largest party with 161 MPs in 1996.

With Atal Bihari Vajpayee practically in charge of the BJP between 1999 and 2004 with the responsibility to run a ruling coalition, the slogan of Jai Shri Ram retreated to form background score. The defeat of the BJP in 2004 and in 2009 forced the BJP to rethink its strategy.

The slogan returned with greater vigour in 2014 even though the party - with Narendra Modi calling the shots - did not give much space to construction of Ram temple at Ayodhya. Jai Shri Ram was a frequently used slogan in BJP's rallies.

As prime ministerial candidate, Modi addressed an election rally in Faizabad, the district that holds Ayodhya, which many believe to be the birthplace of Lord Ram. Though, Modi, in 2014 election rally, did not talk about Ram temple, he did refer to Lord Ram a number of times in his speech with the crowd chanting Jai Shri Ram.

Modi did not go to Ayodhya until May 2019, when he addressed an election rally. Speaking at the outskirts of Ayodhya, Modi talked about defeating terrorism and New India but Jai Shri Ram was the dominant cry in the rally.

The slogan has made to the Lok Sabha now. BJP members heckled Trinmool Congress (TMC) MPs in the Lok Sabha shouting Jai Shri Ram when they came for taking oath as newly elected members of the house in June. This came as a reaction to Mamata Banerjee's opposition to the slogan, which she said was a threat to Bangla culture.

The BJP has made substantial gains in West Bengal where Jai Shri Ram has become the cry for galvanising party cadres against the ruling TMC. The BJP has alleged that one of its workers was lynched by TMC members for chanting Jai Shri Ram.

## BJP'S TRANSITION FROM RAM TO REFORM TO RAM

The year was 1989. The first general election in which the Bharatiya Janata Party's (BJP's) manifesto explicitly talked about reconstructing the Ram temple in Ayodhya. "By not allowing the rebuilding of the Ram Mandir in Ayodhya, on the lines of Somnath Mandir built by the Government of India in 1948, it has allowed tensions to rise, and gravely strained social harmony," the party's manifesto that year stated.

The year 1989 was in many ways the BJP's chance at redemption after its predecessor Bharatiya Jana Sangh got its first shot of power along with its socialist allies after Emergency. In 1984, the party had managed to win just two seats in the parliamentary elections. The Congress, riding high on a sympathy wave following Indira Gandhi's assassination, swept the country by winning 404 out of the 533 seats.

So, BJP's redemption song in 1989 was going to be the Ram Mandir. With mandir on its mind, the BJP won 85 seats, and so began the party's push for a Ram temple in Ayodhya, with none other than L K Advani leading the charge with his Rath Yatra.

The VP Singh-led National Front government that tried to throw a spanner in Advani's Rath Yatra was derailed after the BJP withdrew support following Advani's arrest at Samastipur in Bihar while galvanising foot soldiers for the Ram temple in Ayodhya.

The BJP's egression from the National Front government set the stage for yet another election in 1991. The 1991 elections, widely dubbed as the Mandir vs Mandal elections, was perhaps when the Ram temple pitch in the BJP reached a crescendo.

Yes, 1989 was the year when Mandir found a mention in BJP's manifesto for the first time. But its decibel still hadn't reached the feverish pitch that came in 1991.

The BJP's electoral push was largely powered by the ammunition it had against the then prime minister, Rajiv Gandhi. And Gandhi had given his principal opposition quite a few of them – Bofors, India's humiliation in Sri Lanka and economic regression, among other things.

The BJP minced no words while describing him in the run-up to the 1989 elections in its manifesto, "Everything Rajiv Gandhi touches ends up in a bloody mess. A man who waded to his office through the blood-soaked streets of Delhi will be leaving behind a gory legacy. This country is not safe in the hands of such a man or such a party."

But by 1991 the BJP was selling itself to Indian voters as the only viable alternative to the Congress. And central to this sales pitch was Ram Mandir, firmly entrenched in the party's strategy to make it stand out in India's highly polarised political landscape.

The party's pitch was retrofitted appropriately in 1991 to tell voters that building a Ram temple in Ayodhya was righting of historical wrongs. To build a Ram temple would end the centuries old virulence and distrust between Hindus and

Muslims. The party's election manifesto read: "BJP firmly believes that construction of Ram Mandir is a symbol of the vindication of our cultural heritage and national self-respect.

For BJP it is purely a national issue and it will not allow any vested interests to give it a sectarian and communal colour. The party is committed to build Shri Ram Mandir at Janmasthan by relocating superimposed Babri structure with due respect."

The BJP's attempt to storm to power on the back of such strong assertions of Hindu pride suffered a setback with the assassination of Rajiv Gandhi after the first phase of polling. Election analysis of the time shows that following Rajiv Gandhi's assassination, after the first phase of polling was held on May 20, 1991, the vote polled by the Congress in India's most electorally crucial state improved by five per cent in the second phase.

Riding on the Ram Mandir wave, the BJP won 52 of the 85 seats in Uttar Pradesh – almost half of all the seats it won nationally. This was a significant vindication of BJP's temple politics. In 1989, the party had won just eight seats in Uttar Pradesh.

By the time the 1996 elections approached, the demolition of the Babri Masjid and the ensuing communal riots had singed the nation. For the first time since 1984, the BJP introduced Hindutva in its electoral discourse and started expounding the concept of 'Bharatvarsha' as the true identity of a united India.

In the background of the deadly post-Babri communal riots, the party sold Hindutva as a principle that alone could preserve the unity and integrity of India. In the party's own words, Hindutva was "a collective endeavour to protect and re-energise the soul of India, to take us into the next millennium as a strong and prosperous nation. Hindutva is also the antidote to the shameful efforts of any section to benefit at the expense of others."

For the BJP, the ultimate vision of Hindutva would be realised only after the construction of a Ram temple in Ayodhya.

The BJP's 1996 manifesto set forth the agenda: "We hold that only by recognising the limitless strength of cultural nationalism can the nation be moulded.

When the BJP joined the movement for the construction of the Ram Mandir at Ayodhya, it was to strengthen just these foundations. On coming to power, the BJP government will facilitate the construction of a magnificent Shri Ram Mandir in Ayodhya which will be a tribute to Bharat Mata.

This dream moves millions of people in our land; the concept of Rama lies at the core of their consciousness." A similar vision was set forth by the BJP in its 1998 manifesto as well.

The years of political uncertainty that followed the 1996 elections led the BJP on a different trajectory altogether in 1999 after Atal Bihari Vajpayee's infamous 13-day government failed to muster the numbers in Parliament.

The Kargil war, largely perceived as India's victory over Pakistan's aggression with Vajpayee leading the charge meant that Hindutva and Ram Mandir were completely dropped from the BJP's manifesto for the 1999 elections held a couple of months after the culmination of the conflict.

The BJP's cultural nationalism rhetoric of the past completed disappeared off the party's discourse. For the first time since 1989, Ram and the politics of Mandir were relegated to the background in favour of words like administrative reforms, trade & commerce and price stability.

From a discourse that sought to highlight the failures of the Congress party, the BJP now overwhelmingly focussed on its own model of economic metamorphosis that revolved around an 'India built by Indians'.

But BJP's economic model failed to woo voters. By 2002-03, India's GDP growth plummeted to 3.8 per cent. The BJP government failed to arrest India's rising unemployment rate. By 2004, unemployment rates were above 8 per cent – at the same level it was in the early 1980s. The Babri demolition and Mandir politics that had now faded from public memory found no resonance with Indian voters. Sensing that economic gloom would spell its doom, the party reverted to Ram Mandir – atleast on paper.

The party re-affirmed its commitment to build a Ram temple in Ayodhya in the light of a judicial order to maintain status quo at the disputed site. The BJP's 2004 manifesto stated, "As Maryada Purushottam, Ram is an inspiring cultural symbol of India. His birthplace in Ayodhya is also associated with the religious sentiments of crores of Hindus.

The BJP remains committed to its stand that the judiciary's verdict in this matter should be accepted by all. However, we believe that dialogue, and a negotiated settlement in an atmosphere of mutual trust and goodwill, are the best way of achieving this goal." The BJP sought to re-sell itself through the 'India Shining 'campaign but failed to sell the proposition to Indian voters.

The BJP had no clear answer to what would revive its fortunes. The Congress was at the peak of its socialist powers from 2004 to 2009 with its various social sector programmes redistributing wealth to India's rural population. This meant that the BJP wouldn't get another chance of power at least till 2014.

In 2009, when the United Progressive Alliance – 2 (UPA-2) government led by the Congress stormed back to power, the BJP had already reduced Ram temple to the footnotes of its electoral discourse. The construction of a Ram temple at Ayodhya was now competing with other issues that the BJP wanted to project as preserving India's cultural heritage.

Now Ram Mandir was being spoken in the same terms as cleaning the Ganga, saving India's thorium reserves, saving cows and calves, supporting religious monasteries, saving Waqf properties from illegal encroachments and preventing archeological sites from public vandalism. Hindutva as the party's core philosophy that was last reiterated in 1998 failed to even a find a mention.

In 2014, the BJP's election manifesto committee headed by Murli Manohar Joshi further diluted the Hindutva pitch in the run-up to the elections. Hindutva was never uttered. The BJP would now 'explore all possibilities within the constitutional framework' for the construction of a Ram Mandir.

The BJP's political whirlwind in the 1990s around Ram Mandir looked like having sailed into the doldrums. Instead, the quest of power now revolved around one man – Narendra Modi. Political slogans like 'Sabka Saath, Sabka Vikas' and 'Ek Bharat, Shreshta Bharat' now resounded in the party's corridors. At the core of BJP's new vision of India were administrative, institutional and electoral reforms.

Ram was spoken in hushed voices before the 2014 elections and the construction of his temple in Ayodhya wasn't meant to be a vote generator for the BJP. But these were reiterations before the elections.

Once in power BJP leaders and prominent personalities like Uttar Pradesh chief minister Yogi Adityanath have openly projected the return of *Ram rajya* (rule of Ram).

The BJP may not be shouting from elevated pulpits any more, but rebuilding a temple for Ram allegedly annihilated by India's first Mughal emperor is not a dream the party wants to silently relegate to the background.

## HOW RAM MANDIR MOVEMENT SHAPED INDIAN POLITICS

History is often all about 'what if? The answer to this question determines the course of events that, in turn, determine the course of history. Twenty-five years after Ayodhya became a household word, setting into motion a deep social and profound cultural churn, I wonder what if a slumbering dispute was not awakened by revivalists seeking to set right historical wrongs and restoring to Hindus what belonged to them but was under occupation of, putting it bluntly, squatters? After all, for close to four decades none had agitated for an early resolution of the dispute or demanded the opening of the locked doors of what Muslims called Babri Masjid, a mosque raised on the ruins of a destroyed temple by Mir Baqi, believed to be from Tashkent, to honour Babur the Invader.

Hindus believed the mosque was built after destroying a temple commemorating Ram Janmabhoomi, the birthplace of Sri Ram. The walls of Babri Masjid bore tell-tale signs of the destruction that preceded its construction - disfigured stone engravings and pillars that can be seen at many other sites were razed to build mosques by Islamic invaders and Mughal rulers.

Would LK Advani then have become the legendary hero of the Ram Janmabhoomi movement, the defining moment of independent India's quest for nationhood? Or, we could ask, what if Advani had not pushed the BJP into associating with the Ram Mandir movement through a presidential resolution at the National Executive meeting in Palampur, and then embarked upon a Somnath to Ayodhya Ram Rath Yatra, perched atop a converted Toyota pick-up truck, the first of its kind of political mobilisation for a religious cause?

And what if he had not been arrested at Samastipur but allowed to reach Ayodhya? But as the idiom goes, if ifs and buts were pots and pans there would be no work for tinkers' hands. Idle speculation over what may have been is irrelevant 25 years after popular anger felled the monument meant to glorify Babur, much as statues honouring the memory of tyrants, despots, racists and slave drivers have been and are being pulled down across the world. I was drawn to the Ayodhya dispute, unfolding a long distance away from Kolkata after reading stories on the VHP calling for Ram Janmabhoomi's restoration along with Gyanvapi in Kashi and Krishna Janmabhoomi in Mathura tucked away in the inside pages of Delhi newspapers.

That nascent interest took me to Ayodhya on an exploratory visit. It was also a learning experience. A cocooned existence restricted to urban confines had not quite prepared me for the intensity of faith that existed in the heartland. Through 1988-1991 I kept returning to Ayodhya, writing about the VHP's, and later the BJP's mobilisation of opinion and support for a cause that triggered the biggest mass movement, uniting Hindus across caste and community divisions, overriding language and sectarian barriers.

The VHP would call for kar seva and volunteers would gather in Ayodhya in thousands. The authorities would strike a compromise and convince the VHP to put off their programme. Rajiv Gandhi, sensing the mounting Hindu disquiet after his government subverted the Shah Bano judgment and banned Salman Rushdie's The Satanic Verses, had the locked doors of the disputed structure reopened.

A court decision that was not forthcoming for decades miraculously happened overnight. In 1989, Rajiv Gandhi launched the Congress's election campaign from Ayodhya, signalling his and his party's position on the issue, if only to drown the increasingly strident allegations of corruption against him and his cronies. Bofors was only one of the many deals agitating people those days. It didn't quite help him. He lost the election and VP Singh came to power, supported by both Left and Right, an arrangement that was destined to collapse. It did after Advani was arrested and Singh went back on his comment, "Arrey bhai, wahan masjid hai hi kahan?"

Standing on the Ram Chabutra with Mark Tully and Manoj Raghuvanshi and other members of the Newstrack crew on November 2, 1990, I looked in amazement at the milling crowds. Thousands of people had gathered for kar seva, or temple construction work, in front of the disputed structure.

Over the previous two days, they had poured into Ayodhya, defying prohibitory orders and curfew. Mulayam Singh Yadav, then chief minister of Uttar Pradesh, had boastfully said the security cordon was so tight even a bird would not be able to get through. But that did not deter the faithful.

Many swam across Sarayu, others walked through fields, a continuous stream of people kept entering Ayodhya, some in the dead of night evading security pickets. When the security forces opened fire, we were taken aback. It was like firing at a dense mass of human beings. A sadhu standing next to me was hit by a bullet on his forehead; he crumbled and fell. I doubt I have experienced similar chilling fear as I did that early-winter afternoon.

The crowd went berserk, some kar sevaks clambered atop the main dome of the structure, they were shot and came tumbling down. A helicopter appeared in the sky, hovering over where we stood. Extricating ourselves from the chaos took both time and effort. Later that evening, while telexing my story at the small post office in Faizabad, I was overwhelmed by both anger and grief.

That was the day when the destruction that was wrought two years later on December 6, 1992, became an inevitable denouement of the Ayodhya movement. It was destined to be so in the absence of political wisdom that was in extremely short supply after PV Narasimha Rao ascended the masnad of Delhi. This is also why I totally, wholly disagree with those who sing paeans to Rao as a wise ruler who ruled wisely. He did not. What if he had not tried to stop the kar seva on that fateful December day when India changed forever?

## THE EMERGENCE OF THE HINDU NATIONALISM AND THE SANGH PARIVAR

The origin of the idea of the Hindu Rashtra lies in the mid to late nineteenth century, in the British colonial period and is connected with the names of Vivekananda, Dayanand Saraswati and Aurobindo Ghose. But it must be noted that it is highly problematic to trace the historical origins of Hindu nationalism since Hindu nationalism itself claims legitimacy in the writings of this period. Vivekananda has thus for example become a crucial icon of the Hindu nationalist discourse, though the Ramakrishna Mission he founded has distanced itself from the Hindu nationalism (cf. Bhatt; Mukta 2000). But the birth of Hindutva itself can be dated from 1920s when the founding text of Hindu nationalism and a *definition* of *Hindutva* – Vinayak Damodar Savarkars *Hindutva – or who is a Hindu*? (1923) – was written. *Hindutva* can be translated as 'Hinduness', i.e. *the essence of being Hindu*. "Hindutva is fundamentally an empty signifier that has become extraordinarily politically potent" (Bhatt; Mukta 2000:413) and serves as a great example of the invention of a primordial tradition that is supposed to stand at the core of the contemporary identity politics. *Hindutva* is associated with *common blood* resp. *'race', jati, Vedic-Aryan forefathers*, and makes use of different ethnic, religious, 'racial' and nationalist motives, but does not use any of these exclusively – its nature is thus fundamentally eclectic. In 1924 the most important male nationalistic organization – the Rashtriya Swayamsevak Sangh (RSS) – was founded by Keshav Baliram Hedgewar, while Golwalkar is considered as the ideological father, the great "guruji". This organization is still at the core of organizations that are allied to Hindutva ideology (the so called *Sangh Parivar*), it is a highly centralized semi-paramilitary organization devoted to recruitment and training of young men for service to the Hindu Nation. Later numerous offshoot organizations were created, the most important ones were: the Jana Sangh in 1951, which was the precursor of the current Bharatiya Janata Party (BJP) and the Vishwa Hindu Parishad (VHP) in 1964. This 'family' of organizations which RSS created is often labeled as Sangh Parivar, and these organizations are the largest body of organizations in Indian civil society. The BJP formed in 1998 its first shaky coalition government which was followed by another coalition government in 1999 which was in power until 2004.

## Demonizing the Muslim Other

The *Muslim Other* plays in the Hindutva ideology a crucial role in defining, delineating and creating a boundary around the Hindu community; the Muslim Other is usually portrayed as the absolute opposite of the Hindu, where the Hindu is the educated, civilized, tolerant, rational, modern, caring etc. This polarization is also present in the distinction between semitic and non-semitic religions which is being continually emphasized. The well-known case of the Ayodhya (van der Veer 1994; Talbot 2000), the recovery of Ram's birthplace from the hands of its Muslim "occupants" and the building of a new temple became another strong and potent symbol of the restoration of the Hindu nation and its pride and of demonizing the Other. Muslims are also presented as a "pampered" minority with special reservations and since the era of the 'Mandalisation' of politics, when special reservations were assigned to different groups of the Indian society – which was apprehended as dividing the Hindus – the Muslims began to be perceived as greater a threat to the Hindu nation; the stereotypes and prejudices were strengthened. Secularism is in this context conceived of as overriding Hindu rights (and labeled as 'pseudo-secularism') since it is connected with appeasement of minority claims and favoring of Muslims, secularism is thus "portrayed as a source of national weakness" (Talbot 2000:176). Another way how to create and strengthen the boundary between Hindus and Muslims is the strategy of using Hindu women's bodies and portraying Muslim men as violators of the Hindu women and thus the evil and threat to the Hindu nation. The nuclearization of India serves as another mighty symbol and an agent of Othering between India and Pakistan.

## *Idealized Men and Women as Portrayed in the Ideology of Hindutva*

Men and female bodies hand in hand with cultural representations of femininity and masculinity serve as powerful symbols and metaphors for depicting a nation. In the discourse of Hindu nationalism two images of manliness and masculinity are especially highly celebrated – i.e. the image of Hindu soldier and warrior monk (Banerjee 2006) – and have great impact also on women, who are trying to respond properly to the call of nationalism that glorifies muscular strength, moral fortitude, readiness to go to the battle and defend the nation against the enemy, the Other. Women can thus within the frame of this ideology play either roles of heroic mothers, chaste wives or celibate warriors (Banerjee 2006). The gendered power imbalances as such are not challenged and the patriarchal Hindu family remains in the ideology of Hindutva the primal reference point.

### *Hindu Religiopolitics and Public Rituals*

Since the primary aim of the Hindu Religiopolitics is to unite all Hindus and overcome all possible divisions within the Indian society, the ever-present polytheism and hierarchichal differentiation within *Hinduism* is necessarily perceived as a great problem that must be dealt with. It is highly problematic to translate all the multiple – regional, caste, family – gods and goddesses, beliefs and practices into symbols of unity, when these signify belonging to a definite group or category. The Hindu nationalist leaders are perfectly conscious of this situation and have therefore chosen several deities that appeal to as great number of people as possible and that symbolize best the pan-Hindu unity. The pantheon of the 'celestial nationalists' thus consists of Rama, Ganesha, the 'epic' Krishna, Durga and others (Fuller 2004). The Hindu unity is promoted in public rituals and worships of these gods and in diverse festivals, which also serve as a manifestation of Hindu strength and physical control. "Converting private devotion into demonstrative public worship has been a consistent strategy of Hindu nationalists, whose broader aim is to transform the polity and civil society, and the public sphere as a whole." (Fuller 2004:287).

## ANALYSIS

One of the world's most ancient religions is a force in modern Indian politics. Hinduism, the avowed faith of Prime Minister Narendra Modi, forms the philosophical bedrock of his ruling Bharatiya Janata Party (BJP). It is also the religion of 80 percent of India's nearly 1.3 billion people, making it the third-largest faith tradition globally, after Christianity and Islam. Of course, despite its overwhelming demographic presence, Hinduism never became India's official religion. Instead, India, as outlined in its constitution, has remained an officially secular nation, home to a dizzying array of philosophies and interpretations, movements and sects, and significant communities of religious-minority Muslims, Christians and Sikhs. The architects of the secular and pluralistic concept of Indian nationhood that sought to embrace this diversity were Mahatma Gandhi and Jawaharlal Nehru, India's first prime minister. The Indian National Congress (INC) party that they led has generally followed, if not perfectly, the founders' philosophy to this day.

However, in recent months a surging wave of Hindu nationalism has challenged this bedrock philosophy, touching off a raging national debate about the fundamental nature of India's political identity. This so-called intolerance debate, which has pitted traditional pluralism against a more strident, conservative, religious-based conception of Indian nationhood, has counted among its controversies the February arrest of doctoral student Kanhaiya Kumar, a political activist, on charges of sedition. The arrest sparked nationwide protests, with activists accusing the BJP of undermining democracy and free speech by imposing a divisive and heavy-handed brand of right-wing Hindu nationalism.

According to its more hard-line proponents, Hinduism should supplant secularism as the guiding principle of Indian society. Taken to its extreme, this would entail the political and cultural subordination of the country's Christian and Muslim populations. While this is unlikely to happen in the near term, even a partial implementation of this vision is cause for concern in a country whose history is punctuated by gruesome episodes of religious violence — often between its Hindu majority and Muslim minority. The intensifying clash between the philosophies and the resulting political ramifications will undermine Modi's already languishing reform agenda, deepen the country's political polarization, and temper economic growth this year.

## The Origins of the Current Dispute

One of the most coherent responses to British colonialism in India in the early 20th century came from the Hindu right. Some Hindus believed that the decentralized nature of their religion had enabled outside powers, including the Mughal and British empires, to rule India for a combined 421 years until independence in 1947. In 1925, an Indian doctor named K.B. Hedgewar formed the Rashtriya Swayamsevak Sangh (RSS) to promote a more centralized and assertive interpretation of Hinduism. The RSS believed that the 1947 partition of India that created Pakistan exemplified the inadequacies of Nehru's secular policies, leading India to sacrifice a part of its territory to appease Muslims. The RSS feared that Indian secularists would further partition the nation to give other minorities self-determination, leading to the disintegration of the holy land.

Hedgewar envisioned India as a distinctly Hindu nation in which the populace was united around a common and defensible interpretation of Hinduism. One RSS member, Nathuram Godse, was so incensed by the appeasement of Indian Muslims and the thought of a religiously pluralistic society that he assassinated Gandhi, its leading proponent, on Jan. 30, 1948. Afterward, the ruling INC banned the RSS, a prohibition that lasted only until 1949. Today, the RSS operates thousands of national chapters called shakas and claims 2 million to 5 million members. RSS members complete a 30-day curriculum of activities meant to enhance character, physical discipline, martial skills and religious devotion. The RSS is part of the Sangh Parivar, a conglomerate of Hindu nationalist organizations spanning religion, politics and defense of the faith.

## HINDU NATIONALISM AND MODI'S CHALLENGES

Modi embodies the past, present and future of the Hindu nationalist movement. When he was 8 years old, Modi joined the RSS youth wing and became a full-time volunteer at 17.

The role that Hindu nationalists play in Modi's constituency explains in part the difficulty he has had in advancing his economic reform policies. Broadly, the membership of the BJP can be divided into two wings: those with pragmatic concerns and the ones focused on religion. To maintain the support he needed to reach office, he must balance the interests of the two. Business owners and middle-class party members are generally most interested in economic reform. Ideological and religious-minded Hindu voters, while also concerned with economics, skew toward social and cultural issues. Modi must balance the interests of both groups. If he abandons his message of economic reform, he risks alienating pragmatic voters. Yet if he remains silent on those issues important to the Hindu vote — the slaughter of cattle, the status of Kashmir, the demolition of the Babri mosque — he risks the same outcome. Modi is slow to criticize his party members' more zealous and outlandish comments, such as when Sakshi Maharaj, a BJP lawmaker, characterized Gandhi's assassin as a patriot or when External Affairs Minister Sushma Swaraj called for the sacred Hindu text Bhagavad-Gita to be enshrined as India's national scripture.

In some instances, Modi himself has exploited religious fault lines for electoral gain. For instance, in early 2015 he warned that an INC win in state elections that year would possibly lead to an increase in the slaughter of cattle, which are sacred to Hindus. These comments, which followed an old electoral tactic in Indian politics, were meant to galvanize the Hindu vote by stigmatizing Muslims, who eat beef. The issue continued to simmer, and in October, a mob of Hindu villagers beat 50-year-old Muslim laborer Muhammad Ikhlaq to death with bricks after accusing him of slaughtering a cow and storing beef in his refrigerator (cattle slaughter is illegal in Uttar Pradesh, the state where Ikhlaq lived). Ikhlaq's death was followed by two more lynchings in connection with the issue of cattle slaughter. Around the same time, Manohar Lal Khattar, chief minister of the state of Haryana, said India's Muslims should stop eating beef altogether out of respect for Hindus.

## Implications for India's Future

Modi's strategic exploitation of Hindu nationalism will likely continue. Currently, the BJP holds a majority in the lower house of parliament. But if Modi is to pass the land, labor and tax reform needed to stimulate economic growth and provide jobs for the 1 million people entering the market every month, he needs to increase his party's representation in parliament's upper house, where the opposition holds a large-enough voting bloc to block legislation.

To gain the majority, the BJP must win state assembly elections. There are five such elections scheduled this year. However, the lack of progress on major economic reform means that the BJP will feel compelled to campaign on issues important to Hindu nationalists instead. The BJP has already raised the issue of Muslim migration into Assam state, which holds elections next month. Of course, Modi recognizes that by taking this approach, he will deepen political polarization and empower the INC, which will exploit the inevitable backlash arising from these campaign tactics, using it as political cover to block legislation without appearing to be obstructionist. But this is a price he is willing to pay to win elections.

The euphoria surrounding Modi's 2014 election to prime minister has waned, and the challenges of governing a nation as fragmented and diverse as India have endured. In the end, Modi will choose politics before economics and aim to preserve his voter base by appeasing both his party's pragmatic and ideological wings. He will be unable to advance his key pieces of economic reform this year, suggesting that the Indian economy, which grew at a 7.5 percent annual rate in 2015, will not reach the 8 percent growth desired by some officials this year. Moreover, Hindu nationalist sentiment will not dwindle, but rather flare up during the state assembly election campaigns. Modi will seek to temper these sentiments by offering occasional words of support, such as his remarks on the peaceful nature of Islam at the recent World Sufi Forum.

The pluralistic and tolerant side of Modi's faith is perhaps best expressed through an ancient Hindu verse that reads "truth is one, but the sages call it by many names." But if Hindu nationalism continues to grow under the BJP, Rashtriya Swayamsevak Sangh might be the name that matters most in India.

## SHAPING OF HINDU POLITY & NATIONALISM IN THE 20TH CENTURY

### Sri Aurobindo

Sri Aurobindo was a nationalist and one of the first to embrace the idea of complete political independence for India. He was inspired by the writings of Swami Vivekananda and the novels of Bankim Chandra Chattopadhyay. He "based his claim for freedom for India on the inherent right to freedom, not on any charge of misgovernment or oppression". He believed that the primary requisite for national progress, national reform, is the free habit of free and healthy national thought and action and that it was impossible in a state of servitude. He was part of the revolutionary group Anushilan Samiti and was involved in armed struggle against the British In his brief political career spanning only four years, he led a delegation from Bengal to the Indian National Congress session of 1907 and contributed to the revolutionary newspaper Bande Mataram.

In his famous *Uttarpara Speech*, he outlined the essence and the goal of India's nationalist movement thus:

*"I say no longer that nationalism is a creed, a religion, a faith; I say that it is the Sanatan Dharma which for us is nationalism. This Hindu nation was born with the Sanatan Dharma, with it, it moves and with it, it grows. When the Sanatan Dharma declines, then the nation declines, and if the Sanatan Dharma were capable of perishing, with the Sanatan Dharma it would perish."*

In the same speech, he also gave a comprehensive perspective of Hinduism, which is at variance with the geocentric view developed by the later day Hindu nationalist ideologues such as Veer Savarkar and Deendayal Upadhyay:

*"But what is the Hindu religion ? What is this religion which we call Sanatan, eternal ? It is the Hindu religion only because the Hindu nation has kept it, because in this Peninsula it grew up in the seclusion of the sea and the Himalayas, because in this sacred and ancient land it was given as a charge to the Aryan race to preserve through the ages.*

*But it is not circumscribed by the confines of a single country, it does not belong peculiarly and for ever to a bounded part of the world. That which we call the Hindu religion is really the eternal religion, because it is the universal religion which embraces all others. If a religion is not universal, it cannot be eternal. A narrow religion, a sectarian religion, an exclusive religion can live only for a limited time and a limited purpose. This is the one religion that can triumph over materialism by including and anticipating the discoveries of science and the speculations of philosophy."*

In 1910, he withdrew from political life and spent his remaining life doing spiritual exercises and writing. But his works kept inspiring revolutionaries and struggles for independence, including the famous Chittagong Uprising. Both Swami Vivekananda and Sri Aurobindo are credited with having founded the basis for a vision of freedom and glory for India in the spiritual richness and heritage of Hinduism.

CHAPTER 4

# Ayodhya Ram Mandir and Babri Masjid Dispute

## THE CONTRADICTIONS IN THE AYODHYA VERDICT

Both sides have evidence supporting their claims but the court believes the Hindu evidence is stronger

The court accepts that both Hindus and Muslims have shown evidence of worship at the Masjid after 1857.

Supreme Court judgments should be intelligible and convincing. Those are two qualities I would stress above any other. In their absence, judgments could amount to sophistry. Now, to what extent does this apply to the recent judgment on the Babri Masjid-Ram Janmabhoomi dispute?

In paragraph 796, the court sets out how it came to its verdict. "The dispute is over immovable property. The court does not decide title on the basis of faith or belief but on the basis of evidence." Let's then look at that evidence and ask is it clinching and irrefutable.

The court accepts that both Hindus and Muslims have shown evidence of worship at the Masjid after 1857. However, before that year, the court says whilst "on a preponderance of probabilities", there is evidence of Hindus worshipping in the inner structure, while this is missing in the case of Muslims. Para 786 says: "There is no account by them of possession, use or offer of namaz in the mosque between the date of construction and 1856-57 ... nor is there any account in the evidence of the offering of namaz in the mosque over this period."

For me, this is where the problem starts. Whilst claiming that there isn't "evidence of the offering of namaz", the court accepts this was a mosque that existed for over 450 years. So if it's a mosque, doesn't it follow prayers were held there? And if there is no evidence of that between 1528 and 1857, is the court claiming the mosque was defunct or disused for over 325 years? And if that's implied or assumed, how does the court explain the mosque's use for Islamic worship after 1857? But these questions are not answered.

There is one further issue. The court accepts that in 1856-57, Hindu-Muslim riots occurred over the right to worship at the Masjid and, as a result, the British erected a railing to create separate spaces for the two faiths. But isn't that proof Muslims were worshipping prior to 1857?

Now, the court relies on 18th century writings by European travellers such as Joseph Tieffenthaler, William Finch and Montgomery Martin for evidence that Hindus worshipped at the Masjid prior to 1857. But these accounts also talk of the mosque and none suggest it was defunct or disused. Surely, the accounts which provide evidence for Hindus also provide evidence for Muslims? And yet the court appears to have turned a blind eye to that.

Let me now take my argument to a different level. Since the court claims it is only arguing on the basis of evidence, I'm troubled by the fact its reasoning seems to fly in the face of history.

The court says: "The Muslims have offered no evidence to indicate that they were in exclusive possession of the inner structure prior to 1857 since the date of the construction in the 16th century." But when the mosque was built in 1528, Babar was the conqueror of India and devoutly Muslim. Later, from 1658 to 1707, Aurangzeb was emperor and said to be a bigot. Is it conceivable they would allow Hindus to pray in a mosque? And, in particular, a mosque named after Babar? Or would they have ensured exclusive Muslim possession?

If the court wants us to accept Muslims did not have "exclusive possession of the inner structure prior to 1857 since the date of the construction in the 16th century", it has to respond to this apparent clash with history.

Finally, look at this sentence from the conclusion in paragraph 800: "On a balance of probabilities, the evidence in respect of the possessory claim of the Hindus to the composite whole of the disputed property stands on a better footing than the evidence adduced by the Muslims." That clearly means that both sides have evidence supporting their claims but the court believes the Hindu evidence is better. Wasn't that grounds for splitting the site between them rather than giving it entirely to the Hindus?

Now, I admit, I'm not a lawyer and certainly not an expert on deciphering Supreme Court judgments. But, if as a citizen, I find these issues troubling, can you call the judgment intelligible and convincing? Since it's said to be based on evidence, shouldn't that, at the very least, be beyond reasonable doubt? Is it in this case?

## AYODHYA DISPUTE

The decade of 1980 will be remembered as a bloody decade with communal clashes all over the country. In a surprise development, the Supreme Court on 21st March 2017 urged the rival parties in the Ram Janamabhoomi – Babri Masjid (RJBM) case to negotiate and resolve the dispute in a spirit of give and take. The Chief Justice of India offered himself to be a mediator should both the parties agreed. The observations came on application of Subramanian Swamy seeking urgent hearing of the appeal against the order of Allahabad High Court dated 30th September 2010 in the RJBM title suit. Subramanian Swamy, a BJP leader, has no locus standi in the case and he is not a party in the Appeal. Yet the Supreme Court exercised its discretion and even asked the BJP leader to talk to all parties to the case and bring them to negotiating table.

It is not clear whether Swamy was prompted by the Prime Minister but the application seems to be made in the background of massive victory of the BJP in UP Assembly elections. Though the mandate was primarily sought for development – or *sab ka saath, sab ka vikas*, the BJP might have seen this as most opportune moment to push the construction of Ram Temple on the site where Babri Masji once stood for 464 years before it was unlawfully demolished. The parties to the Appeal before the Supreme Court did not feel the need to move the Court for urgent hearing of the case. Many other cases are pending before the Apex Court and which may be of real urgent nature. What persuaded the Court to spend its valuable time on this contentious case wherein one party to the case is in stronger position in the prevailing scenario while the other is more defensive and feeling diffident will be for the Court to satisfy itself. Litigants defending Babri Masjid title are naturally feeling extremely vulnerable and in a very weak position. Not agreeing to settle on the terms desired by the litigants who already have 2/3rds of the land in dispute according to the judgment of the Allahabad High Court and are seeking the entire land would endanger the security of the community at worst and open to charge of being intransigent at best. Several attempts were made to arrive at negotiated settlement and all of them failed.

One attempt was made by the Shankaracharya and religious leaders from Muslim community. Muslim religious leaders gave favourable statements and nod at the initiative. They were hopeful of the initiative leading to an amicable settlement with the spirit of give and take. However, the Sangh Parivar which felt that a settlement would be reached without them being involved opposed the initiative. Statements were planted in the media that Shankaracharya was a devotee of Shiv rather than Lord Ram. Shankaracharya withdrew from the initiative and the settlement did not materialize. The inhabitants of Ayodhya would have long settled the issue in the spirit of give and take had the dispute been left to them. The Head Priest of Hanumangarh, the largest temple in Ayodhya, Mahant Gyandas has organized *iftaars* for Muslims inside his temple and repaired Mosque situated on the land owned by his temple with their funds. Muslims have invited Mahant Gyandas, inside their mosques. Such was the amicable relations between Hindus and Muslims of Ayodhya during the peak of Ram temple agitation. The agitators were mobilized from outside.

The priest of Ram Janmabhoomi Temple – Mahant Lal Das too opposed the VHP-BJP led Ram Janmabhoomi movement. Mahant Lal Das was assassinated and his assassins have remained a mystery. The final attempt to settle the issue was made by Hashim Ansari, the oldest litigant in the dispute, a simple man living in hut. Hashim Ansari died a few months ago after the Judgment of the Allahabad High Court. He was disillusioned with the Judgement and wanted to settle the issue. Hashim Ansari and the rival litigant Mahant Ramchandra Das Paramhans of the Ram Janamabhoomi Nyas were good friends and remained so till the Mahant died in 2003. Hashim Ansari told this author that they would not only eat from the same plate, they would also travel in the same vehicle to and fro Lucknow Bench of Allahabad High Court where the title suit was being heard. Had it been left to the people of Ayodhya, they would have in all likelihood resolved the dispute in the spirit of give and take. The inhabitants of Ayodhya enjoy the bonds of brotherhood and sisterhood and were vary of Sangh Parivar's mobilization for construction of Ram Janambhoomi Temple as it disturbed peace of the town for days and they would lose their livelihood. The earlier negotiations failed primarily due to intransigence of the Sangh Parivar for whom the issue was more of a political weapon which they would pull out during elections rather than issue of faith.

If negotiations are held today, those defending the title of Waqf Board would be under extreme political and social pressure to give up whatever little they have got from the judgement of the Allahabad High Court. Whereas Nirmohi Akhada and Ram Lalla, who have got 2/3rds of the land parcel would be negotiating for the rest of the 1/3rdof the land with the political might of the State and Centre backing them. Does the Supreme Court want a "settlement" between hugely unequal parties or justice in accordance with the law? One of the legal doctrine is "he who wants justice should approach the courts come with clean hands" Those who mobilized and demolished the Babri Mosque cannot be said to have approached the court with clean hands. A demand to construct a protective roof against the vagaries of nature on the *chabutra* outside the Mosque but within the precincts in the year 1885 enlarged to demanding the entire Mosque land and construction of Ram Janmabhoomi Temple on it not on the basis of law of the land, but on the basis of faith. While the claims did not succeed with the British Colonial government, it is the secular state that progressively gave in to the demands of manipulated faith of the cultural and political elite claiming to represent the entire majority community. The Allahabad High Court too ruled on the basis of unproven faith rather than on the basis of law of adverse possession.

## From Ram Chabutra to claim over Babri Masji: failure of Justice

Let us examine this story. There are no two opinions that in the year 1528 a mosque was built by Mir Baqi, one of the Governors of the Mughal Emperor Babar. The Sangh Parivar maintains that this mosque was built after destroying a Ramjanmabhoomi temple, which existed on the land whereas the Muslim political leaders as well as most reputed historians of integrity insist that there is no credible proof that there was any Ramjanmabhoomi temple.

The District Gazetteer of 1905 notes that till 1855, Hindus and Muslims prayed in the same premises that is now contentious Ramjanmabhoomi-Babri Masjid site. After 1857 rebellion, an outer enclosure was put in front of the mosque and the Hindus who were forbidden access to the inner yard raised an outer platform (chabutra). The first signs of the dispute sometime in 1861 appear too close after the 1857 rebellion to warrant such a conclusion. A British officer who was officiating as a Commissioner and Settlement Officer, Faizabad, in 1861 wrote a book *A Historical Sketch of Fyzabad Tehsil Including the Former Capital Ayodhya and Fyzabad.* The book was based on what he found was "locally affirmed" and his own surmises - Ayodhya must at least have possessed a fine temple in the Janmasthan. The dispute was initially only regarding Chabutra adjoining the Babri Masjid. He further wrote: *"It seems that in 1528 Babar visited Ayodhya and under his orders this ancient temple was destroyed".* There is slender evidence to conclude that Babar ever passed Ayodhya.

Hindu priests wanted a temple constructed on the Chabutra to be able to conduct their worship without vagaries of weather, as Chabutra was an open platform.

In the year 1885, one Mahant Raghubar Dass, claiming himself to be the Mahant of Janam Asthan had filed a suit on 19-1-1885 in the Court of Sub-Judge Faizabad, Pandit Hari Kishan (Suit No. 61/280 of 1885). It was alleged in the said Suit that Chabutra of Janam Asthan was a platform of 21 feet towards East and West and 17 feet towards North and South. It was further alleged in the said Suit that as there was no building over it and the Mahant and other priests had to face grave vagaries of the weather. The Mahant therefore wanted permission to construct a temple over the said Chabutra of 21 X 17 feet, which had been prohibited by the Deputy Commissioner of Faizabad. The Suit 61/280 of 1885 was dismissed on 24-12-1885 by Pandit Hari Kishan, Sub-Judge of

Faizabad. Relying upon the site plan prepared by Gopal Sahai, the Learned Sub-Judge observed:

*"The entrance to the enclosure is under a gateway on which appears the superscription of "Allah". Immediately on the left is the platform or chabutra of masonary occupied by the Hindus. On this is a small superstructure of wood in the form of a tent. This chabutra is said to indicate the birthplace of Ram Chander. ...*

*"... in between the mosque and Chabutra, there is a wall...and it is clear that there are separate boundaries between the mosque and Chabutra and this fact is also supported by the fact that there is boundary line built by the Government before the rent dispute".*

It was further observed that if temple was allowed to be constructed on the Chabutra at such a place, then there would be sound of bells of the temple and *sankh*, when both Hindus and Muslims passed from the same way. If permission was given to Hindus for constructing temple then one day or the other there would be rioting and thousands of people would be killed.

Thus, the learned Sub-Judge opined that awarding permission to construct the temple at this juncture is to lay the foundation of riot and murder, hence in view of the policy and also in view of justice the reliefs claimed should not be granted. The Sub-Judge also rejected the reliefs sought on the ground of adverse possession and observed that:

*"It is most unfortunate that a masjid should have been built on the land specially held sacred by the Hindus. But as that occurred 356 years ago, it is too late now to remedy the grievance. All that can be done is to maintain the parties in status quo."*

The Appeal of Mahant Raghubar Dass against the judgement of the Learned Sub-Judge before the District Judge of Faizabad and the Judicial Commissioner, W. Young (Civil appeal No. 27 of 1886) was also dismissed. In his judgement dated November 1, 1886 observed:

*"This spot is situated within the precinct of the grounds surrounding a mosque erected some 350 years age owing to the bigotry and tyranny of the emperor who purposely chose this holy spot, according to Hindu legend as the site of his mosque. The Hindus seem to have got very limited rights of access to certain spots within the precinct adjoining the mosques and they have for a series of years been persistently trying to increase those rights and to erect buildings on two spots in the enclosure namely (1) Sita ki rasoi (kitchen of Sita) and (2) Ram Chander ki Janmabhoomi (birthplace of Lord Rama)... I am further of the opinion that the civil courts have properly dismissed the plaintiff's claim."*

Two things are to be noted here. The suit as well as the Appeal was rejected on grounds of adverse possession. The dispute was about the Chabutra situated in the precinct on which a building was sought to be erected and never the mosque itself. As set out in the judgement, certain elements from the Hindu community tried to persistently increase their rights - in the second and third round to the entire mosque itself. Even though the reliefs prayed for were not granted, the judgement tried not to antagonise the Hindu Community entirely by mentioning the atrocities of the tyrannical and bigot emperors (from whose tyrannical rule the colonial rulers claim to have "liberated" the sub-continent). It is not clear on what supporting evidence did the judges observe that the tyrannical Mughal Emperor out of bigotry demolished a temple 350 years ago to build a mosque in his name. Thus in spite of the judgements, the Ramjanmabhoomi-Babri Masjid controversy remained very much alive.

In 1934 riots, which were triggered off by the slaughter of a cow in the village of Shahjahanpur near Ayodhya, riotous mobs demolished part of the wall surrounding the mosque and damaged the domes. However, the mosque was restored at the cost of the Government.

Till 22nd December1949, Muslims offered namaz in the Babri Masjid. However, on the night of 22nd December 1949, idols of Bhagwan shri Ramchandra were surreptitiously smuggled and installed inside the mosque. Constable Mata Prasad at Ayodhya Police Station reported the incident next day morning and the District Magistrate K.K. Nayar sent the following message to the Chief Minister and Chief Secretary by radiogram:

*"A few Hindus entered Babri Masjid at night when the masjid was deserted and installed a deity there, DM and SP and force at spot. Situation under control, Police picket of 15 persons was on duty at night but did not apparently act."*

K. K. Nayar, who later contested elections on the then Jan Sangh ticket, wrote in his diary:

*"The crowd made a most determined attempt to force entry. The lock was broken and policemen rushed off their legs. All of us, officers and men, somehow pushed the crowd back and held the gate. The gate was secured and locked with a powerful lock brought from outside and the police force was strengthened."*

Nayar also wrote to the Chief Secretary that in grave risk of large-scale riots it would not be desirable to attempt the removal of the idols through governmental agency. He also advised against stopping *bhog* and *aarti* but advised that the present *pujari* should be changed. Markandey Singh, Magistrate, First Class, and Additional City Magistrate, Faizabad-cumAyodhya after being "fully satisfied from information received from police sources and from other credible sources that a dispute between Hindus and Muslims of Ayodhya over the question rights of proprietorship and worship in the building claimed variously as Babri Masjid and Janmabhoomi Mandir, Mohalla Ram Kot, within the local limits of my jurisdiction, is likely to lead to a breach of peace," ordered the attachment of the "said buildings" under Section 145 CrPC and appointed Priya Dutt Ram, Chairman, Municipal Board, Faizabad-cum-Ayodhya, as receiver to arrange for the care of the property in dispute on December 29, 1949.

Then a civil suit number 2 of 1950 was filed on January 16, 1950 by Gopal Singh Visharad in the court of the civil judge,

Faizabad, praying for a declaration that he is entitled to worship and visit without obstruction or disturbance Shri Bhagwan Ram Chandra and others installed in the Janmabhoomi and a perpetual injunction restraining the defendants from removing these idols. Amongst the eight defendants were five Muslims and the state of Uttar Pradesh, the Deputy Commissioner and the Police Superintendent of Faizabad.

The civil judge N.N. Chadha, granted an interim injunction on 16/1/1950 allowing *puja* and *darshan* though the rights were in dispute. The Order was later modified on 19/1/1950 as follows:

*"The parties are hereby restrained by means of the temporary injunction to refrain from removing the idols in question from the site in dispute and from interfering with the puja etc. as at present carried on."*

In addition to the above suit, three more suits relating to disputes over receivership and waqf were filed during the intervening period. The Nirmohi Akhara also staked its claim for ownership of the disputed land.

A lawyer of Ayodhya, Umesh Chandra Pandey quietly moved an application on 25/1/86 in the Court of Sadar Munsif, Hari Shakar Dubey seeking directions restraining the respondents from imposing any sort of restrictions or hurdles in the *darshan* and *puja*, etc. of Lord Rama and others in the Janambhoomi offered by him and other members of the Hindu community. The Application was in regular Suit no. 2 of 1950.

The Munsif refused to pass orders on the ground that the file of the leading case along with which the above suit was consolidated was requisitioned in the High Court. Umesh Chandra had no *locus standi* in the above suit, and had not even impleaded all the defendants in the suit as party respondents in the application. Umesh Chandra filed an appeal against the order of the Munsif before the District Judge, Faizabad, K.M. Pandey on 31/1/86. The district judge rejected the application of the Mohammed Hashim to be impleaded as a party in the appeal. The District Judge recorded the statements of District Magistrate, Indu Kumar Pandey and Senior Superintendent of Police, Karma Vir Singh to the effect that:

*"...it is not necessary to keep the locks at the gates for the purpose of maintaining law and order or the safety of the idols. This appears to be an unnecessary irritant to the applicant and other members of the community. There does not appear o be any necessity to create an artificial barrier between the idol and the devotees. It appears that the opposite parties have remained a prisoner of indecision for the last 35 years. Somebody in his wisdom thought fit to put locks at the gates at any point of time and nobody since then has seen whether there is any necessity to retain locks or not".*

The District judge then observed:

*"after having heard the parties it is clear that the members of the other community, namely the Muslims, are not going to be affected by any stretch of imagination if the locks of the gates were opened and the idols inside the premises are allowed to be seen and worshipped by the pilgrims and devotees. It is undisputed that the premises are presently in the court's possession and that for the last 35 years Hindus have had an unrestricted right or worship as a result of the court's order of 1950 and 1951. If the Hindus are offering prayers and worshipping the idols, though in a restricted way for the last 35 years, then the heavens are not going to fall if the locks of the gates are removed. The district magistrate has stated before me today that the members of the Muslim community are not allowed to offer any prayers at the disputed site. They are not allowed to go there. ... If this is the state of affairs then there is no occasion for any law and order problem arising as a result of the removal of the locks. It is absolutely an affair inside the premises. There is no justification for retaining locks after the positive statements of the district magistrate and the SSP Faizabad that the law and order situation can be very well kept under control by other means as well and for that end it is not necessary to keep the locks on these gates."*

The appeal allowed and the respondents - district magistrate, the city magistrate and the police superintendent of Faizabad were directed to open the locks forthwith and not to impose any restrictions or cause hurdle in the*darshan* and *puja*, etc. of the applicant and other members of the community in general. With the order of the District Judge, the site, which was in the register of waqf as a mosque for over over 400 years as a mosque was converted into a de facto temple. The procedure adopted by the district judge of recording the statement of the District Magistrate and the Senior Superintendent of the Police was very unusual to the say the least. Application of Umesh Chandra Pandey was incompetent as he was not a party in the suit.

The suit itself was not pending. Gopal Singh Visharad, the Plaintiff in the Regular Suit No. 2 of 1950 had died years ago and no substitution had been made in his place and as such the suit had automatically abated. Such an order could not be passed altering the situation after 36 years. Also, contrary to the general procedure and practice was the fact that the District Judge rejected the application of the Muslims who were originally party to the suit to be impleaded as a party. The District Judge had no basis to conclude that Muslims would not be adversely affected and that too without hearing the applicants to be impleaded as a party.

The District Judge in effect adjudicated the rights of the contending parties without hearing all the parties to the suit on a very narrow and negative ground that there would not be any law and order problem if the locks were removed.

The adjudication was not on strength of respective claims and the case of the parties, as all the parties concerned and the strength of their claims were not heard were not heard at all. Law and order problem is never a consideration while adjudicating rights of the party. If the courts adjudicate rights of the parties to litigation on consideration of law and order, what we will have is not rule of law but rule of might.

The background in which the judgement was delivered will not be out of place here. The SSP and the DM would not have given the statement about their confidence in being able to maintain law and order, without approval of the State and Central Government. The Rajiv Gandhi Government was on the one hand trying to appease the Muslim Fundamentalists on the issue of Sahabano and intended legislation for denial of maintenance to divorced Muslim women under S. 125 of Cr.P.C. On the other hand, the Government was also trying to appease the Hindu community by getting the locks of Ramjanambhumi-Babri Masjid opened for *darshan* and *puja*.

## AYODHYA VERDICT: WHY IT WOULD WORRY US FOR YEARS TO COME

The Supreme Court claims that its Ayodhya verdict is not based on faith and belief of the Hindus but on credible and admissible evidence. But that is clearly not the case and it raises many serious questions for jurists and social scientists to ponder. The unanimous Supreme Court (SC) verdict on Ayodhya dispute brings in several factors into play -legal, historical and archaeological evidence, land and revenue records, faith and belief, travelogues, scriptures, the Constitution of India and the rule of law - to decide the title of the site where the Babri Masjid once stood for 464 years until it was demolished in 1992. The verdict is in favour of the "deity of Lord Ram" and the Muslims have been asked to build their masjid elsewhere for which the state (Central or state government) would provide five acres of land.

A week after the verdict was delivered by a five-member bench in a widely broadcast event, a heated debate continues: What exactly was the basis of it? While some experts point at faith and belief of the Hindus, others disagree; a few even express their inability to decipher saying that the verdict contains many contradictions and ambiguities. Questions have also been raised about the application of several legal principles relating to limitations, adverse possessions and other such.

Before exploring all these aspects, here is a reality check on what weighed in the minds of the judges while deciding the case. (Page numbers have been given for easy referencing since the verdict runs into 1,045 pages.)

Is it based on legal evidence and the rule of law? The judges set the ground rules very clearly about deciding the title. One, they rule out getting into the Mughal era events (the Babri masjid was built in 1528) by saying: "This Court cannot entertain claims that stem from the actions of the Mughal rulers against Hindu places of worship in a court of law today." (page 707)

Then they lay out the rules to play by: "The dispute is over immovable property. The court does not decide the title on the basis of faith or belief but on the basis of evidence. The law provides us with parameters as clear but as profound as ownership and possession. In deciding title to the disputed property, the court applies settled principles of evidence to adjudicate upon which party has established a claim to the immovable property." (emphasis added, page 920)

The following two are the most significant legal evidence the Supreme Court has examined in its "Analysis on title". Both are post 15 August, 1947 - the date set by the Places of Worship (Special Provisions) Act of 1991 for not allowing any change in the religious character of a place of worship "as it existed on that day", except for the Ayodhya dispute.

## Placing the idols inside the Babri masjid in 1949

About the placement of the idols in the masjid's inner sanctum in 1949, the verdict says: "...on the night between 22/23 December 1949, when a group of fifty to sixty persons installed idols on the pulpit of the mosque below the central dome. This led to the desecration of the mosque and the ouster of the Muslims otherwise than by the due process of law." (emphasis added, page 913)

A few pages later it says: "The exclusion of the Muslims from worship and possession took place on the intervening night between 22/23 December 1949 when the mosque was desecrated by the installation of Hindu idols. The ouster of the Muslims on that occasion was not through any lawful authority but through an act which was calculated to deprive them of their place of worship." (emphasis added, page 922)

## Demolition of the Babri masjid in 1992

The verdict says: "On 6 December 1992, the structure of the mosque was brought down and the mosque was destroyed. The destruction of the mosque took place in breach of the order of status quo and an assurance given to this Court. The destruction of the mosque and the obliteration of the Islamic structure was an egregious violation of the rule of law." (emphasis added, page 913-914).

This was repeated a few pages later: "The Muslims have been wrongly deprived of a mosque which had been constructed well over 450 years ago" and "There was no abandonment of the mosque by the Muslims." (emphasis added, page 922 and 923)

The verdict could not have been based on such evidence as it points out that the acts of sneaking in the idols into the masjid and then demolishing the masjid amount to "desecration of the mosque" and constitute "egregious violation of law", respectively.

Is it based on archaeological findings?In 2003, the Archaeological Survey of India (ASI) had submitted its Allahabad high court-mandated scientific investigation of the disputed site. After analysing the ASI's findings, the verdict says it "must, however, be read contextually with the following caveats":

1. "While the ASI report has found the existence of ruins of a pre-existing structure, the report does not provide: (a) The reason for destruction of the pre-existing structure; and (b) Whether the earlier structure was demolished for the purpose of the construction of the mosque.
2. "Since the ASI report dates the underlying structure to the twelfth century, there is a time gap (original

emphasis) of about four centuries between the date of the underlying structure and the construction of the mosque. No evidence is available to explain what transpired in the course of the intervening period of nearly four centuries;

3. "The ASI report does not conclude that the remnants of the pre-existing structure were used for the purpose of constructing the mosque (apart, that is, from the construction of the mosque on the foundation of the erstwhile structure); and
4. "The pillars that were used in the construction of the mosque were black Kasauti stone pillars. ASI has found no evidence to show that these Kasauti pillars are relatable to the underlying pillar bases found during the course of excavation in the structure below the mosque." (all emphasis added, except the one specified, pages 906, 907)

And then it concludes: "A finding of title cannot be based in law on the archaeological findings which have been arrived at by ASI" because "no evidence is available in a case of this antiquity on (i) the cause of destruction of the underlying structure; and (ii) whether the pre-existing structure was demolished for the construction of the mosque." (emphasis added, page 907).

Is it based on travelogues, gazetteers, land or revenue records? The verdict examines many travelogues but emphasises chiefly on the accounts of Father Joseph Tieffenthaler, a priest, and Robert Montgomery Martin, an Anglo-Irish author and civil servant, of 18th and early 19th century.

The verdict says the travelogues indicate four things: (i) "...the existence of faith and belief of the Hindus that the disputed site was the birthplace of Lord Ram" (ii) "Identifiable places of offering worship by the Hindus including Sita Rasoi, Swargadwar and the Bedi (cradle) symbolising the birth of Lord Ram in and around the disputed site" (iii) "Prevalence of the practice of worship by pilgrims at the disputed site including by parikrama and the presence of large congregations..." (iv) "The historical presence of worshippers and existence of worship at the disputed site even prior to the annexation of Oudh by the British and the construction of a brick-grill wall in 1857." (page 908)

And then, the verdict adds the following caveats: That "the accounts of the travellers must be read with circumspection"; "their personal observations must be carefully sifted from hearsay - matters of legend and lore" and that "Consulting their accounts on matters of public history is distinct from evidence on a matter of title.

An adjudication of title has to be deduced on the basis of evidence sustainable in a court of law, which has withstood the searching scrutiny of cross-examination". (emphasis added, page 908)

About the gazetteers, it says: "Similarly, the contents of gazetteers can at best provide corroborative material to evidence which emerges from the record." (page 908) Taken together, the travelogue and gazetteers, the verdict concludes: "Title cannot be established on the basis of faith and belief above." (emphasis added, page 908)

The land and revenue records had already been disposed of as of no significance earlier: the revenue records by keeping in mind "the fundamental principle of law that revenue records do not confer title" (page 886) and the land records from the emperor Babar's time being undated, "on the basis of testimony" and about "land free grant" of Rs 302, 3 ana and 6 pai "for meeting the expenses and the salary of "Muezzin and Khateeb", not a title to the land. (page 793)

## THE SUPREME COURT JUDGMENT

The Supreme Court, adjudicating on the title dispute in 2019, takes note of the many unlawful acts of Hindus. The court says, "The damage to the mosque in 1934, its desecration in 1949 leading to the ouster of the Muslims and the eventual destruction on 6 December 1992 constituted a serious violation of the rule of law" [para 788, clause XVIII (vii) of the judgment]. And yet, the court proceeds to hand over the entirety of the disputed land to the Hindu parties.

One of the foremost principles of natural law is, *"He who comes into equity must come with clean hands,"* or as otherwise expressed, *"He that hath committed inequity shall not have equity."* Both a historic as well as legal assessment of this dispute renders it amply clear that the conduct of Hindu parties has been inequitable. On what basis, then, does the court proceed to hold in their favour?

The first thing to clarify here is that the court was not adjudicating on the question of whether a Ram temple once existed where the Babri Masjid stood. Based on the ASI report, the court comes to the following conclusions,

"The excavation indicates the presence of an underlying structure below the disputed structure;" "The underlying structure was not of Islamic origin;" "There is no specific finding that the underlying structure was a temple dedicated to Lord Ram;" "Since the ASI report dates the underlying structure to the twelfth century, there is a time gap of about four centuries between the date of the underlying structure and the construction of the mosque. No evidence is available to explain what transpired in the course of the intervening period of nearly four centuries."

*-(paras 509, 788)*

The court therefore refused to determine questions of possession based on archaeological findings.

The judgment seeks to remind us that this is in fact a title dispute, and that such dispute ought not be adjudged by religious yardsticks.

"The adjudication of civil claims over private property must remain within the domain of the secular if the commitment to constitutional values is to be upheld."

*-(para 204)*

India's first Prime Minister, Jawaharlal Nehru was not a big fan of boasting about India's secular commitments. Speaking in the Constituent Assembly, he had said,

"Another word is thrown up a good deal, this secular state business. May I beg with all humility these gentlemen who use this word often to consult some dictionary before they use it. It is brought in at every conceivable step and at every conceivable stage. I just do not understand it. It has a great deal of importance, no doubt.

But, it is brought in all contexts, as if by saying that we are a secular state we have done something amazingly generous, given something out of our pocket to the rest of the world, something which we ought not to have done, so on, and so forth. We have only done something which every country does, except a very few misguided and backward countries in the world. Let us not refer to that word in the sense that we have done something very mighty."

*-(Constituent Assembly Debates, volume 10, pages 398-401)*

While speaking these words, it must have seemed to Nehru that secularism was the only natural way for India to exist, and that any reiteration of the greatness of this value is unnecessary bravado. But that is not true for the India of today, where the secular fabric of our polity faces an existential threat.

In this context, the Supreme Court was aware of the highly sensitive task of adjudication that lay before it. Hence, the court undertook several steps to reiterate the fact that it was committed to secularism in this adjudication process. The court repeatedly emphasized that secularism is a basic feature of the Indian constitution. In doing so, the court also extolled the values of The Places of Worship Act. "Above all, the Places of Worship Act is an affirmation of the solemn duty which was cast upon the State to preserve and protect the equality of all faiths as an essential constitutional value, a norm which has the status of being a basic feature of the Constitution" (para 83).

The court remarks that,

*"...title cannot be established on the basis of faith and belief above" (para 788). Despite such reassurances, the court seems to defer to faith at several points in the judgment. "Whether a belief is justified lies beyond ken of judicial inquiry;" "Once the witnesses have deposed to the basis of the belief and there is nothing to doubt its genuineness, it is not open to the court to question the basis of the belief."*

-(para 555)

To this Prof. Mustafa points out the court's inconsistent position,

*"But did not this very court interpret Koran on maintenance in the Shah Bano case (1985) and on triple divorce in the Shayara Bano case (2017)? Did it not reject the Hanafi interpretation?"*

The judgment makes a cardinal deference to Hindu faith when it seeks to overlook the significance of the dividing wall set-up by the British. This allows the court to disregard the crucial bifurcation of the disputed land between an inner courtyard (where Muslims offered namaz) and an outer courtyard (where Hindus prayed).

"Despite the setting up of the grill-brick wall in 1857, the Hindus never accepted the division of the inner and the outer courtyard. For the Hindus, the entire complex as a whole was of religious significance. A demarcation by the British for the purposes of maintaining law and order did not obliterate their belief in the relevance of the 'Garbh-Grih' being the birth-place of Lord Ram"

*-(para 773)*

At this point, it must be mentioned that the court's position here is factually untenable. As mentioned earlier, the Hindu litigation in this entire dispute had originated with the claim that Ram chabutra (located in the outer courtyard) is the birthplace of Ram. The suit that Mahant Raghubar Das had filed on January 19, 1885, sought permission to build a temple on the chabutra. The district judge, dated March 26, 1886, ruled,

"This chabutra is said to indicate the birthplace of Ramchander."

Surely, if for the Hindus the entire land was meant to be Ram's birthplace, the original litigants wouldn't have restricted their title claims to just the chabutra.

The consequences that follow from the court ignoring such distinction between inner and outer courtyards (and treating them as a composite whole) are of paramount importance. The court made two important conclusions that underpin its final orders,

*1. "The Hindus have been in exclusive and unimpeded possession of the outer courtyard where they have continued worship."*

2. "The inner courtyard has been a contested site with conflicting claims of the Hindus and Muslims."

*-(para 788, clause XVIII)*

Therefore, as opposed to granting the Hindu representatives possession to the outer-courtyard, and then proceeding with a balancing act with respect to the possessory title for the inner courtyard, the court could eventually conclude that,

"on a balance of probabilities, the evidence in respect of the possessory claim of the Hindus to the composite whole of the disputed property stands on a better footing than the evidence adduced by the Muslims..."

-(para 800; emphasis supplied)

And hence the court determined that the,

"Possession of the inner and outer courtyards shall be handed over to the Board of Trustees of the Trust or to the body so constituted."

The trustees shall have the powers for the construction of a temple and all necessary incidental and supplemental matters.

This final decree of the court raises another question on its adjudication. Can a secular State be ordered to facilitate the construction of a temple, which is an essential part of the Hindu belief? Does this not amount to a secular State fostering a particular religion?

Eminent legal scholar Upendra Baxi said the Centre was already empowered under Section 6 of the Acquisition of Certain Area at Ayodhya Act, 1993 to vest the disputed land in a trust or authority.

Justice K. Chandru, former Madras High Court judge, however argued that the Ayodhya Act was upheld only as an,

*"interim measure so that land was not tampered with or frittered away when the case of its title and possession was still under litigation."*

He questioned why the apex court directed the Centre – which was not a party to the Ayodhya title suits or appeals – to formulate a scheme for the land. The court could have very well asked the local civil court under Section 92(g) of the Code of Civil Procedure to settle a scheme for the land.

The judgment has also been criticized for imposing differential evidentiary standards. A crucial factor that weighs with the court in deciding against the Sunni Waqf Board is the inability of the Muslim claimants to show that namaz was offered in the mosque before 1856.

"But, a crucial aspect of the evidentiary record is the absence of any evidence to indicate that the mosque was, after its construction, used for offering namaz until 1856-7."

*-(para 678)*

However, in its recognition of the Hindu claim over the inner courtyard, the court holds,

"Even after the construction of the dividing wall by the British, the Hindus continued to assert their right to pray below the central dome."

*-(para 788, clause VII; emphasis supplied)*

This is a manifestly inconsistent standard. While the Muslims claimants are required to prove that namaz was in fact offered in the mosque before 1856 (a fact which would be clear as day to any observer), the burden on the Hindu claimants is merely that they "continued to assert" their right to pray.

It must be noted that the fact that finally settles the dispute in favor of the Hindus is their unimpeded possession of the outer courtyard, whereas what goes to the detriment of the Muslim parties is that there were repeated conflicts regarding the possession of the inner courtyard.

"The riots of 1934 and the events which led up to 22/23 December 1949 indicate that possession over the inner courtyard was a matter of serious contestation often leading to violence by both parties and the Muslims did not have exclusive possession over the inner courtyard."

*-(para 781)*

Perhaps the greatest indictment of the judgment would be that it uses the repeated acts of disruption and interference on part of the Hindus to eventually hold in their favour. The court conveniently forgot the cardinal principle of equity mentioned above,

*"He who seeks equity must do equity."*

The fact that Muslims across generations had solemnly, and in a dignified manner, respected the rights of Hindu claimants to pray at the Ram chabutra and Sita ki rasoi was eventually held against them, insofar as it was used to prove exclusive possession of the Hindus over the outer-courtyard. Had Muslims not offered this courtesy, would the verdict have been different?

I seek to conclude with AG Noorani's words of cautionary wisdom,

*"When the communal pitch and opportunism are gone, Indians themselves will look back in shame on a structure built with force and deceit."*

## UNDERSTANDING THE RAM MANDIR-BABRI MASJID CONFLICT

Who are the litigants? What were some of the arguments made? What to expect today?

The Supreme Court is expected to pronounce its verdict on the vexed Ram Janmabhoomi-Babri Masjid today. The demolition of the Babri Masjid at the disputed Ram Janmabhoomi site in Ayodhya on December 6, 1992, had sparked communal riots across the country. Here is a short primer:

### *Who are the litigants?*

Fourteen appeals were filed in the apex court against the 2010 Allahabad High Court judgment, delivered in four civil suits, that the 2.77-acre land in Ayodhya be partitioned equally among the three parties—the Sunni Waqf Board, the Nirmohi Akhara and Ram Lalla.

On the Hindu side, Nirmohi Akhara—a denomination of Ram-worshipping sadhus—claim historical worship rights over the shrine. Ram Lalla (infant Ram) was represented in court (deities can appear as minors by law) by Devaki Nandan Agarwal, a retired High Court judge, in 1989; Now, Trilok Nath Pandey is Ram Lalla's "friend". Ram Janmabhoomi Nyas, also a litigant on the Hindu side, is a VHP-backed organisation that has been aggressively pushing for the construction of a temple at the site. Hashim Ansari, a Muslim man who lived in Ayodhya, was the oldest litigant in the Babri mosque case, and his son Iqbal Ansari has since taken over the helm. Sunni Waqf Board is the major litigant on the Muslim side, arguing that they have full possession of the title.

## What were some of the arguments made?

The five-judge Constitution bench, headed by Chief Justice Ranjan Gogoi, hearing the Babri Masjid-Ram Janmabhoomi dispute, on the penultimate day, asked former attorney general and senior advocate K. Parasaran, who appeared for the Hindu party: "They say, once a mosque always a mosque, do you support this?" "No. I do not support it. I will say once a temple always a temple," Parasaran replied. In essence, this statement summed up the impasse on the sensitive issue. Rajeev Dhavan, appearing for the Muslim parties, argued that Muslims had title over the land since 1528 when mosque was built and there have been evidence that Mughals, Nawab of Awadh and then Britishers gave grants.

Moreover, Hindu parties, from 1885 to 1989, did not claim title. Dhavan said he was "cautioning" the bench against re-writing history as lawsuits cannot be decided on the basis of archeological evidence and by deciding whether Babur created a wakf. Cases have to be decided under legal parameters and courts cannot be persuaded to decide that 500 mosques, built by conquering emperors, be dug up to establish that temples were existing before the mosques, he said.

Conflicting archaeological reports—especially one in the 1990s which claimed there was no temple structure underneath the mosque—had figured in the hearings. He said that Quran, Hadith and other Islamic law cannot be used in "bits and pieces" to establish that the place was not a valid mosque in view of the fact that Islamic law is "very complex" and has evolved in last 1500 years.

Parasaran, appearing for the Hindu parties, argued that there were several mosques in Ayodhya where Muslims can pray but Hindus cannot change the birth place of Lord Ram.

"Please do the reparation of a historical wrong committed by foreign ruler Babur who came here and said that I am the emperor and my fiat is the law," the senior lawyer, appearing for Mahant Suresh Das, who is a defendant in a law suit filed by Sunni Waqf Board and others in 1961. "Muslims can pray in any other mosque in Ayodhya. There are 55-60 mosques in Ayodhya alone. But, for Hindus, this is the birth place of Lord Ram...which we cannot change," he said.

Hindus have been fighting for centuries for the birthplace of Ram which cannot be changed and for Muslims all mosques are equal, Parasaran said, adding that foreigners like Mughals, Portuguese, French and Britishers came to rich India and plundered it which led this country to poverty.

Parasaran said it has been said that "ancient mosque" was built by Babur more than 433 years ago after his conquest of India and hence the title of the mosque is "traceable to the conquest and occupation of Emperor Babur" but it has not been proved by the Muslim parties. He then referred to the findings of a Faizabad court in 1886 on a lawsuit filed by Mahant Raghubar Das and said it was held the mosque was built on the land held sacred by Hindus.

## What to expect today?

Though all parties—Hindu and Muslim—have called for peace ahead of the verdict, security measures across the country are at an all-time high. Elaborate security arrangements have been made across the country ahead of the Supreme Court judgement in the communally sensitive Ayodhya land dispute case on Saturday, while the temple town remained on the edge and political leaders, including Prime Minister Narendra Modi, and religious leaders urged people to maintain peace and respect the verdict.

Authorities said social media posts will be monitored to ensure that no attempt is made to vitiate the atmosphere by spreading fake or inflammatory content. Arrangements have also been made to ensure the safety and security of religious places across the country.

The Uttar Pradesh government ordered closure of all educational and training institutes till Monday.

The demolition of the Babri Masjid at the disputed site on December 6, 1992, had sparked communal riots. On Friday morning, Chief Justice Gogoi held an hour-long meeting with Uttar Pradesh Chief Secretary Rajendra Kumar Tiwari and Director General of Police Om Prakash Singh, who apprised him about the security arrangements made to maintain law and order in the state. A multi-layered security has been put in place in the temple town of Ayodhya, turning it into a fortress with deployment of 60 companies (90-125 personnel each) of PAC and paramilitary forces. Vehicle checking has been intensified near the Ramjanmabhoomi police station, "karyashala" of Ram Janmabhoomi Nyas and other parts of the town.

The Delhi government has advised all private schools to remain closed on November 9 as a precautionary measure. The Madhya Pradesh government has declared a holiday for all educational institutes in the state on Saturday. Police have been put on alert in Mumbai and the rest of Maharashtra. In Mumbai, police have issued prohibitory orders against gathering of five or more persons till November 18.

Rajasthan Chief Minister Ashok Gehlot directed senior police officers to ensure law and order in the state. He asked the officers to make additional deployment in sensitive areas. In the Union Territory of Jammu and Kashmir, prohibitory orders under Section 144 of the CrPC have been issued, banning assembly of more than four people, DGP J&K, Dilbag Singh told PTI.

Schools and colleges in the UT have been ordered shut on Saturday and all examinations scheduled for November 9 have been postponed. The Karnataka government on Friday declared that all schools and colleges in the state will remain closed on November 9 in view of the Supreme Court verdict in the Ayodhya land dispute case.

A cross-section of people in Ayodhya said they want to move on and leave the past behind. Shiv Sakal, who lives near Badhi Devkali bypass in Ayodhya, said, "I sincerely pray to Lord Ram that this dispute be resolved at earliest, so that the element of uncertainty is gone from our minds once and for all.

"Many of my relatives who live in Bundelkhand are sceptical of coming to Ayodhya and say that they will come here only after the Supreme Court judgement is delivered," he said.

## DEMOLITION OF THE BABRI MASJID

On 6 December 1992, a large group of Hindu activists of the Vishva Hindu Parishad and allied organisations demolished the 16th-century Babri Mosque in the city of Ayodhya, in Uttar Pradesh. The demolition occurred after a political rally organised by Hindu nationalist organisations at the site turned violent.

In Hindu tradition, the city of Ayodhya is the birthplace of Rama. In the 16th century a Mughal general, Mir Baqi, had built a mosque, known as the Babri Masjid at a site identified by some Hindus as *Ram Janmabhoomi*, or the birthplace of Rama. The Archaeological Survey of India states that the mosque was built on land where a non-Islamic structure had previously existed. In the 1980s, the Vishva Hindu Parishad (VHP) began a campaign for the construction of a temple dedicated to Rama at the site, with the Bharatiya Janata Party (BJP) as its political voice. Several rallies and marches were held as a part of this movement, including the *Ram Rath Yatra* led by L. K. Advani.

On 6 December 1992 the VHP and the BJP organised a rally at the site involving 150,000 volunteers, known as *kar sevaks*. The rally turned violent, and the crowd overwhelmed security forces and tore down the mosque. A subsequent inquiry into the incident found 68 people responsible, including several leaders of the BJP and the VHP. The demolition resulted in several months of intercommunal rioting between India's Hindu and Muslim communities, causing the death of at least 2,000 people. Retaliatory violence against Hindus also occurred in Pakistan and Bangladesh.

## Background

In Hinduism the birthplace of the deity Rama, known as "Ram Janmabhoomi", is considered a holy site. This site is often believed to be at the place where the Babri Masjid stood in the city of Ayodhya in Uttar Pradesh: historical evidence to support this belief is scarce. There is a rough scholarly consensus that in 1528, following the Mughal conquest of the region, a mosque was built at the site by the Mughal general Mir Baqi, and named the "Babri Masjid" after the Mughal emperor Babur. Popular belief holds that Baqi demolished a temple of Rama to build the mosque; historical basis for the belief is debated. Archaeological evidence has been found of a structure pre-dating the mosque. This structure has been variously identified as a Hindu temple and a Buddhist structure.

For at least four centuries, the site was used for religious purposes by both Hindus and Muslims. The claim that the mosque stood on the site of a temple was first made in 1822, by an official of the Faizabad court. The Nirmohi Akhara sect cited this statement in laying claim to the site later in the 19th century, leading to the first recorded incidents of religious violence at the site in 1855. In 1859 the British colonial administration set up a railing to separate the outer courtyard of the mosque to avoid disputes. The status quo remained in place until 1949, when idols of Rama were surreptitiously placed inside the mosque, allegedly by volunteers of the Hindu Mahasabha. This led to an uproar, with both parties filing civil suits laying claim to the land. The placement of the idols was seen as a desecration by the users of the Masjid. The site was declared to be in dispute, and the gates to the Masjid were locked.

In the 1980s, the Vishva Hindu Parishad (VHP) began a campaign for the construction of a temple dedicated to Rama at the site, with the Bharatiya Janata Party (BJP) as its political voice. The movement was bolstered by the decision of a district judge, who ruled in 1986 that the gates would be reopened and Hindus permitted to worship there. This decision was endorsed by Indian National Congress politician Rajiv Gandhi, then the Prime Minister of India, who sought to regain support from Hindus he had lost over the Shah Bano controversy. Nonetheless, the Congress lost the 1989 general election, and the BJP's strength in parliament grew from 2 members to 88, making its support crucial to the new government of V. P. Singh.

In September 1990, BJP leader L. K. Advani began a *Rath Yatra*, a political rally travelling across much of north India to Ayodhya. The *yatra* sought to generate support for the proposed temple, and also sought to unite Hindu votes by mobilizing anti-Muslim sentiment. Advani was arrested by the government of Bihar before he could reach Ayodhya. Despite this, a large body of kar sevaks or Sangh Parivar activists reached Ayodhya and attempted to attack the mosque. This resulted in a pitched battle with the paramilitary forces that ended with the death of several kar sevaks. The BJP withdrew its support to the V. P. Singh ministry, necessitating fresh elections. The BJP substantially increased its tally in the union parliament, as well as winning a majority in the Uttar Pradesh assembly.

## Demolition

On 6 December 1992, the RSS and its affiliates organised a rally involving 150,000 VHP and BJP *kar sevaks* at the site of the disputed structure. The ceremonies included speeches by BJP leaders such as Advani, Murli Manohar Joshi and Uma Bharti. During the first few hours of the rally, the crowd grew gradually more restless, and began raising slogans. A police cordon had been placed around the structure in preparation for attack. However, around noon, a young man managed to slip past the cordon and climb the structure itself, brandishing a saffron flag. This was seen as a signal by the mob, who then stormed the structure. The police cordon, vastly outnumbered and unprepared for the size of the attack, fled. The mob set upon the building with axes, hammers, and grappling hooks, and within a few hours, the entire structure, made from mud and chalk, was levelled.

A 2009 report, authored by Justice Manmohan Singh Liberhan, found 68 people to be responsible for the demolition of the Masjid, mostly leaders from the BJP. Among those named were Vajpayee, Advani, Joshi and Vijay Raje Scindia. Kalyan Singh, who was then the Chief Minister of Uttar Pradesh, also faced severe criticism in the report. Liberhan wrote that he posted bureaucrats and police officers to Ayodhya, whose record indicated that they would stay silent during the mosque's demolition.

Anju Gupta, a police officer who had been in charge of Advani's security on that day, stated that Advani and Joshi made speeches that contributed to provoking the behaviour of the mob. The report notes that at this time several BJP leaders made "feeble requests to the kar sevaks to come down... either in earnest or for the media's benefit". No appeal was made to the Kar Sevaks not to enter the sanctum sanctorum or not to demolish the structure. It further noted: "This selected act of the leaders itself speaks of the hidden intentions of one and all being to accomplish demolition of the disputed structure." The report holds that the "icons of the movement present [that day]... could just as easily have... prevented the demolition."

## Conspiracy allegations

In a March 2005 book, former Intelligence Bureau head Maloy Krishna Dhar claimed that Babri mosque demolition was planned 10 months in advance by top leaders of the Rashtriya Swayamsevak Sangh ("RSS"), BJP and VHP, and criticised the manner in which the then Prime Minister P. V. Narasimha Rao handled the issue.

Dhar claimed that he was directed to arrange security for a meeting between individuals from the BJP and other constituents of the Sangh Parivar, and that the meeting "proved beyond doubt that they (RSS, BJP, VHP) had drawn up the blueprint of the Hindutva assault in the coming months and choreographed the *pralaya nritya* (dance of destruction) at Ayodhya in December 1992. The RSS, BJP, VHP and the Bajrang Dal leaders present in the meeting amply agreed to work in a well-orchestrated manner."

Claiming that the tapes of the meeting were personally handed over by him to his boss, he asserts that he has no doubts that his boss had shared the contents with the Prime Minister (Rao) and the Home Minister (Shankarrao Chavan). The author claimed that there was silent agreement that Ayodhya offered "a unique opportunity to take the Hindutva wave to the peak for deriving political benefit."

In April 2014, a sting operation by Cobrapost claimed that the demolition was not an act of frenzied mobs but an act of sabotage planned with so much secrecy that no government agency got wind of it. It further said that the sabotage was planned several months in advance by Vishva Hindu Parishad and Shiv Sena, but not jointly.

## Communal violence

The destruction of the Babri Mosque, as well as the destruction of numerous others that day, sparked Muslim outrage around the country, provoking several months of inter-communal rioting in which Hindus and Muslims attacked one another, burning and looting homes, shops and places of worship. Several of the BJP leaders were taken into custody, and the VHP was briefly banned by the government. Despite this, the ensuing riots spread to cities like Mumbai, Surat, Ahmedabad, Kanpur, Delhi, Bhopal and several others, eventually resulting in over 2000 deaths, mainly Muslim.

The Mumbai Riots alone, which occurred in December 1992 and January 1993 and which the Shiv Sena played a big part in organising, caused the death of around 900 people, and estimated property damage of around 9,000 crore ($3.6 billion). The demolition and the ensuing riots were among the major factors behind the 1993 Mumbai bombings and many successive riots in the coming decade. Jihadi groups including the Indian Mujahideen cited the demolition of the Babri Mosque as a reason for their terrorist attacks.

## Investigation

On 16 December 1992, the Union home ministry set up the Liberhan Commission to investigate the destruction of the Mosque, headed by retired High Court Judge M. S. Liberhan. After 399 sittings over sixteen years, the Commission submitted its 1,029-page report to Indian Prime Minister Manmohan Singh on 30 June 2009.

According to the report, the events of 6 December 1992, in Ayodhya were "neither spontaneous nor unplanned". In March 2015, the Supreme Court of India admitted a petition alleging that, with a BJP government in power, the CBI would not pursue conspiracy charges against senior BJP leaders including L. K. Advani and Rajnath Singh. The Court asked the CBI to explain its delay in filing an appeal. In April 2017, a special Central Bureau of Investigation court framed criminal conspiracy charges against Advani, Murli Manohar Joshi, Uma Bharti, Vinay Katiyar, and several others.

## International reactions

### *Pakistan*

In Pakistan, the government closed offices and schools on 7 December to protest against the demolition of the Babri Masjid. The Pakistani Foreign Ministry summoned the Indian ambassador to lodge a formal complaint, and promised to appeal to the United Nations and the Organisation of the Islamic Conference to pressure India to protect the rights of Muslims. Strikes were held across the country, while Muslim mobs attacked and destroyed as many as 30 temples in one day by means of fire and bulldozers, and stormed the office of Air India, India's national airline, in Lahore. The retaliatory attacks included rhetoric from mobs calling for the destruction of India and of Hinduism. Students from the Quaid-i-Azam University in Islamabad burned an effigy of the then-Prime Minister of India, P.V. Narasimha Rao, and called for "Jihad" against Hindus. In subsequent years, thousands of Pakistani Hindus visiting India sought longer visas, and in some cases citizenship of India, citing increased harassment and discrimination in the aftermath of the demolition.

### *Bangladesh*

Following the demolition, Muslim mobs in Bangladesh attacked and burned down Hindu temples, shops and houses across the country. An India-Bangladesh cricket match was disrupted when a mob of an estimated 5,000 men tried to storm the Bangabandhu National Stadium in the national capital of Dhaka. The Dhaka office of Air India was stormed and destroyed. 10 people were reportedly killed, 11 Hindu temples and several homes destroyed. The aftermath of the violence forced the Bangladeshi Hindu community to curtail the celebrations of Durga Puja in 1993 while calling for the destroyed temples to be repaired and investigations be held into the atrocities.

### *Middle East*

At its summit meeting in Abu Dhabi, the Gulf Cooperation Council strongly condemned the Babri Masjid demolition. It adopted a resolution which described the act as a "crime against Muslim holy places." Among its member states, Saudi Arabia severely condemned the act. The United Arab Emirates, home to large expatriate communities of Indians and Pakistanis, conveyed a more moderate reaction. In response, the Indian government criticised the GCC for what it regarded as interference in its internal affairs. Ayatollah Ali Khamenei condemned the demolition, and called upon India to do more to protect its Muslim population. Although its government condemned the events, the UAE experienced severe public disturbances due to the demolition of the Babri Mosque. Street protests broke out, and protesters threw stones at a Hindu temple and the Indian Consulate in Dubai. In Al-Ain, 250 km east of Abu Dhabi, angry mobs set fire to the girls wing of an Indian school. In response to the violence, UAE police arrested and deported many expatriate Pakistanis and Indians who had participated in the violence. The Commander-in-Chief of the Dubai police force, Dhahi Khalfan, condemned the violence by foreign nationals in his country.

## In popular culture

Malayalam author N. S. Madhavan's story *Thiruthu* is based on the Babri masjid demolition. The Ayodhya dispute and the riots following the demolition of the Babri Masjid form part of the backdrop to Antara Ganguly's 2016 novel, *Tanya Tania*. *Lajja* (Shame), a 1993 novel by Bangladeshi author Taslima Nasrin, was partially inspired by the persecution of Hindus in Bangladesh that intensified after the demolition of the Babri Masjid.

The documentary *Ram ke Naam* (In the name of God) by Anand Patwardhan examines the events preceding the demolition. The Bollywood film *Mausam* is based on the events surrounding the demolition. The events riots that followed the demolition are an important part of the plot of several films, including *Bombay* (1995) set in the Bombay riots. *Daivanamathil* (2005) explores the repercussions of the demolition on Muslims in Kerala. Both *Bombay* and *Daivanamathi* won the Nargis Dutt Award for Best Feature Film on National Integration at the respective National Film Awards. The 2007 film *Black Friday* was based upon the 1993 Bombay bombings which were considered to be the after effect of the demolition of the mosque.

## Regional impact

Riots in the aftermath of Babri Masjid's demolition extended to Bangladesh, where hundreds of shops, homes and temples of Hindus were destroyed. Widespread retaliatory attacks against scores of Hindu temples also took place across neighbouring Pakistan. Reprisal attacks against Hindus in both countries, in turn, entered the discourse of right-wing Hindu nationalists – some of whom in 1995 appealed to the United Nations to protect Hindus in Bangladesh and Pakistan. The impact of Babri Masjid's demolition and its repercussions negatively effects relations between India and Pakistan until the present day.

## Liberhan Commission

The Liberhan Commission set up by the Government to investigate the demolition later blamed 68 people including senior BJP, RSS and VHP leaders for the demolition. Among those criticised in the report were Atal Bihari Vajpayee, the party's chief LK Advani, and chief minister Kalyan Singh. A 2005 book by the former Intelligence Bureau (IB) Joint Director Maloy Krishna Dhar claimed the senior leaders of RSS, BJP, VHP and Bajrang Dal had planned the demolition 10 months in advance. He also suggested that the Indian National Congress leaders, including prime minister P V Narasimha Rao and home minister S B Chavan, had ignored warnings about the demolition for deriving political benefits.

## REFOCUS ON THE DEMOLITION OF BABRI MOSQUE

27 years ago, Indian Constitution which claims India to be a secular state was torn into pieces when on December 6, 1992, a large crowd of Hindu Karsevaks (Volunteers) entirely demolished the 16th-century Babri Masjid (Mosque) in Ayodhya, Utter Pradesh in a preplanned attempt to reclaim the land known as RAM Janmabhoomi–birthplace of the god.

The demolition of the Babri Masjid sparked Muslim outrage around the country, provoking several months of inter-communal rioting between Hindu and Muslim communities, causing the death of at least 2,000 people, the majority of whom were Muslims. The governments of several neighboring countries, including those of the Islamic World condemned the

Indian government for failing to stop the destruction of the historical mosque.

In a 2005 book, India's former Intelligence Bureau (IB) Joint Director Maloy Krishna Dhar wrote that Babri mosque demolition was planned 10 months in advance by top leaders of the Rashtriya Swayamsevak Sangh (RSS), BJP BJP/Sangh Parivar, VHP, Shiv Sena, the Bajrang Dal and the then Prime Minister P.V. Narasimha Rao. Dhar elaborated, "He had drawn up the blueprint of the Hindutva (Hindu nationalism) assault at Ayodhya in December 1992."

However, on December 6, 1992, the RSS and its affiliates organized a rally involving 150,000 VHP and BJP Karsevaks at the site of the mosque. The ceremonies included speeches by BJP leaders such as L.K. Advani, Murli Manohar Joshi and Uma Bharti. During the first few hours of the rally, the crowd began raising militant slogans. A police cordon had been placed around the mosque in preparation for an attack. Nevertheless, around noon, a young man managed to slip past the cordon and climb the mosque itself, brandishing a saffron flag. This was seen as a signal by the mob, who then stormed the structure. The police cordon, vastly outnumbered, fled. The mob set upon the building with axes, hammers, and grappling hooks, and within a few hours, the entire mosque was leveled. Hindu fanatics also destroyed numerous other mosques within the town.

A 2009 report of the inquiry commission, authored by retired of High Court Justice Manmohan Singh Liberhan, found 68 people to be responsible for the destruction of the Babri Masjid, mostly leaders from the BJP. Among those named were Vajpayee, Advani, Joshi, Vijay Raje Scindia and Kalyan Singh who was then the Chief Minister of Uttar Pradesh. Liberhan wrote that he posted bureaucrats and police officers to Ayodhya, whose record indicated that they would stay silent during the mosque's demolition. Anju Gupta, a police officer who had been in charge of Advani's security on that day, stated that Advani and Joshi made speeches that contributed to provoking the behavior of the mob to accomplish demolition of the mosque. However, the commission clearly identified BJP, RSS and VHP as the organizations responsible for the incident and also nominated L.K. Advani, Lalu Parsad Yadav and Murli Manohar Joshi as main culprits behind this incident. But no action was taken against them.

By showing prejudice in favour of Hindus, on September 30, 2010, the Allahabad High Court ruled that the 2,400 square feet (220 m2) disputed plot of land, on which the Babri Masjid had stood would be divided into three parts. The site at which the idol of Rama had been placed was granted to Hindus in general, the Sunni Wakf Board got one-third of the plot, and the Hindu sect Nirmohi Akhara got the remaining third. The excavations by the Archaeological Survey of India were heavily used as evidence by the court to support its so-called finding that the original structure at the site was a massive Hindu religious building.

The anti-muslim biased approach could be judged from the verdict of the Supreme Court of India. While announcing its judgement on the disputed land regarding the Babri mosque, the court ruled in favour of the Hindus and said that a temple will be constructed on the Ayodhya land. The court noted that the demolition of the 460-year-old Babri Mosque in 1992 was a violation of the law and ordered that five-acre alternative land in a suitable, prominent place be provided to Muslims for a mosque. The land for the mosque will be acquired by the government.

Muslims in India protested against the Supreme Court's decision which is likely to have a significant impact on fraught relations between India's Hindus and Muslims, who constitute 14 percent of its 1.3 billion people.

Muslim group's lawyer, Zafaryab Jilani said: "This is not justice." India's Chief Justice Ranjan Gogoi stated: "This court must accept faith and accept the belief of worshippers."

The court's verdict was a huge victory for Hindu nationalists under Indian Prime Minister Narendra Modi, who had promised to build the temple in 2014 elections that brought him to power.

It is notable that in the Indian general elections of 2019, BJP and National Democratic Alliance (NDA) won a huge majority in the Lok Sabha, with the BJP sweeping up 303 seats on its own—21 seats more than it won in the 2014 elections. Hindu majority was mobilized on 'hate Muslim' slogans and 'anti-Pakistan' jargon, while the incessant and unjust Indian propaganda against the Muslims and Pakistan was beyond anybody's cognition, which still keeps ongoing. Indian Prime Minister Modi's extremist party BJP had also got a land sliding triumph in the Indian elections 2014 on the basis of anti-Muslim and anti-Pakistan slogans. Hence, since Prime Minister Modi came to power, he has been implementing anti-Muslim and anti-Pakistan agenda with the support of fanatic coalition outfits.

In this regard, various developments like unprecedented rise of Hindu extremism, persecution of Muslims, assaults on Muslims, including their places of worships and property by the fanatic Hindu mobs, inclusion of Hindu religious books in curriculum, forced conversion of Muslims into Hindus and ban on beef and cow slaughter clearly showed that encouraged by the Hindu fundamentalist groups such as BJP, RSS VHP, Bajrang Dal and Shiv Sena, including other similar parties have been promoting religious and ethnic chauvinism in India by propagating the ideology of Hindutva which is the genesis of Hindu terrorism.

Owing to the huge mandate of the BJP in the elections of 2019, violence has been let loose, with "Jai Shri Ram"–a slogan that roughly translates to "Hail Lord Ram". As Modi was named as the leader of the NDA for a second time, minority communities especially Muslims have made to live in fear by the extremist Hindus.

In the aftermath of the elections, news reports have highlighted different cases in which Dalits and particularly Muslims were violently targeted for reasons as varied as allegedly possessing beef, protesting against caste-based discrimination or simply being Muslim. Especially, various incidents of arrests and violent assaults on the Muslims by the Hindus have been recorded.

As regards Modi's victory in the elections 2019, India's many politicians and analysts opined, "Modi's election win is a victory for far-right Hindu nationalism...India's secular democracy is under threat...BJP's record in 2015-2019 has been divisive, to say the least. The party has marginalised religious minorities, especially Muslims, from public life with many, as a result, being lynched by Hindu nationalists in the name of cow protection...Jingoism and Islamophobia have propelled the BJP to an even stronger showing than in 2014. A Modi victory puts India's 200 million Muslims in danger...Modi is part of the large Hindu supremacist family...In his home state of Odisha, he furthered India's sectarian divide, pushed the idea of Hindu supremacy and with that, violence against Muslims, Christians and other minorities...Modi is radicalising Muslims."

It is mentionable that almost 120 days have passed. Indian forces have continued lockdown and curfew in the Indian Occupied Kashmir (IOK). On August 5, 2019, New Delhi unilaterally annexed the IOK, revoking articles 35A and 370 of the Constitution which gave a special status to Kashmir. While, Indian fanatic rulers are also escalating tensions with Pakistan to divert attention from the drastic situation of the Indian Held Kashmir, and have continued shelling inside Pakistani side of Kashmir by violating the ceasefire agreement in relation to the Line of Control (LoC).

Besides, implementing the August 5 announcement, the Indian central government issued a notorious map on October 31, this year. In accordance with it, Jammu and Kashmir was bifurcated into two union territories—Jammu and Kashmir and Ladakh.

Although apparently, India claims to be the largest democracy, acting upon the principles of liberalism and secularism, yet in practice, all political, economic and social fields of the country are divided on the caste lines. It is surprising that theoretically, the Indian Constitution safeguards the rights of minorities, but in practice, the ideology of Hindutva prevails. Hindu majority led by the BJP has shown complete disregard to the Constitution and continued committing excesses and cruelties against Muslims, Sikhs, Christians and Dalits with impunity.

Nonetheless, apart from other frenzy events, the demolition of the Babri Masjid will remain a major scar on Indian so-called secularism, as on the very day (6th December); Indian fundamentalist leaders broke all the records of Hindutva terror by deliberately hurting the feelings of the Muslims. The atrocities and tyranny let loose on that day in Ayodhya continue unabated against the Muslims in one form or the other, under the Modi regime.

CHAPTER 5

# The Hindu Renaissance

The nineteenth century witnessed a remarkable and largely unexpected renaissance in Hindu thought, Yoga, Veda and Vedanta that brought back to life and placed in the modern context, the world's oldest spiritual heritage. An ancient religion that seemed on the verge of extinction was suddenly awake and able to express and assert itself on the stage of the modern world, providing a new view of humanity, culture and religion that could enrich all cultures and countries.

Many western educated Hindus went back to their own traditions and sought to create new movements within Hinduism that reflected a deeper interpretation of their older teachings as well as a new projection of it for the modern age. They sought to restore, reform and universalize Hindu thought. They did not see a need to abandon their traditions for the trends in western thought or religion that they were exposed to — though that had come to dominate their country and its educational institutions — but rather began to recognize in their own traditions something more spiritual and more comprehensive than the products of the western mind, which seemed to them mired in materialism and dogma.

Swami Dayananda of the Arya Samaj in the late nineteenth century brought about an important call to return to the Vedas and provided strong critiques of western religions and philosophies, which had put Hinduism under siege and in defense. He personally debated with western missionaries and educators and was able to show that Hindu thought had a depth that they could not dismiss or even counter when it was clearly articulated.

Then at the turn of the twentieth century, Swami Vivekananda of the Ramakrishna Mission took the message of

Hinduism, Yoga and Vedanta to the western world itself, where he was enormously successful, setting up missions in Europe and North America that continue to the present day. Vivekananda also helped revive the ancient traditions in India, setting the stage for the modern Hindu, Yoga-Vedanta movement.

Whereas Swami Dayananda sought to preserve the Vedic message to protect Hindu society from colonial efforts to undermine it, Swami Vivekananda sought to universalize the Yoga-Vedantic message to transform the world. Hindu thought suddenly had not only a renewed value for India but a new message for the entire world. Many other teachers and thinkers of India took up similar views and activities.

## INFLUENCE OF INDIAN INDEPENDENCE MOVEMENT

The late nineteenth century saw the beginning of another major movement in Indian thought and society, the Indian independence movement. It started under the inspiration of the Hindu renaissance through Vivekananda, Dayananda, B. G. Tilak, and Sri Aurobindo and others like them, who looked to Hindu thought through the Vedas, Bhagavad Gita and Vedanta for the foundation of the national struggle.

The Hindu renaissance naturally became strongly aligned with the Indian independence movement as India was a Hindu majority country. However, the Indian independence movement proved over time to be both a boon and a curse to the Hindu renaissance, expanding it in some areas but contracting it in others.

Many Hindus joined the movement and brought Hindu values and practices into it. Mahatma Gandhi, who later came to lead the independence movement, wore the garb of a Hindu sadhu, spoke of the Bhagavad Gita as the greatest book, criticized the missionaries, and called himself a Hindu.

However, a tendency arose to modify Hindu thought for the sake of the independence movement. In particular, the need to bring religious minorities into the movement went against the need of Hinduism to awaken and reclaim its ancient glory. The Hindu reconversion movement that Swami Dayananda set in motion was almost brought to a standstill largely by Hindus themselves. It eventually became politically incorrect from the standpoint of the Indian independence movement for Hindus to defend much less promote their religious identity, so as not to politically alienate the non-Hindus in the country.

Because of the political necessities of the Indian independence movement, the effort in Hindu thought to articulate its own unique identity as well as to expand its reach gradually receded. The Hindu renaissance took a back seat for the Indian independence movement.

The fearless and bold self-confidence of Vivekananda, Rama Tirtha and Swami Dayananda in relating the Vedic and Vedantic teachings gave way to an almost timid and apologetic seeking for consensus against the British.

## REPERCUSSIONS OF INDIAN INDEPENDENCE MOVEMENT

The muting of the Hindu voice that occurred in the Indian independence movement became hardened in independent India, largely to maintain political support of the same minorities. Politicians of a Hindu background found that they could get more easily elected by playing to minority religious vote banks and appealing to their religious identities and insecurities.

Hindus remained hesitant to project their own tradition in a positive way, much less criticize other religions, in order to avoid offending religious minorities that might vote against them or feel unwanted in the country. In some respects the situation became worse. For example, very few Indian politicians today would make the same statements against the missionaries that Mahatma Gandhi made during his lifetime, or even quote these, so as to maintain their Christian vote banks.

After the achievement of independence, the history, philosophy and global relevance of Hinduism failed to get properly articulated or taught. Vedic and Hindu schools did not come up. Hinduism did not take its place, much less its seniority and depth in the world's presentation of religious and spiritual traditions. It did not create its own global voice but remained under foreign, alien and often hostile outside interpretations.

While people in the world generally look at Christianity and Islam according to Christian and Islamic sources, Hinduism remains looked at primarily according to non-Hindu sources which have not changed significantly since the colonial era. While India achieved its freedom from colonial rule, Hinduism remained in the colonial and missionary shadow. It was not freed along with the country, nor did independent India seek to remove the distortions about the majority religion of its peoples, which it continued to allow to be taught in its schools, even though it collects money from Hindu temples taken over by government control.

Another negative result of the lack of proper formulation of Hindu thought was that Indians of an intellectual bent went over to other systems, notably Marxism, which had more to offer by way of an intellectual point of view and a future to strive for. People were not given any Hindu identity or sense of worth, so they naturally sought a non-Hindu or anti-Hindu identity. They embraced intellectual critiques of Hinduism and had no Hindu intellectual response to provide any balance.

## THE GLOBAL SPREAD OF HINDU THOUGHT

Global Hinduism has had a similar result, becoming both a help and a hindrance for the Hindu renaissance. In spreading their message globally, Hindu teachers found it easier to promote their own guru or sect of Hinduism and leave Hinduism itself behind or at home. The perceived ethnicity of Hinduism, its being limited to India and those born as Hindus was one side of the issue. The other side was the difficulty of communicating the Hindu tradition as a whole compared to the ease in promoting one particular guru or lineage.

Vivekananda himself, who was the first real global guru from India, found that the greatest interest in the West was in the figure of the guru-avatar, Yoga practices, meditation and a generalized Vedantic thought, while the missionary inspired fear of Hinduism as polytheistic and superstitious was deeply entrenched.

The result was that Hindu gurus in the West tried to appear as universal figures that accepted all religions and were Hindus only by accident of birth. This may have been necessitated by the anti-Hindu propaganda and even racism that they had to face initially — which was still strong in the West particularly in the early twentieth century — but it also became hardened into a trend of its own.

Rather than seeking to reformulate, articulate or defend Hinduism as a whole, Hindu gurus have usually given priority to developing their own particular group and its following, which they then seek to expand in its own right. If you ask western followers of such Indian gurus what religion they follow, they often say that they follow the universal religion of their guru, not that they are Hindus. This may be the case even if the individuals have Hindu names or are Swamis rooted in traditional Hindu orders.

One could say that Hindus are very universal in their sectarianism. Hindu sects have gone global and universal. Some have formulated themselves as new universal religions, with their guru as an avatar. Others claim to have gone beyond religion to a universal spiritual tradition. Yet few have taken the effort to openly honor the greater Hindu tradition or Sanatana Dharma as the universal tradition it has always formulated itself to be, even though they rely upon the Vedas, Upanishads, Bhagavad Gita, Yoga Sutras and other standard teachings of Sanatana Dharma for their particular approaches. There may have been historical or cultural necessities for this phenomenon but its long term limitations must be recognized.

## THE HINDU DIASPORA

The global spread of Hinduism has a human dimension, with many Hindus migrating to the West over the past several decades and some having arrived during the colonial era itself. What they find is that the people in their new countries regard them as Hindus, even if they would rather define themselves according to a particular Hindu sect or in some way as universal. Such Hindus in the West have found a need to define themselves as Hindus not only for westerners to understand them but for their children to continue their traditions.

However, when they look to define what it means to be a Hindu, they find that the Hindu tradition is amorphous and they often don't know exactly what it is. They are torn between a vague universalism, on one hand, and an ethnic identity on the other. They find a lack of educational material in Hinduism to direct their children toward in order to resolve this problem. The lack of any real articulation of Hinduism as a whole has left them at a disadvantage, which other groups have been quick to exploit, especially among the Hindu youth that is vulnerable to peer pressure.

## RELATIVE TO OTHER RELIGIONS

The lack of a proper and accessible definition of Hinduism by Hindus themselves has confused other religions and religious scholars. They may think that Hinduism is not a religion at all but a collection of disparate sects and cults with nothing really in common. Some western scholars see Hinduism as a conglomeration of a Vaishnava, Shaiva and other religions with no common teaching behind them. After all, each Hindu sect has an extensive literature about itself but little to say about or to define Hinduism as a whole.

For many such non-Hindus, the Hindu claim to accept all religions is regarded as a kind of 'me-too' following, a currying of favor from a colonized people, not a sign of a mature analysis or critical understanding of disparate religious doctrines. It seldom helps other religions understand Hinduism and its particular teachings. Though Hindus have been the main religious group today to promote a tolerance of all religions, it is curious to note that the other religions of the world do not respect Hinduism in turn. This may be because Hindus in trying to be all things to everyone do not project a self-confidence or self-definition that others can recognize.

While this urge is understandable and important, there needs to be a clear formulation of how to proceed in a way that is credible and expansive. Many Hindus who want to reclaim the different facets of the Hindu tradition that have been taken over by other groups may not understand Hinduism in the broader sense and how to explain it to the world as a whole.

## THE HINDU BACKLASH

This compromised and co-opted state of Hinduism has naturally had its backlashes, which have similarly had both positive and negative sides as backlashes usually do.

On the positive side, many Hindus are seeking once more to redefine Hinduism as Sanatana Dharma or the universal teaching and the different sampradayas or sects of Hinduism, including the modern universalists, as its branches. While they are recognizing the importance of India as the repository of Santana Dharma, they are also discovering a global Vedic heritage that reaches to every part of the planet.

There are now westerners who are happy to formally become Hindus. Hindu as a religious option is arising all over the world as it is after all the world's third largest religion! In addition, the idea of the Vedic sciences, which includes Yoga, Vedanta, Vedas and Ayurveda under one umbrella, is gaining credibility. People are beginning to discern the outlines of Sanatana Dharma behind its many facets, though a clear understanding of Hinduism as a whole remains rare.

On a social level in India, there has been an arising of political parties and social movements that address Hindu sentiments to counter the favoritism extended to religious minorities in the country that is unparalleled in the rest of the world. However, owing to a great extent because of this same lack of articulation of Hinduism in the broader sense, they can be unclear as to what they are really promoting as Hinduism or as Hindutva, which has itself become a negative term in the global media.

They appear to others as Hindu nationalists, not as universalists portraying Hinduism as relevant to the entire world. They have lacked the intellectual voice to bring out what Hinduism really is and give it a futuristic vision, which has shadowed and limited their efforts.

There is yet another type of Hindu backlash arising among Hindus in the West. Many Hindus are disturbed to find that Hindu teachings through Yoga, Ayurveda and Vedanta have been taken over by various movements in the West without adequate credit given to the original tradition that these come from. Some Hindus now want to take back Yoga, for example, which they find that many people in the West are regarding as a tradition only accidentally or superficially connected to Hinduism.

## CRISIS IN THE HINDU RENAISSANCE

The Hindu renaissance for all of its wonderful gains, whether in spreading Hindu teachings, or aiding in India's independence and resurgence, has suffered from the lack of a clear articulation of Hinduism or Sanatana Dharma as a whole. In spite of the great Hindu renaissance in India and the spread of Hindu gurus and their teachings globally over the last two centuries, there remains a crisis of identity in the Hindu tradition and among Hindus themselves.

Hindus as a whole don't know who they are, what in particular they follow or why. Some Hindu groups have defined their tradition in such a universal and vague manner that it has lost any structure. They are unable to articulate a cogent

Hindu point of view on the pressing issues of our times even where traditional Hindu and Vedic texts have a tremendous amount to offer.

While different Hindu teachings have spread worldwide, an understanding and appreciation for Hinduism as Sanatana Dharma or the universal tradition has not kept pace with this. Meanwhile the different modern Hindu sects that have gone global lack a broader perspective to defend themselves from the challenges of the world around them. Some western Yoga groups – who have avoided any direct association with Hinduism – when attacked as 'cults' have been forced to call themselves Hindus in order to gain credibility at a legal level. It remains to be seen how many generations their particular sects or movements will last without the broader Hindu tradition to defend and support it.

We note a kind of opposite type of imbalance in how Hinduism has developed in the India context versus the global context, two extremes that need to be brought back into harmony. In the India context, Hinduism has remained trapped in an Indian identity with political limitations on how that can express itself or what it appears to be. This can make Hinduism appear backward and unprogressive even to Hindus.

In the global context, Hindu teachers have largely abandoned any Hindu identity and gone universal, ignoring or hiding their roots in Sanatana Dharma, even though it is the Hindu based teachings of Yoga, Ayurveda and Vedanta that have given them their appeal. It is the same problem behind both instances: a failure to articulate Hinduism as Sanatana Dharma in a clear, coherent, comprehensive and consistent manner.

We can contrast this with how Buddhism has presented itself. Buddhist teachers in the West have not denied their Buddhist backgrounds and have tried to give their followers some sense of what this is above and beyond the particular Buddhist sect that they may follow. Perhaps this is because

Buddhism is stronger in more than one country and not so linked with one country's affairs. But it is also because Buddhists have been more willing to take up the intellectual challenge and to recognize a common dharma in the process.

The result of this lack of intellectual articulation and self-defense is that Hinduism all around has remained under attack from conversion seeking religions, political interests, the commercial media, and foreign powers, with little to defend much less promote itself. Hindu society has been misguided, confused and unclear as to how to handle the situation. Even most Hindu gurus have not wanted to address the anti-Hindu propaganda out of fear of exposing themselves to the resultant criticism or the label of being called a Hindu. Hindus have hoped these problems would go away if they ignored them, but have only found that their identity has become increasingly a target of distortion, if not denigration. It is relative to this complex and compromised background that Ram Swarup arose, steadily addressed all the issues and brought about a revolution in Hindu thought which, if followed, can correct this difficult condition.

## RAM SWARUP

Ram Swarup Though he never had an organization, a mission or an ashram and preferred to remain in the background, Ram Swarup nevertheless became one of the dominant figures in modern Hindu thought. He brought an important new point of view into the Hindu renaissance of the past two centuries which can move it in a new positive direction. He not only wrote about Hinduism in the India context but relative to the world as a whole and the major movements and ideologies of our times. He articulated a Hindu point of view in a clear, succinct, cogent and comprehensive manner that makes it compelling for all those who have an open mind and an inner vision.

Ram Swarup represents the deeper response of the Hindu mind to the critical cultural and religious challenges of today. His work has had a strong impact in India already but its main impact is likely to be for the future, for generations yet to come, as he was a thinker ahead of his time. His impact in the West, though crucial in regard to a number of individual thinkers, is yet to come and may prove more significant. Starting with his main disciple and colleague Sitaram Goel, he has inspired a whole group of thinkers and writers East and West, who are disseminating his ideas and inspirations in various ways. In introducing his writings, I will try to first put the Hindu movement into a broader perspective, reflecting my study of his writings.

Ram Swarup provides a compelling intellectual and spiritual defense as well as a universal projection of Hinduism that articulates Hinduism or Sanatana Dharma as a whole, and can help put the Hindu renaissance back on track. He is a unique thinker who has addressed all the main issues of Hindu dharma and has charted a way forward through all potential limitations and distortions. He was willing to stand up and make his voice heard as early as the nineteen fifties, facing the Marxists who then were the darlings of the Indian media, when no individual or group seemed to understand the gravity of the situation or how to deal with it.

Ram Swarup has first of all reclaimed Hinduism as a positive term through his consistent articulation of Hindu thought. Even many Hindus today object to the term Hindu, though they don't seem to have a better name for their great tradition. Ram Swarup has shown that the term Hindu needs to be honored and redefined as Sanatana Dharma or the universal tradition that has always been its real meaning. Though Hinduism as a term still has many negative connotations, largely of a missionary and Marxist nature, terms like Hindu thought, Hindu mind and Hindu Yoga are coming out in a positive way to a great extent because of his influence.

Ram Swarup developed redefinition of Hinduism that has inspired such an important spiritual movement as the Hinduism Today magazine in the West. Following the inspiration of Ram Swarup, Sivaya Subramuniya Swami of Hinduism Today magazine boldly proclaimed, "Hinduism is unique among the world's religions. I boldly proclaim it the greatest religion in the world." The great Swami, with the spiritual confidence of another Vivekananda, goes on to explain all that Hinduism has to offer in terms of mystical teachings and profound Yoga practices that cannot be found actively expressed or represented in any other religion in the world today. He lauds Hinduism for its diversity and abundance of deities, temples, festivals, teachings, gurus, monks and practices. His words are not a sectarian call or a political statement but a sincere appreciation of the greatness of Sanatana Dharma that many people will feel once they understand the overall tradition and its universality that is not limited to a book, savior, prophet, chosen people or dogma.

## RAM SWARUP'S CRITIQUE OF RELIGION

Ram Swarup pioneered a new Hindu examination of other religions, notably Christianity and Islam, that is balanced, clear and rational, based upon higher ideals and insights. He aims towards a universal truth, higher consciousness and yogic values that all religions need to honor. He points out differences between the teachings of Hinduism and Vedanta and those of current Christian and Islamic theology, which inevitably take their followers in different directions. He does much of this by simply contrasting their actual teachings with those of Hinduism, whether in regard to karma and rebirth, higher consciousness, or an understanding of the nature of Atman and Brahman, the higher Self and the Absolute.

If we put the teachings of different religions as their followers commonly know them to be side by side, the distinctions become obvious. All religions are not the same and don't teach the same thing. We need to be as discriminating about religious and spiritual teachings as we are about food, work, relationship, culture or any other major part of life. Ram Swarup has brought that profound yogic discrimination or viveka back into Hindu thought and into the Hindu examination of religious teachings.

He uses yogic psychology to examine the religious experience. In the process he exposes the biases behind conversion based monotheism and shows its idea of deity to be tainted by human prejudices, not a truly spiritual formulation of unity or universality.

His discriminating insight is particularly important in exposing how Christians in India will use Hindu teachings, ideas or images to promote their conversion efforts. Even when liberal Christians in India talk of oneness and Advaita, they will not accept karma and rebirth, much less make any Hindu teacher equal to Christ, or try to stop the conversion of Hindus. Their non-duality, though borrowed from Hindu teachings, is not a unity of truth beyond religious identities but an effort to make Christianity more appealing to the Hindu mind so as to facilitate the conversion process. It is an effort to Christianize Hindu ideas not to take us to a unity beyond all conversion, which is a denial of the sacred nature of the Atman or true Self.

Such a Hindu critique of other religions is necessary and helpful and can serve to balance the criticism of Hindu dharma, most of which is unfounded, that is already out there. It can promote the mystical side of other traditions and help people who want to go beyond the limitations of belief based approaches to an inner experiential yogic spirituality.

Different religions, like different philosophies, will take those who embrace them in specific directions according to their specific prescriptions. We need to be honest with people about that, not sugar coat religious differences in an aim to create social harmony. Social harmony should be based upon free thinking and an acceptance of religious differences — including atheists and agnostics – not an effort to pretend that religious differences do not matter or do not exist.

A mature society can allow religious differences just as it does differences in science, art or culture. A social order that cannot accept religious differences, but must pretend they are not real, must remain limited, artificial and stifling to the spirit. Hinduism is a religion can find unity in diversity, which is a unity of truth beyond the boundaries of all beliefs and organizations. In this way any free thinker can find a place within it. Ram Swarup reveals this pluralistic understanding behind the Hindu sense of unity, which is the real meaning of the harmony of all dharmas.

No one criticizes a Christian or a Muslim for praising their particular religion. It is only the modern Hindu who seems to have lost that self-respect, even though his tradition is far more grandiose and comprehensive. Christians and Muslims are not expected to accommodate Hindu beliefs, whether they live in India or elsewhere in the world, while expressing their views. Yet Hindus are often afraid or perhaps unable to explain what Hinduism is relative to the other religions, which they seldom study or analyze according to the tenets of Hindu thought.

Ram Swarup was a very gentle, kind and soft spoken person, yet he did not compromise the truth or seek favor by trying to please everyone around him. He has shown that Hindus can be tolerant and respectful of others and yet do not have to give up their own critical voice or compromise their own identity in the process. Hindus must learn to hold to the inner truth of their tradition even when relating to people of contrary views that they must seek to counter in order to defend the higher dharma in the global arena.

Perhaps because Ram Swarup was not trying to promote a particular guru or become one himself, he has not fallen into the trap of making his own teachings supreme and distancing himself from the greater Hindu tradition. At the same time, he has always emphasized the flexibility of Hindu thought to provide the vision to discover new solutions to all human problems. He has not simply repeated the old formulas of the past that refer to a time and culture that is no more. He has brought back the Hindu mind and its deeper timeless intelligence, not just promoted old books or old interpretations of them. He has shown how Hindus can reform their own community by a return to the teachings of Sanatana Dharma.

Ram Swarup has provided a new voice to the Hindu mind that brings back its earlier inspiration both for India and for the world as a whole. Yet in the process, he has not merely rubber stamped Hinduism or particular Hindu groups but has recommended both reform and revitalization in reclaiming and expressing the greater Hindu heritage that even many Hindus have forgotten.

## HINDUISM'S FORGOTTEN FRIENDS

Ram Swarup projected a strong Hindu defense, not just of the Hindu tradition but of all related native, indigenous and pagan traditions which have similarly been denigrated by missionary and colonial influences. Most modern Hindu teachers in their rush to gain acceptance by the western monotheistic establishment have tried to make Hinduism appear monotheistic and have avoided any association with non-monotheistic traditions, much less any effort to defend them, though these are their true brothers and sisters facing the same daunting challenges. It is these indigenous and pagan traditions that most resemble Hinduism which itself is the largest pagan religion in the world. They are looking to Hinduism for help and guidance. Ram Swarup has been the main Hindu teacher to hear their call.

Ram Swarup inspired western pagan thinkers and shown that the same denigrations and distortions that are cast on Hinduism are cast on their religions as well (starting with the derogatory terms of pagan, polytheist and animist). He has provided an insight and a self-articulation that they can adapt. He has brought back the role of Hinduism as the defender of all native and consciousness based spiritual traditions that have been similarly attacked by missionary influences and exclusive, belief-oriented dogmas. This new alliance must be pursued and allowed to grow in a natural way. It can change the face of world religion for centuries to come because it can bring humanity back to the Divine presence hidden in nature and her formations of lands, plants, animals, clouds and stars

— the sacred world of Brahman that both monotheistic religions and modern political ideologies rarely see or honor.

## CONCLUSION

The coming decades are bound to bring critical challenges for the world and for India. The powers of materialism, consumerism and terrorism seem stronger than ever. In this context the message of Ram Swarup and the relevance of Hindu thought will become more crucial.

It is important for the Hindu movement to move forward and redefine itself based upon the many-sidedness of its vision. This involves taking a global approach, presenting Sanatana Dharma in the context of the greater Vedic and yogic sciences and culture. The connection of Hinduism with Indian politics that dominated both the independence movement and the post-independence era in both positive and negative ways needs to be put in a broader perspective, which is a greater need to promote Hinduism as Sanatana Dharma for the world overall.

While India will likely play a central role in that projection of the universal Dharma, the effort cannot be limited to the issues of India. At the same time, while Hindu Dharma has a universal vision, this cannot be owned or limited by any sect, teacher or person who uses, adapts or claims any of its teachings. It is Hinduism that is the universal tradition, not any of its ancient or modern offshoots that are but its expressions.

A true Hindu or Sanatana Dharma follower will always take a global view but adapted locally, wherever he or she may live. India is important for its having preserved the global Hindu heritage, not simply for what may occur outwardly in the country. The current Hindu movement in India tends to lose that global perspective and can appear narrow. Hindu teachings like Yoga outside of India are largely in denial of their common Hindu or Sanatana Dharma connections. However useful these approaches may have been at one time, they need to be adjusted today.

The universality that has been applied to various Hindu gurus and sects needs to be applied to and credited to Hinduism as a whole. There need to be a new examination of what Hinduism has been traditionally and what its relevance can be for the future, not by outside scholars but by Hindus themselves. We need new books on Hinduism, its teachings and its history, as well as new Hindu schools to promote Sanatana Dharma and its various branches, arts and sciences. Hindus cannot rely upon the non-Hindu world to do this. They must take the lead and bring the Hindu renaissance back to the forefront. The writings of Ram Swarup can provide the cornerstone for this effort. These should be available in every Hindu temple, ashram, school or institution, particularly where English is the dominant medium of expression.

## MODERN AGE AND THE HINDU RENAISSANCE IN THE 19TH CENTURY

Many Hindu reform movements originated in the nineteenth century. These movements led to the fresh interpretations of the ancient scriptures of Upanishads and Vedanta and also emphasised on social reform. The marked feature of these movements was that they countered the notion of western superiority and white supremacy propounded by the colonizers as a justification for British colonialism in India. This led to the upsurge of patriotic ideas that formed the cultural and an ideological basis for the independence movement in India.

### Brahmo Samaj

The Brahmo Samaj was started by a Bengali scholar, Ram Mohan Roy in 1828. Ram Mohan Roy endeavoured to create from the ancient Upanishadic texts, a vision of rationalist 'modern' India. Socially, he criticized the ongoing superstitions, and believed in a monotheistic Vedic religion. His major emphasis was social reform. He fought against Caste discrimination and advocated equal rights for women. Although the Brahmos found favourable response from the British

Government and the Westernized Indians, they were largely isolated from the larger Hindu society due to their intellectual Vedantic and Unitarian views. But their efforts to systematise Hindu spirituality based on rational and logical interpretation of the ancient Indian texts would be carried forward by other movements in Bengal and across India.

## Arya Samaj

Arya Samaj is considered one Hindu renaissance movements of the late nineteenth century. Arya Samaj is often considered as a social movement, many revolutionaries and political leaders of the Indian Independence movement like Ramprasad Bismil, Bhagat Singh, Shyamji Krishnavarma, Bhai Paramanand and Lala Lajpat Rai were to be inspired by it.

## Swami Vivekananda

Another 19th century Hindu reformer was Swami Vivekananda. Vivekananda as a student was educated in contemporary Western thought. He joined Brahmo Samaj briefly before meeting Ramakrishna, who was a priest in the temple of the goddess Kali in Calcutta and who was to become his guru. Under the influence of Orientalism, Perennialism and Universalism, Vivekananda re-interpreted Advaita Vedanta, presenting it as the essence of Hindu spirituality, and the pinnacle indeed of the development of human's religiosity. This project started with Ram Mohan Roy of Brahmo Samaj, who collaborated with the Unitarian Church, and propagated a strict monotheism. This reinterpretation produced neo-Vedanta, in which Advaita Vedanta was combined with disciplines such as yoga and the concept of social service to attain perfection from the ascetic traditions in what Vivekananda called the "practical Vedanta". The practical side essentially included participation in social reform.

He made Hindu spirituality, intellectually available to the Westernized audience. His famous speech at the Parliament of the World's Religions at Chicago on 11 September 1893, followed huge reception of his thought in the West and made him a celebrity in the West and subsequently in India too. His influence can still be discerned in popular western spirituality, such as nondualism, New Age and the veneration of Ramana Maharshi.

A major element of Vivekananda's message was nationalist. He saw his effort very much in terms of a revitalisation of the Hindu nation, which carried Hindu spirituality and which could counter Western materialism. The notions of White supremacy and Western superiority, strongly believed by the colonizers, were to be questioned based on Hindu spirituality. This kind of spiritual Hinduism was later carried forward by Mahatma Gandhi and Sarvepalli Radhakrishnan. It also became a main inspiration for the current brand of Hindu nationalism today. One of the most revered leaders of the Rashtriya Swayamsevak Sangh (RSS), Babasaheb Apte's lifelong pet sentence was "Vivekananda is like Gita for the RSS." Historians have observed that this helped the nascent Independence movement with a distinct national identity and kept it from being the simple derivative function of European nationalisms.

# CHAPTER 6 The Hinduism

Any one at the first attempt to define Hinduism by recognizing in it the totality of religious forms which originated and developed on Indian soil. It would then be necessary to exclude Buddhism, which in ancient days spread across a large part of Hindustan and still remains very much alive in some areas of the continental borderlands. It would also be necessary to exclude Jainism, which has today about one and a half million followers although in the past it was, relatively at least, more widespread.

Other religious groups would also have to be barred: six million Christians, Jews and Zoroastrians, and some twenty-five million fetishists and animists, who one might say participate in varying degrees in certain elementary forms of Hinduism. In relation to the mass of the Indian population, which at present numbers approximately four hundred million, these groups are practically negligible both statistically and culturally. This is not the case, however, with Islam. Since the eleventh century Islam has steadily drawn millions of persons from the Hindu community; and even today, in spite of the creation of Pakistan as a Muslim state within the subcontinent,

Islam has some thirty-five million followers in the Indian Union. It is not regarded a heresy as for Sikhism, or the religion of the Sikhs, it may be regarded a religious movement at the uttermost limits of Hinduism.

To bound Hinduism within the boundary of India, however, would be to bypass the missionary character of this religion in the past. In the so-called Hinduization of southeast Asia, Indian religious influences combined with indigenous elements and in the course of time were assimilated by Buddhism, Islam or some form of national religion. In this way Hinduism has had a unplumbed influence, especially in Cambodia, ancient Champa and Bali. One should also recall that there are Hindus in Ceylon (among the Dravidian population), in Nepal, in Pakistan (an inestimable number) and in Indian settlements scattered all over the world. Can one rather define Hinduism by its elements?

In real, this will have to be done; but in attempting to find such a unifying definition we run the risk of generalizing to such an extent that we fail to grasp the infinite diversity of forms which constitute Hinduism.

The primitive origin of Hinduism was in part of Indo-European origin; the framework at least was such, while the content was largely indigenous or was modified on the spot. The Aryan tribes which invaded India during the second millennium before our era brought with them a body of religious belief which was already well organized and which survived in classical Hinduism — at the cost of A number of modifications. This "Aryan" religion (that is, Indo-European on Indian soil) had already been sifted out during the so-called Indo-Iranian intermediary period. It was at the end of this period that a separation occurred between the original religion of Iran (pre-Zoroastrian) and what was to become the Vedic religion in north-western India. To this ancient foundation was added a succession of influences which made Hinduism a religion quite various from that of the Aryan invaders. Most of these new developments took place during historical time. The primary stages were the seem ance of great philosophical speculations and the fixation of the Smti (at the beginning of the Christian era), the first fragmentation into sects (first and second centuries A.D.), the seem ance of bhakti (600-800 A.D.), and Tantrism (since 800 A.D.). However all these movements existed, as early as the Vedic period.

It is possible, too, and even likely that Hinduism assimilated some pre-Aryan, or at least non-Aryan institutions which were inherited from regional cults and modified with the primitive Indian data as the basis. The prehistorical civilization of the Indus basin (Mohenjodaro and Harappa), which dates from the beginning of the second millennium before Christ, testifies to some of the characteristics by which we can identify a proto-Hinduism: an image of the Mother Goddess, a horned god in the posture of a Yogin, and ritual emblems of vegetal or animal character. Hinduism is indeed a complex and rich religion. No founder's initiative, no dogma, no reform have imposed restrictions on its domain; on the contrary, the contributions of the centuries have been superimposed without ever wearing out the previous layers of development. In fact, as per the what phenomena one considers, Hinduism can seem either as an extrovert religion of spectacle, abundant mythology and congregational practices or as a religion which is profoundly interiorized.

To the first opinion belong the activities of the sects, the bhakti movement, and the worship of the cow, in which some find the concrete symbol of Hinduism; here, too, could be included the principle of non-violence, at least in its social application. To the view of Hinduism as an interior life belong the paths of spiritual progress, the quest for liberation, the tendency to renunciation, and ultimately the intensive concentration on problems which in other cultures are more often reserved for theologians or philosophers. Hinduism, which is eminently popular in its practices and external expressions, is essentially also a religion of the learned: it cannot be understood if the Vedanta and the Samkhya have not been fully comprehended or if, at the outset, there is no idea of the immense network of symbolism which underlies and links together all Indian thought. Ultimately, Hinduism characterizes society as a whole. The caste system with its various "stages" of existence is part of Hinduism. Life is looked upon as a rite; there is no absolute dividing line between the sacred and the profane. In fact, there is no Hindu term corresponding to what we call "religion." However there are numerous "approaches" to the spiritual life; and there is dharma, or "maintenance" (in the right path), which is at once norm or law, virtue and meritorious action, the order of things transformed into moral obligation — a principle which governs all expressions of Indian life.

When, it may be asked, did Hinduism begin? An answer to this question can only be indirect: Hinduism began at the time when the original activity of the Vedic ritual came to an end, when the old Vedic framework was lost. We may date this occurrence, perhaps, between the sixth and fourth centuries B.C. From this perspective, a text or a religious expression is designated as Hindu as long as it does not reveal any trace of division into schools or of the ancient liturgical patterns. Before our era of the Epics, the ethico-juridical literature and the Aphorisms (Sutras) which served as the basis for grand speculations similar was the situation.

Indeed after all the situation, however, is not quite so clear, for just as there was an undercurrent of Hinduism in Vedism, so there is Vedic survivals in classical Hinduism. The name of "Brahmanism" is sometimes given to the oldest of the learned forms of Hinduism. But taking everything into consideration, it is preferable to look upon Hinduism as a whole without looking for superficial subdivisions. On this interpretation Vedism is regarded the most ancient form of Hinduism. Certainly Vedism cannot be neglected since all that follows it is inexplicable without it. If we are to look for a global characterization of Hinduism, we could (as was recently suggested) consider it the very type of a religion of renunciation. Certainly Hinduism could exist without those who renounce, but it would remain singularly impoverished and would be as if deprived of its crest. Various elements of the religion seem to have been created for the man who has withdrawn from mundane life, or they were later modified for his needs. This could explain the evolution of the theory of Karman and of transmigration, perhaps too the development of bhakti and (by a kind of reversal) of Tantrism. On a common ground, we can consider as effects of renunciation both Indian pessimism and the escapist tendency, which may go so far as to reject the elementary exigencies of religion. It is all an affair of the individual. Hinduism does not know the opposition which is found in Buddhism between a well-developed monastic milieu and a secular environment.

## Uniqueness of Hindu Religion

Among all the great Religions of the world Hinduism is unique as it had no single founder or Messiah nor a single book as a source but grew gradually over a period of several thousand years. The Hindu society is the product of A number of races and A number of cultures with several forms of practice. It evolved out of the varying faiths in various groups of the community as it was absorbing and assimilating all the diversified social movements and cultural practices of India. Consequently, it does not have a single Holy book as a source to guide all, like a Bible or Koran or Dhammapadam. Most of their beliefs and practices are based on the teachings of the Vedas, Agamas, Upanishads and several books written, based on these texts. Large portions of these texts are lost. Hindus believe that their religion is without beginning, even preceding the creation of human race and the creation of the universe. They believe that creation of the universe and their life are without beginning or end and is a continuous process, a cycle of creation and dissolution.

The Vedas are the very breath of this process with which Lord Brahma, the creator, creates the universe and all its lives. The name "Hindu" is said to have been derived from the name given by the Western and Persian scholars to the people settled on the River Sindhu. Some believe the name has a much older origin in the scriptures. Scholars often referred to this as the Brahmanical faith. Hindus called it "Vaideeha Dharma" or "Sanathana Dharma". Philosophers often do not want to refer to it as a mere religion, as that will narrow it down to a blind faith of prayers to God. It permits free thinking, questioning and facting. It allows both philosophy and rituals. As it accepts various forms of worship it accepts even atheists and agnostics.

Simplicity and complexity are the most favourable factors and characteristics contributing to the greatness of Hindu Religion. It permeates totally the life of every Hindu from the moment of his birth, throughout his life, whether he is a believer or not, whether a scholar or an illiterate. It is followed more as a way of life. However, Hindu Religion is a rare faith with very few "dogmas, dos and don'ts." It accepts the reality that all people, with the variations in their intellectual maturity, cannot understand and accept to follow the same path though the goal will be the same. It has A number of teachings showing the various spiritual paths available to various types of people. It permits the greatest freedom of worship, as each person is guided by his or her own spiritual experience. Hindu Religion does not accept a single dogma or a dictatorial religious guidance. It has tremendous tolerance for other religious faiths and beliefs. Lord Krishna in Bhagavat Geetha says, "Who-so-ever follows any faith and worships me in what-so-ever form with steadfastness and with devotion, his faith in that form shall I indeed reinforce". The religion permits worship and rituals in various forms for several Deities, though; every worshipper knows that he or she is offering the prayers only to the one great Almighty who will come to them in every form they pray. Very few religions of the world have such a tolerant approach. Hinduism has attracted thinkers from all over the world through the ages. However, even educated Hindus are often unaware of what this religion really stands for or teaches, though a number of people do some prayers blindly following the customs left by their family. One among the several causes was the subjugation by alien rulers of Islamic and Christian faiths for many years.

Among all the religions of the world Hinduism is the oldest religious faith. It is the faith of the diverse groups of people of this area, in India, Nepal and Indonesia, over 900 million people. There are A number of other ancient cultures in these areas that were influenced by the Hindu faith. It is believed to have been practiced in the Indian subcontinent, in the west Asia and Southeast Asia for over 6000 years.

Western Historians, often limited by their Biblical theories, said that it originated from the cultural practices of "Aryan invaders" to the Indus valley in 2500 BC. A simple story told over the years becomes an accepted part of history. Hindu Scholars discounted this view and say that it was present for over 7 to 10 thousand years all over India and West Asia. The ancient India had several groups of farmers and nomadic hunters. They all had a number of various faiths and beliefs and followed their own methods of prayer rituals. All these got absorbed with Hindu religion.

Researchers and the historians always find it hard to fix the specific dates of the origin of the faith or the time in which various religious texts were written. Even the early Puranas refer to "Devas" and "Asuras" often fighting wars. It is possible these stories are based on such historical incidents. It is interesting to note that while in our mythology Devas were the good ones and Asuras were the bad, early Persians referred to their good gods as "Ahuras" and "Ahura Mazda" and bad ones as "Daevas," though all of them were also religious and prayed to God and performed rituals to Fire, like the rituals in Rig Veda. In all these Puranas, very little information is given about the time or the name of the author. For a long time a number of these works were passed on as recitation, by mouth. Later, a number of sages arranged them in proper orders. Any records of the historical dates of these events are obviously artificial, though attempts have been made to divide the period into some convenient time-frames.

The mythology of Hinduism is rich, multifarious, and inclusive. It portrays the terrible alongside the benevolent, the trivial alongside the cosmic, and the grotesque alongside the sublime. The earliest source of Hindu mythology is the Vedic literature, the oldest texts of which are the four Vedas, or "Books of Knowledge": Rigveda, Yajurveda, Samaveda, and Atharvaveda. These books are the oldest Indian documents and represent the religion of the Aryan invaders of the subcontinent over the period from 1400 to 500 BC. Because it integrates a variety of heterogeneous elements, Hinduism constitutes a complex but largely continuous whole; and, because it covers the whole of life, it has religious, social, economic, literary, and artistic aspects. Hinduism thus can't be defined precisely.

## HINDU RELIGION AND THE ETERNAL TRUTH

There are literally thousands of books, spiritual literature and scriptures to guide both the beginners and the scholars. There are several pathways given to the followers. It is not based on any single book or the words of any single teacher or prophet. It does not follow any blind doctrine. Everyone is allowed to study, question, and doubt, analyse, fact and then accept the teachings after their own spiritual experience. The first sets of books are known as "Sruthis" or "Vedas." They are "of Superhuman or Divine origin".

They are unchangeable, highest spiritual knowledge of the Eternal Truth ever known. They are older than creation itself. In the beginning of each era (Kalpa), the Supreme God, Brahmam, creates Himself as Brahma, and gives Him the knowledge of Vedas as His own breath. The Universe and all its beings are created by Brahma out of the sound of Pranava Manthra "OM" and the knowledge of Vedas. Vedas are the primary authority and the very soul of Hinduism. They were revealed to the Rishis, the sages or seers, who received them as an intuition by direct revelations from God. Sage Veda Vyasa codified and organized the four Vedas, Rig, Yajur, Saama and Atharva.

His disciples Paila, Vaisampaya, Jobjectiveini and Sumanta taught them to their disciples and the latter in turn to their pupils. This way, the knowledge of Vedas was passed on through generations by memorizing and reciting the verses for thousands of years. The Rig Veda consists of 1028 Sookthas collected as 21 sections or Sakhas with hymns in praise of the Divine. Yajur Veda, with 109 sakhas, mainly consists of Hymns used in religious rituals and rites. Saama Veda has 1000 sections, and it is made of Verses from Rig Veda set to music. Atharva Veda has 50 sakhas with 598 hymns, gives a number of rites and rituals to guide man in his daily activities and materialistic life, to ward off evil and destroy enemies.

In the same manner Advaitha philosophy like Veda, describe the Supreme formless God as Nirguna Brahmam. He manifests with His veil of Maya as Saguna Brahmam, in the hundreds of forms that are worshipped in our Temples and houses, so that the common man can understand. Each individual is allowed to pray to any of the expressions explained in our Agamas, Ithihasas and Puranas. Every Hindu who worships these forms knows very well this truth that all these forms lead to the One Divine Force and the various Images used in the worship are only for the sake of concentration to a figure for rituals. "Ekam Sat Vipra Bahudhah Vadhanthi" — Truth (The Supreme Reality) is One but the Sages call It (Him) by a number of names. They all know that God in His true form or nature is far beyond comprehension. The Vaishnavites refer to "Him" as Savisesha Brahmam, as the supreme God who is not without form but without attributes and beyond our understanding. In this manner all the religions of the world in one or other form accepts Hinduism a distinct and unique religion. All the individuals are allowed to pray to any form after accepting that form as their personal Deity, Ishta Devatha. They develop all the devotion and love to God in that form. They get the rights to perform the rituals after getting trained in the rules by "Adhikaras". Each one gets these training from a guru, teacher, a parent or an elder member in the family.

When Hindus pray to their Deities at home or in Temples, they pray to images, statues or pictures. They are often criticized by the ignorant outsiders as senseless "Idol worshippers." However, for the Hindu, it makes all the sense as they worship the formless Divine as Vigrahas. It may be a human figurine, a lamp, fire, water, Sun, a stone or clay shaped like a cone or Linga or just the formless space. It is no various from National Flag for a soldier in war, Cross for a Christian, Kaba for a Muslim or the Holy book for any religion.

They are all just various forms of representation of a faith, to respect and worship. The basic principle of Hinduism is the belief in one supreme being who is without forms or attributes, worshipped in any one of several of His forms of expressions. They believe that God accepts every one's prayer to every form they worship.

They believe in non-violence or Ahimsa, in vegetarian food habits, and in compassion to all lives. They believe in Divine duty or Dharma and activity without attachment or Karma yoga and the need for a devotion and surrender to God or Bhakthi. They believe in the indestructibility of the soul, cycle of rebirth and the ultimate liberation of the Soul or Moksha. The basic philosophies are given in the various Upanishad and portions of the Vedas.

Ancient Sages wrote the six Dharsanas as explanatory texts for these Upanishads. Vaiseshika, Sankhya and Vedantha Dharsanas deal with theoretical aspect of the religious faith, prayers and the philosophy. Nyaya, Yoga and Poorva Mimamsa systems explain the practice of the faith with analysis, logic and pure rituals. Nyaya system is the science of debate, logic and discussion with facting and arguing as described by Rishi Gauthama. Vaiseshika by Rishi Kanada arranges its inquiries into categories such as substance, quality, action, property and non-existence. They were the analytical Systems. Sankhya by Rishi Kapila is called a synthetical system starting from a primordial principle called prakrithi which evolves and brings forth everything, when it comes in contact with Purusha. The

Yoga system by Sage Patanjali is a supplement to Sankhya, laying emphasis on the practical side of self discipline and concentration. Poorva Mimamsa of Sage Jobjectiveini lays stress on the Vedic rituals and sacrifices as the ultimate for the liberation and eternal happiness. They did not deny a God but just ignored His existence. Other Mimamsakas modified Sri Jobjectiveini's theory later to introduce the concept of God in rituals. Uttara Mimamsa or Vedantha of Sage Vyasa or Krishna Dvaipanya explained the Hindu Philosophy.

Like any scientific theory the Philosophical teachings of Hinduism, are of no use to the common man unless it is applied for their daily practice. It has survived the test of time for a number of thousand years and still remains popular due to the sound principles on which its practice is based. It gives various rules of ethics and conducts for various categories of people. The Dharma Sasthras and Smrithis teach us of normal conduct in performing our work. Dharma, Artha, Kama and Moksha are the four Purusharthas that govern out activity. Dharma is the proper rules of one's duty, which literally means "that which holds" the universe and its beings. They are classified as SaA number ofa Dharma or the general and universal rules and Visesha Dharma or specific personal rules for each individual. They give peace, joy, strength and tranquillity. Artha and Kama are the materialistic desire and passion that also govern our actions. Unless one seeks the material benefits and pleasures within the scope of Dharma, it will cause grief with greed and lust. The relief from pain and suffering and ultimate liberation that is the chief fact for all our actions is Moksha or Liberation.

The four Yogas give us the spiritual discipline of our conduct. Karma Yoga is the correct path of performing work without greed or desire and the action performed without looking for the fruits of benefit or loss. As rituals became popular and were being regarded as the sole path for the eternal bliss, the soundness of its philosophy and ethics of practice were reestablished by the sages. Raja Yoga is the discipline of control of our body and mind. It teaches concentration, meditation, breathing and physical exercise and a state of equanimity of the mind as a natural reaction to all activities. Bhakthi Yoga is the spiritual discipline of absolute devotion and love of God. It teaches prayers and surrender to God at all times. It teaches to see and feel God in all people and all actions.

In the Vedas and Agamas rituals at the Temple and at home are given. Hinduism dictates several rituals for various occasions based on days, Stars and phase of the Moon. Every one needs to perform certain Karmas and rituals as part of their daily duties to the family, to the community, to animals, to ancestors and to God. They are called "Runa" and "Nithya Karma". At home, rituals are conducted for birth, stages of life, first feeding, starting of education, starting of religious study, for marriage and during pregnancy for the child. Funeral rituals and annual rites are conducted for the departed souls. A number of other rituals are conducted based on star positions and New Moon days. The offerings are given in front of Fire or water in a temporarily prepared area in the house or in a community hall or river bank. Vedic prayers are recited by priests and the person performing the service.

Offerings (such as food, cloth, coconut, clarified butter, fruits) are put into Fire as a sacrifice offered to the celestial forces, called Devas, often mistaken by outsiders as "A number of gods". In addition to these rituals, devotional prayers are also conducted to various images of a personal God in any of His expressions, called Ishta Devatha. It is believed that a person should get proper knowledge and training from a religious teacher or Guru before he or she can get the rights or "Adhikara" to perform these prayers. In these rituals, God in one of His forms is invited as a guest to the house, honoured with a ceremonial bath and washing of feet. Then He is offered dress, sandal paste, jewellery and food and then prayers are recited in praise of him. The deity is ceremonially installed and these prayers are offered every day in the temples.

In Hinduism it is believed that the Nirguna Brahmam is without forms or attributes and is Impersonal. It is hard to visualize and comprehend for ordinary people due to their ignorance and limitations. Therefore, to make this Universal Spirit easily understandable, we have Saguna Brahmam, God with a number of forms and attributes that are known as the One Great God or Ishwara. Thus the average man or woman is able to offer their prayers to the Divine in any one of the several forms He has manifested to protect the universe and the humanity from great calamity, whenever the rule of righteousness declines and injustice triumphs. Every Hindu knows that, when they pray to any one of the several forms, God will accepts their prayers in that form and He will manifest again and again to protect the pious ones and destroy the evils and evil doers and establish the "Dharma."

Ithihasas basically are the historical narrations of ancient times explaining such incarnations of Maha Vishnu as Sri Rama in Ramayana and Sri Krishna in Mahabharatha. We also have various expressions of Siva, Vishnu, Sakthi and several others explained in the Puranas. Agamas explain the rules of building temples for God in various expressions and the rules of rituals to be performed for these Deities. Jnana and Karma path deal with the Formless Brahmam. Bhakthi pathway supports the love, devotion and ultimate surrender to God in one of His A number of forms. Historically, the evolution of the system of Bhakthi and prayers to various Deities is very ancient and is as old as the Vedas.

## Vedism

Many historians are of the view that Hinduism turned its back on Vedic beliefs. If this is true, it is just as factable to claim that Hinduism is a continuation of the Veda. Not only did the Veda offer in an embryonic state the majority of the characteristics which developed with the passage of time, but also classical Indian mythology would scarcely be digestible without the Veda, in which private rites as well as much Hindu speculation have their source. The Vedic religion consisted first of all of a very highly developed mythology. Its pantheon lacked an absolute sovereign and distributed gods as per the the regions occupied by them, as per the their relation with rites, and as per the the functions which they represented.

The general tendency was to attribute highest significance to the god who was being invoked by conferring on him those attributes which generally belonged to other gods. Still, there were gods who permanently occupied an honoured and lasting place. First among these was Indra was a doer of warlike deeds who drove back darkness, killed the demon, and protected the Aryas, being the "Arya" god par excellence. Then, among the major gods, there were two complementary deities personifying sacrifice: Agni, god of fire with its diver's forms, and Soma, god of plant and liquor. Man addressed prayers to the gods, asked of them material goods and a long life. He knew, however, that in and above the gods there were abstract forces which were active. Notable among these was Zta, the force of order which correlated the cosmic and the human. The profound meaning of Vedic prayer was precisely to maintain order: to watch carefully the normal course of natural phenomena so that by following these patterns, the ritual courses can guarantee perenniality in its realm.

Through the Rig-veda, a hard text which comprises hymns addressed to the gods this mythology and its underlying speculations are known. This text, which may be dated from the middle of the second millennium B.C., is the most ancient literary document of India and one of the most ancient of the Indo-European world. It is composed in very archaic Sanskrit. Texts later than the Rig-veda reveal other aspects of the religion. Magic, or more correctly prayers of a compelling motive, is the subject of poems contained in the Atharva-veda, a text which is probably a little later than the Rig-veda in origin. This text also comprises the most ancient traces of cosmogonic speculation. Yet even in the comparatively recent portion of the Rig-veda is to be found the theme of the primitive man, a sort of cosmic giant who was immolated at the time of the First Sacrifice. Out of his limbs originated the human and animal species, notions and things. This is the archetype of Indian myths of creation. Other collections contain formulas to be recited during the course of ceremonies. And along with these formulas (which are often borrowed from the verses of the Rig-veda), there are explanations and commentaries to clarify their usage. The most important commentary is the Brahmagyans out of the chief subject of the texts called Brahmagyans the Hundred Paths.

In addition there are formulas and commentaries adapted to more secret practices, which take place in the silence of the forest. It is in these that we find the beginning of that esoteric teaching which later was to play such an important part in India. In these, too, is found the path toward the world of those dedicated to Renunciation. However most of the texts, beginning with the Rig-veda, were composed with a view toward sacrifice. Sacrifice was at the centre of the Vedic religion: a succession of oblations and prayers, fixed as per the strict liturgy, in which the culmination was reached when the offering was placed in the fire. The objective of the ritual was to enter into communication with the divine world and thence to acquire certain advantages which profane initiative could not enjoy. Sometimes vegetables and animal, the offering comprises predominantly of the Soma plant, from which is extracted a liquor which possesses intoxicating qualities.

No prayers were disassociated from cult; there were neither temples nor idols; but there existed a body of paid priests who during the performance of the ceremony put themselves at the disposal of the patron and his wife while they participated in the ceremonial. The scenario varied greatly from a simple daily oblation in the fire to the sacrificial sittings in which the king celebrated his victories in majestic manner or was anointed at the time of his coronation (Rajasuya).

Private rites were performed by the head of the family with a restricted liturgy at the family hearth. Description of all these practices is preserved in the Sutras, which are texts of aphoristic style (solemn or private, strictly religious or semi juridical). These texts, like the whole of Vedic literature, are the property of special schools, each of which have its own practices and refer to various portions of the ancient canon. We can form only an imperfect idea of such a religion whose past extends over centuries without any clear evidence of an evolution. Certain aspects of the religion, especially its socio-cultural context, remain obscure. Although it does not disregard interior ritual or asceticism, it is primarily a ritualistic religion in which the believer defines faith as the conviction he has of the exactitude and effectiveness of the rite. Moral obligation demands the exercise of good acts, of giving ("Give in order to receive").

A number of the primitive values of restraint and of the exchange of goods have been preserved in the Vedic religion. On ultimate ends and future life there is no clear perspective: during the period of the Brahmagyan men beg that they may not "die again." Toward the end of what is generally called the Vedic period, that is, toward the fifth or fourth century B.C., there seem ed new texts, the Upanishads or "Equivalences." Without abandoning ancient modes of thought, these texts reveal a sort of Gnosticism which attempts to explain by way of parables that the atman or individual soul is identical with Brahman or the universal soul. "Thou art That": that is to say, "Thou, the individual, art identical with the ultimate principle of things." This is the supreme truth which leads to Liberation. Thenceforth the world of the gods, the external apparatus of cult, which had already been strongly reduced in the Brahmagyan, tended to disintegrate. We discover an allegorical ritualism, a religious form of an introspective type. This form endured in the background of later religious expressions in India and nourished whole Hinduism. In its birth ground it was a sort of avant-garde among the circles of the professional ritualists.

A popular Hinduism flourished after the Upanishads. Suddenly we encounter a religion open to all tendencies, one which in a number of respects was more akin to primitive Vedism with its luxuriant mythology than to the semi esoteric Vedism of the Upanishads and Aranyakas.

## THE EVIL OF CASTE IN HINDU SOCIETY

Hindu society is plagued by the ills of caste system and of late, this problem has taken the proportions of Goliath and is threatening the very integrity of the nation. The society in India is rather divided on the basis of caste and not a single day passes without an incident where caste becomes the focal point. Recently in Maharshtra State a Dalit family of four was done to death by the upper caste Hindus and there was big riot and arson in the State.

Similar incidents also take place in other State from time to time. Trains were burnt, shops were looted and life came to stand still. A caste war is a regular phenomenon in Bihar and Jharkhand States.

For western people, this issue appears rather very strange and weird. The extreme end of caste problem is the case of untouchability that was once predominant in Hindu society.

This practice although has died out outwardly, is still raising its head at some place or other in the country and causing serious heart burns.

These issues have been examined. The caste system and the practice of untouchability have lowered the image of Hinduism in the eyes of the world. Eminent social reformers in all ages tried to fight the system and could not eliminate the evil. The modern stalwarts like Mohandas Karamchand Gandhi, Babasaheb (Respectful addressing in Hindi) Dr Bheem Rao Ambedkar (Much publicized as an architect of Indian Constitution and an eminent Barrister), Mahatma Phule, the social reformer are some of the noted social reformers who struggled to eradicate the evil. But they could not succeed. Frustrated Ambedkar finally shifted over to Buddhism from Hinduism.

The problem was also recognized in 12th century in the present State of Andhra Pradesh by eminent social reformer Brahma Naidu (Brahmanna), the Prime Minister of King Nalagama Raja who ruled at Gurajala in the present Guntur District and was a very valiant military commander.

His policies also resulted in the great Palanati Battle fought in 1182 ~1186 in which scores were slain and almost all the South Indian Kings took part in the battle that was mostly the outcome of a family feud.. Hindu society is divided into four castes. These are firstly Brahmin (Priestly class, secondly Kashatriya (War like or ruling class), Thirdly Vaisya (Merchant Class) and lastly Shoodra (Servent class).

The shoodra category has innumerable sections and tribes and at the lowest end are the untouchables. These were named Harijans by the Late Mohandas Karamchand Gandhi (Father of Nation) who did not want to address them as untouchables and gave a respectful word and called them Harijans meaning God's men. This term is under disuse now and Harijans are being addressed as Dalits. The first three castes which are called upper castes have many sects, all falling in their respective class. The most important question is whether the caste system was sanctioned by the scriptures and was it an authorized practice. Caste System or Varna Ashrama has been one of the most misrepresented, misinformed, misunderstood, and misused and the most maligned aspects of Hinduism.

If one wants to understand the truth, the original purpose behind the caste system, one must go to antiquity to study the evolution of the caste system. Caste System, which is said to be the mainstay of the Hindu social order, has no sanction in the Vedas. The ancient culture of India was based upon a system of social diversification according to spiritual development, and enlightenment, not by birth, but by his karma.

Lord Krishna in his discourse Bhagavad-Gita proclaimed:

"Chaturvaranm maya shrushtam Gunak Karmaha Vibhagasya"

It means the Lord has created the system of four Varna (Castes) according to one's own traits and Karma. Thus the Varna system has not been sanctioned as per birth. However over a period of time the system has degenerated in to the present State and continues to plague the society.

One could attain higher Varna by gaining higher knowledge and conducting in enlightened way. An example of eminent Sage Vishwamitra is quoted. He was originally a distinguished Kshatriya king named Gadheya. Once, he went to a hermitage and there he and his retinue were treated by the most revered and illustrious sage Vashishta by the grace of the divine cow Surabhi that could bestow any thing at request.

Knowing the divine powers of the divine cow, the king wanted to take away the Cow from the hermitage and this was resisted viciously by the cow and Vashishta. Inspite of great army at hand, the King could not take possession of the divine cow and had to retreat in defeat and utter shame. He realized that his kingly powers were of no use against the spiritual powers of Sage Vashishta. He then took a vow that he would attain the status of Brahamrshi by undergoing penance and accordingly, he relinquished his throne and retired to the forests where he underwent great penances.

Although he attained great powers, these were of no use against Vishwamitra as he could not overcome his ego that was a trait of the ruling class and was addressed as Rajarshi (stature lesser than Brahmarshi).

Finally, he could attain his goal with great determination and sacrifice and self illumination and Vishwamitra accepted him a Brahmarshi and as Brahman as the one who attained highest knowledge. This goes to show that one could attain higher position in the structure of Varna by gaining higher and superior knowledge and by exemplary conduct. Similarly, the one at higher level could downgrade himself by his poor conduct in the society.

However the system became hereditary and over the course of many centuries degenerated as a result of exploitation by some priests, and other socio-economic elements of the society. It is also believed that the ruling class in league with the priestly class modified the scriptures to suit them and have complete control over the lower castes. The scriptures Smritis were written by Brahmins who were overwhelmed by Kshatriyas. Brahmins by nature are averse to warfare and were thus confined to living by patronage and begging. The Kshatriya community to keep the most intelligent class of Brahmins in good humour patronized them, bowed to them and made them royal priests. People have to bow to them after giving alms to Brahmins.

Thus their superiority was confirmed as a class and their ego was not hurt. Or else, the most intelligent community would have turned against Kshatriyas that they could ill afford. There is no reference of untouchability in Vedas and it is believed that the original inhabitants of India were called Dasyas and were conquered by the invading Aryans and these were subsequently downgraded to the class of untouchables.

Taittereeyaranyaka Bramamedhe Purusha Sooktam a very important and revered scripture states in Sanskrit :

"Om sahasra seersha purushaha sahasraksha ssahasrapaath

Ssa bhoomin vishwatho vruthwa atyathishta ddasaangulam

Brahmanosya Mukha maaseeth Baahu Rajanyaha Krutaha

Ooroo tadasya Yadvyasyaha padbhyagam Soodro Ajayatha"

It describes that Brahmins were born out of the mouth of the God while Kshatriya were the outcome of the shoulders. Vaisya was born out of the thighs and Shoodra emanated from the feet of the lord. As per the above verses, the Lord who is omnipresent and omnipotent occupies entire universe with thousand hands, thousand eyes, and thousand feet.. He occupies entire universe and measures ten inches. The word Ajayata indicates birth. Unfortunately, the verse was wrongly interpreted.

The God who is having thousand heads has only thousand arms, feet and thousand eyes while it should have been double of them. How can he measure only ten inches? This looks absolutely untrustworthy. It should have been interpreted that the God is capable of watching with thousands of eyes and capable of occupying with thousands of feet and hands. It shows his vastness in the universe and indicates infinite character. The descriptions should be considered in a metaphorical way and not word by word through grammar. Brahmins recite the Vedas and scriptures through mouth and are embodiment of knowledge.

Therefore they were considered to be the facial portions representing the face of the God. It does not amount to have taken birth through the mouth of the Lord. Kshatriya lives by the power of their arms and therefore represents the arms of the Lord. Vaisya sit at one place and do trading. Therefore they are identified with the thighs of the Lord. Shoodra live by serving the others by doing various jobs and trades and thus they are identified with the feet of the Lord.

It is tragic that inspite of interpreting the verse in the above fashion some elements took literal meaning causing great commotion in the Hindu society leading to hatred and sectarian fissures. The Dalits are up in arms against these writings. It is a usual practice that in the demonstrations of Dalits, these scriptures are burnt on the streets along with Manu smriti and Parashara smriti another treatise on Hindu code that has survived for centuries. These writings can not stand scientific logic and has no evidence like many other writings in scriptures of other religions. It goes by faith.

However, as Alain Danielou, son of French aristocracy, author of numerous books on philosophy, religion, history and arts of India, says: "Caste system has enabled Hindu civilization to survive all invasions and to develop without revolutions or important changes, throughout more than four millennia, with a continuity that is unique in history.

Caste system may appear rigid to our eyes because for more than a thousand years Hindu society withdrew itself from successive domination by Muslims and Europeans. Yet, the greatest poets and the most venerated saints such as Sura Dasa, Kabir, Tukaram, Thiruvalluvar and Ram Dasa; came from the humblest class of society." In the words of Sarvepalli Radhakrishnan, "In spite of the divisions, there is an inner cohesion among the Hindu society from the Himalayas to the Cape Comorin."

Caste system has been exploited against the Hindus, for the last two centuries by the British, Christian Missionaries, Secular historians, Communists, Muslims, Pre and Post-Independence Indian politicians and Journalists for their own ends. The selfish political leaders in the country have misused the caste system to generate further passions between communities and propagated sectarian fissures and these are striking at the very roots of the society and threatening the integrity of the nation. The society is at loggerheads with each other threatening the existence of the nation.

The corrupt and selfish political and community leaders leave no stone unturned to derive personal benefit and to attract the masses in to their vote bank and thereby causing very great damage and destabilization to the society and the country. The liberties such as freedom of expression under the constitution have been thoroughly misused in India to flame up passions and mutual hatred. No other society in the world is plagued by this problem in the form of defined caste. The caste feuds have also resulted in the rise of Naxalism a type of communist armed struggle in India. Social exploitation and discrimination and atrocities in the villages by the upper castes and landed gentry have resulted in this rise of militancy and this is predominant in states such as Bihar and newly formed State Jharkhand.

Naxalism has strong roots in Telangana province of Andhra Pradesh State (Ex Nizam State, the princely province in the heart of India that was a protectorate of former British Government in India. Nizam tried to be independent in 1947. But finally ceded to India in 1948 when Indian Army invaded it from all corners of the State and this action was called Police action, but not military action.). Some critics however are of the opinion that the caste system in Hinduism has been unduly highlighted by the media and state that one way to discredit any system is to highlight its excesses, and this only adds to the sense of inferiority that many Indians feel about their own culture.

Caste system is often portrayed as the ultimate horror, in the media, while social inequities continue to persist in theoretically Egalitarian Western Societies.

The Caste system is judged offensive by the Western norms, yet racial groups have been isolated, crowded into reserves like the American Indians or Australian Aborigines, where they can only atrophy and disappear. In these western societies, the caste system may not exist as defined norm as in Hinduism while they discriminate the natives, the black and aborigines as inferior class. For centuries, the black Americans suffered discrimination and were slaves of white Americans. There is an element of truth in these statements too. In European and

American society, names represent the profession such as carpenter, smith, cowman etc.

However there is no organized discrimination in other societies as Hinduism has in its society. The slight bright hope is that the discrimination has slightly reduced now while untouchability has been drastically reduced if not fully eliminated and raises its ugly head in some form or other. The Indian Government has catered for various reservations in Government jobs, educational Institutions, Professional colleges such as medicine, Engineering, Architecture, pharmacy and Dental Courses. Reservations have also been laid down in various parliamentary constituencies and legislatures of States apart from various local and municipal bodies.

The constitution although has catered for such reservations for a limited period after independence, these facilities have been extended year after year and even after 60 years of independence from the British yoke, there by causing severe social strain. It is widely alleged that merit has been kept aside and thrown into a dust bin while mediocre and poor stuff are being promoted in all fields of life thereby causing severe damage to the governance in the country. Fortunately, Defence services in India have not been affected by these reservations where merit counts to some extent although sycophancy too allegedly dominates in ones rise in Rank and status and securing higher brass on shoulders. Some States and political parties vie with each other in extending more and more reservations based on the castes to become popular and gain vote banks. These gimmicks have resulted in serious unrest among youth and agitations that have resulted in further cleavages between various castes and sects in the society.

But the political leaders and the ruling governments are least bothered and are busy in finding ways and means to circumvent and overcome the various judgments of the highest court of the land against some of the reservation policies of the governments. Some political parties and leaders at full throat and pitch voice their condemnation against Supreme Court judgments thus making mockery of justice in India and it has been reduced to a laughing stock in the world on this account in recent times. These leaders get away Scot free from the law for contempt of court.

Thus it is seen that caste system although was not sanctioned by Vedas made inroads into the society and got entrenched. With Government policies, further irreparable damage has been done to the society and it would be impossible to eradicate the evil.

Vested interests have developed due to various reservations where merit is thrown to winds. Reservations in political appointments, ministries, governorships, and professional courses, top central government services such as Indian Administrative and police and foreign services have made reservations more lucrative and all efforts are made to continue and institutionalize these reservations.

The most important aspect of caste system is its influence on Christians and Muslims too who converted from Hinduism. Even after conversion, they maintain identity with the original caste and others in the religion are not accepting them as their equals. Christianity and Islam do not discriminate among men.

But Christian convertees maintain titles such as Mala Christian and Madiga Christian in Andhra Pradesh indicating their original status. The policy of reservations has become lucrative to them and clamor for these facilities based on their own original caste. Similarly, Muslims have sects as Laddaf (Those who whip cotton to make pillows) and Mehetars (Scavengers).

Thus Caste system is going to stay permanently in India and all slogans denouncing the system is a pure and mere eye wash. It is the most tragic phenomenon in India to note the politics of caste that are played whenever President has to be elected in India. Caste card plays a great role in his election apart from the card of religion.

Although Caste system is outwardly shown as the biggest villain in Indian social and political scene, it is encouraged more and more at every level and is being institutionalized, regularized and being promoted.

There is no element of doubt that Hinduism has to live by this system outwardly called evil and internally is being strongly promoted by virtue of vested interests. Although caste was not originally intended to be acquired by birth, it has become hereditary in character and Hindu society has to reconcile to it. The society is facing serious challenges and conflicts on account of this system, yet people have to live by the system. Although officially untouchability has been banned, there is a strong resentment against these communities particularly in rural societies, and the present turmoil in the society is attributable to the administrative policies since independence and no solution appears on the scene.

In the meantime, Indian society is slowly inching towards caste war that could prove catastrophic to the Indian nation and also could lead to its own destruction. If at all India is to be destroyed, it will not be out of any enemy action or from Muslims and it would be out of the caste war that could spell doom to the nation perpetuated by its own selfish leaders.

# HINDUISM TODAY AND ITS INCURSION INTO THE MODERN WORLD

We've discussed the incursion of the West into Hindu life in India. Let's turn to discuss the reciprocal reaction: the movement of Hindus and Hinduism into the West. The history of this movement is far briefer than the other. By the late 19th century, the main vehicle for the transport of Hinduism to the West was literary. Some of the most important Hindu scriptures had been translated into European languages in the 18th century and were available to intellectuals in the West.

Because western impressions were based principally on these translations from the Hindu scriptural traditions, many thinkers had a rather obscure understanding of Hinduism that neglected its more popular expressions.

At the same time, westerners who actually visited India saw a different side of Hinduism: the many colourful festivals and images, the astrologers and fortune tellers, the caste system and the rituals. They were more often than not repelled by what they saw. To these western visitors, Hinduism wasn't more than superstition, idolatry and cultural backwardness.

These impressions, based on translations of its philosophy on one end, and the observation of its popular practices on the other, contributed to an extremely ambivalent western view of Hinduism. Some who knew Hinduism through scripture regarded it as morally and spiritually superior to the western traditions. Many who knew it from popular practice regarded it as vastly inferior to western ways.

## The First Missionary

It was in this context of western ambivalence that the first significant representative of Hinduism came to the West. Swami Vivekananda is sometimes known as the first Hindu missionary to the West. He appeared in Chicago in 1893, at the First World Parliament of Religions. Vivekananda's address to this international gathering of delegates from the major religious traditions was extremely well received and widely celebrated. Vivekananda subsequently established centers for the study and practice of Advaita Vedanta, the monistic Hindu philosophy that he embraced. Vivekananda was followed by numerous Hindu gurus to the West. Many of their names or the names of their orders are familiar to westerners today. We should mention the International Society for Krishna Consciousness. The name Maharishi Yogi became well-known to many in the West as the guru of the Beatles in the 1960's, and as the promoter of a spiritual practice called transcendental meditation.

The names of these modern teachers continue to evoke ambivalent feelings among many westerners. Many celebrate these teachers and their messages and many consider them dangerous. It is unclear at this point what will be the future of Hinduism beyond the Indian subcontinent. In India and the surrounding area Hinduism remains firmly established and its future seems secure, although how Hinduism would negotiate the challenges of westernization is not certain. Nor is it clear how the West would negotiate the challenges of Hinduism. Already western culture is beginning to accommodate Hindu immigrants as great number of temples and Hindu societies multiply throughout the United States and Europe.

It is evident that many westerners find much in Hinduism worth of adoption and admiration. Ultimately, what effects the advent of Hindus and Hinduism would have on the religious practices of the west remains to be seen.

## EQUALITY OF HINDUISM

In the scheme of Manu the Brahmin is placed at the first in rank. Below him is the Kshatriya. Below Kshatriya is the Vaishya. Below Vaishya is the Sudra and Below Sudra is the Ati-Sudra (the Untouchables). This system of rank and gradation is, simply another way of enunciating the principle of inequality so that it may be truly said that Hinduism does not recognize equality. This inequality in status is not merely the inequality that one sees in the warrant of precedence prescribed for a ceremonial gathering at a King's Court. It is a permanent social relationship among the classes to be observed-to be enforced-at all times in all places and for all purposes. It will take too long to show how in every phase of life Manu has introduced and made inequality the vital force of life. But it will illustrate it by taking a few examples such as slavery, marriage and Rule of Law. Manu recognizes Slavery. But he confined it to the Sudras.

Only Sudras could be made slaves of the three higher classes. But the higher classes could not be the slaves of the Sudra. But evidently practice differed from the law of Manu and not only Sudras happened to become slaves but members of the other three classes also become slaves. When this was discovered to be the case a new rule was enacted by a Successor of Manu namely Narada.

This new rule of Narada runs as follows: "In the inverse order of the four castes slavery is not ordained except where a man violates the duties peculiar to his caste. Slavery (in that respect) is analogous to the condition of a wife." Recognition of slavery was bad enough. But if the rule of slavery had been left free to take its own course it would have had at least one beneficial effect. It would have been a levelling force. The foundation of caste would have been destroyed.

For under it a Brahmin might have become the slave of the Untouchable and the Untouchable would have become the master of the Brahmin. But it was seen that unfettered slavery was an equalitarian principle and an attempt was made to nullify it. Manu and his successors therefore while recognising slavery ordains that it shall not be recognised in its inverse order to the Varna System. That means that a Brahmin may become the slave of another Brahmin. But he shall not be the slave of a person of another Varna i.e. of the Kshatriya, Vaishya, Sudra, or Ati-Sudra. On the other hand a Brahmin may hold as his slave any one belonging to the four Varnas. A Kshatriya can have a Kshatriya, Vaisha, Sudra and Ati-Sudra as his slaves but not one who is a Brahmin. A Vaishya can have a

Vaishya, Sudra and Ati-Sudra as his slaves but not one who is a Brahmin or a Kshatriya.

A Sudra can hold a Sudra and Ati-sudra can hold an Ati-Sudra as his slave but not one who is a Brahmin, Kshatriya, Vaishya or Sudra. Challenge Conversion and Hindu Response: Again at a moment of history of our ancient nation when the Hindu foundation of the nation is being challenged and sought to be undermined. But never before in our history has the challenge been as dangerously deceptive, pernicious, and sophisticated as it is now. It is therefore difficult to respond to this challenge since it cannot be easily perceived.

Hence, the response to this challenge and the implicit threat has to be well thought out and profound, but as before in our history, the response to be fruitful has to be designed and structured by the confluence of spiritual guidance and political resolve. Such a confluence has been the fundamental basis of our past responses to such challenges in history, from the installation by rishis of Adi Raja Prithu as King of Bharatvarsh, Chanakya's founding of the Mauryan kingdom, the establishment of the Vijayanagaram empire at Hampi by Sringeri Shankaracharya, to inspiring the fighting armies of Shivaji by Swami Ramdass. Even Mahatma Gandhi and Jayaprakash Narayan in their respective struggles for independence of the nation from colonialism, and for the restoration of democracy in a nation that was drowned in the darkness of the Emergency, had followed this unique Hindu model of spiritually guiding a political movement without seeking the fruits of office for themselves. The Hindu foundation of modern India is why India has been and is even today referred to, in India and abroad, as Hindustan. Hindustan is defined as a nation of Hindus and those who accept that their ancestors are Hindus. The concept also includes refugee minorities who accept the core values of the Hindu culture and therefore recognised as a part of the Hindustan nation. Thus, when the Dwarka Mutt Shankaracharya gave the arriving Parsi refugees in Sanjaan [Kutch coast] a five-point requirement for settling in the country, they readily accepted and have not deviated from it even today.

These five points were: Giving up Persian language and adopting Gujarati; wearing Indian clothes instead of Persian; treating the cow as sacred; reciting some select Sanskrit shlokas in their marriage ceremony; and laying down of weapons. Despite being the smallest minority, with disproportionate share in offices of power and national wealth, and perhaps also the wealthiest community, there is and has been no tension or conflict between Hindus and Parsis. Today Hindus despite de facto in power and in the organs of the state, are victims of that same targeting, but of course in a very subtle and sophisticated manner. In furthering the objective of this targeting, Islam and Christianity, more so the latter, have been able to leverage the influence of prominent Hindus themselves.

Parsis and Jews do not threaten the Hindu character of the nation. They do not seek to proselytise or convert Hindus by monetary inducements or by obscurantist preachings such as curing persons who convert, of incurable terminal diseases. But on the other hand, the preachings of the religious leaders of Islam and Christianity in India, altogether for a thousand years, had targeted Hindus and sought the religious conversions to their faiths by creating deprivation and loss of self-esteem, through the abuse of the power of the state against Hindus.

They were not subtle about it. For example, in 1545, King John III of Portugal gave a command to the then Governor of Goa that neither public nor private 'idols' of Hindu heathens be tolerated on the island of Goa and that severe punishment be meted out to those who persist in keeping them. Thereafter, a terrible inquisition followed during which Hindus were killed, brutalised and their temples razed to the ground. Still we must not forget only a minority of Hindus converted to Christianity.

No other religious community other than Hindus suffered such prolonged and atrocious persecution and survived as a religion of a vast majority on their own soil. Let us not forget this defiance in our past. Today Hindus despite de facto in power and in the organs of the state, are victims of that same targeting, but of course in a very subtle and sophisticated manner. In furthering the objective of this targeting, Islam and Christianity, more so the latter, have been able to leverage the influence of prominent Hindus themselves, who wittingly for money or unwittingly because of a programmed mindset of being defensive about being a Hindu [thereby ready to ape the West] are tools of this targeting. What is the nature and scope of this targeting, and is there a way for us to end it by conciliation with Christians and Muslims? In other words, can we seek to end religious conversion in India today by the ancient Hindu way of shashtrarthas as Hindu saints did, as for example Adi Sankara did with Buddhism and Uttara Mimamsa theologies and Azhwars and Nayanars saints in the south did with Jainism? Will indeed Christians and Muslims recognise the sanctity of shashtrarthas?

There is a serious problem here because as an interesting study of Sarah Claerhout and Jakob De Roover titled: The Question of Conversion in India concludes, Hindus and Christians have fundamentally different and mutually exclusive concepts of religion and thus also in their approaches to the question of conversion. Hence, say the authors, for Hindus and Christians to dialogue on conversion would be fruitless because they will have "great difficulties making sense of each other's statements and arguments". This is because Hindus do not consider any religion as wholly false, and as Gandhiji put it, all religions have some errors in them. Since all religions lead to God, hence there is no need for forcing a conversion. Christians [and Muslims] think that their's is the only true religion, and it is God's work to convert heathens and kafirs to their only true religion. Therefore, either Hindus will have to capitulate on this question by permitting religious conversion in India, or in the alternative be united and assertive to ensure that laws are enacted and effectively enforced against religious conversion of Hindus. There is no third way.

It is urgent now that Hindus be mobilised to assertively oppose any further conversion from Hinduism to any other non-Indian religion. There is no room for indifference here. This is because that status quo is damaging to the Hindu faith, since the Christian missionaries and Muslim mullahs are already fully at work, funds being no constraint, to convert Hindus.

If conversions are not explicitly opposed, then Hindus are implicitly acquiescing in the atrocity. There is a fundamental disconnect between the religious outlook of Hindus and the Christians and Muslims which makes it impossible for a fruitful debate and mutual understanding on the question of religious conversion.

CHAPTER 7

# Hindutva and Hindu Rashtra

## Savarkar

Savarkar was one of the first in the twentieth century to attempt a definitive description of the term "Hindu" in terms of what he called *Hindutva* meaning Hinduness. The coinage of the term "Hindutva" was an attempt by Savarkar who was an atheist and a rationalist, to de-link it from any religious connotations that had become attached to it. He defined the word Hindu as: "He who considers India as both his Fatherland and Holyland". He thus defined Hindutva ("Hindu-ness") or Hindu as different from Hinduism. This definition kept the Abrahamic religions (Judaism, Christianity and Islam) outside its ambit and considered only native religious denominations as Hindu.

This distinction was emphasised on the basis of territorial loyalty rather than on the religious practices. In this book that was written in the backdrop of the Khilafat Movement and the subsequent Malabar Rebellion, Savarkar wrote "Their [Muslims' and Christians'] holy land is far off in Arabia or Palestine. Their mythology and Godmen, ideas and heroes are not the children of this soil. Consequently, their names and their outlook smack of foreign origin. Their love is divided".

Savarkar, also defined the concept of Hindu Rashtra (translated as "Hindu polity"). The concept of Hindu Polity called for the protection of Hindu people and their culture and emphasised that political and economic systems should be based on native thought rather than on the concepts borrowed from the West.

## Mookerjee

Mookerjee was the founder of the Nationalist Bharatiya

Jana Sangh party, the precursor of the Bharatiya Janata Party. Mookerjee was firmly against Nehru's invitation to the Pakistani PM, and their joint pact to establish minority commissions and guarantee minority rights in both countries. He wanted to hold Pakistan directly responsible for the terrible influx of millions of Hindu refugees from East Pakistan, who had left the state fearing religious suppression and violence aided by the state.

After consultation with Shri Golwalkar Guruji of RSS, Mookerjee founded Bharatiya Jana Sangh on 21st Oct. 1951 at Delhi and he became the first President of it. The BJS was ideologically close to the Rashtriya Swayamsevak Sangh and widely considered the political arm of Hindu Nationalism. It was opposed to appeasement of India's Muslims. The BJS also favored a uniform civil code governing personal law matters for both Hindus and Muslims, wanted to ban cow slaughter and end the special status given to the Muslim-majority state of Jammu and Kashmir. The BJS founded the Hindutva agenda which became the wider political expression of India's Hindu majority.

Mookerjee opposed the Indian National Congress's decision to grant Kashmir a special status with its own flag and Prime Minister. According to Congress's decision, no one, including the President of India could enter into Kashmir without the permission of Kashmir's Prime Minister.

In opposition to this decision, he entered Kashmir on 11 May 1953. Thereafter, he was arrested and jailed in a dilapidated house. Syama Prasad had suffered from dry pleurisy and coronary troubles, and was taken to hospital one and a half months after his arrest due to complications arising from the same. He was administered penicillin despite having informed the doctor-in-charge of his allergy to penicillin, and he died on 23 June 1953. Mookherjee's martyrdom later compelled Nehru to remove Permit system, post of *Sadar-e-Riayasat* and of Prime Minister of Jammu & Kashmir.

Along with Vinayak Damodar Savarkar, Mukherjee is considered the godfather of Hindu nationalism in India, especially the Hindutva movement. Though Mukherjee was not associated with RSS, he is widely revered by members and supporters of the RSS and the Vishwa Hindu Parishad.

## Golwalkar

M. S. Golwalkar, the second head of the Rashtriya Swayamsevak Sangh (RSS), was to further this non-religious, territorial loyalty based definition of "Hindu" in his book *Bunch of Thoughts*. Hindutva and Hindu Rashtra would form the basis of Golwalkar's ideology and that of the RSS.

While emphasising on religious pluralism, Golwalkar believed that Semitic monotheism and exclusivism were incompatible with and against the native Hindu culture. He wrote:

"Those creeds (Islam and Christianity) have but one prophet, one scripture and one God, other than whom there is no path of salvation for the human soul. It requires no great intelligence to see the absurdity of such a proposition."

He added:

"As far as the national tradition of this land is concerned, it never considers that with a change in the method of worship, an individual ceases to be the son of the soil and should be treated as an alien. Here, in this land, there can be no objection to God being called by any name whatever. Ingrained in this soil is love and respect for all faiths and religious beliefs. He cannot be a son of this soil at all who is intolerant of other faiths."

He further would echo the views of Savarkar on territorial loyalty, but with a degree of inclusiveness, when he wrote "So, all that is expected of our Muslim and Christian co-citizens is the shedding of the notions of their being 'religious minorities' as also their foreign mental complexion and merging themselves in the common national stream of this soil."

Golwalkar nominated for the post of General Secretary in the General Election of Hindu Mahasabha in 1939, but Golwalkar faced defeat and he left Hindu Mahasabha with quick decision, he decided to maintain distance from Hindu Mahasabha.

1940-1946 Golwalkar maintained distance with Hindu Mahasabha and boycotted every meeting and events in which Hindu Mahasabha was participating. Golwalkar instructed Swayam Sewaks not to join Politics, but suddenly in 1946, Golwalkar issued a statement to Swayam Sewaks and urged to participate in the National Elections from Hindu Mahasabha. Later, Savarkar distributed most of the election ticket to RSS's Swayam Sewaks. Everything was going fine, but on the very next day of ending nomination date, Golwalkar isseud new statement that "We had a successful talk with Gandhi Ji, Gandhi Ji assured us that partition would not happen. So we will not oppose Gandhi Ji and Congress, we will not participate in the Elections." All the Swayam Sewaks were asked to surrender their nominations, as all were nominated from Hindu Mahasabha. Due to this biggest back-step by the chief of RSS, Hindu Mahasabha was unable to participate in the National Elections on the major level.

Later, in the Parliament of 1946, the Proposal of Partition of India was passed with 157 votes of Congress, Muslim League and Communist Party of India. Hindu Mahasabha won 13 seats and Ram Rajya Parishad won 4 seats, were not sufficient to oppose the Bill of Partition of India.

After the assassination of Gandhi, Golwalkar and Hindu Mahasabha's senior leaders such as Shyama Prasad Mukharji founded a new political party as Jan-Sangh, many of Hindu Mahasabha members joined Jan-Sangh.

## Deendayal Upadhyaya

Deendayal Upadhyaya, another RSS ideologue, presented the Integral Humanism as the political philosophy of the erstwhile Bharatiya Jana Sangh in the form of four lectures delivered in Bombay on 22–25 April 1965 as an attempt to offer a third way, rejecting both communism and capitalism as the means for socio-economic emancipation.

## Contemporary descriptions

Later thinkers of the RSS, like H. V. Sheshadri and K. S. Rao, were to emphasise on the non-theocratic nature of the word "Hindu Rashtra", which they believed was often inadequately translated, ill interpreted and wrongly stereotyped as a theocratic state. In a book, H. V. Sheshadri, the senior leader of the RSS writes "As Hindu Rashtra is not a religious concept, it is also not a political concept. It is generally misinterpreted as a theocratic state or a religious Hindu state. Nation (Rashtra) and State (Rajya) are entirely different and should never be mixed up. State is purely a political concept. The State changes as the political authority shifts from person to person or party to party. But the people in the Nation remain the same. They would maintain that the concept of Hindu Rashtra is in complete agreement with the principles of secularism and democracy.

The concept of "'Hindutva" is continued to be espoused by the organisations like the RSS and political parties like the Bharatiya Janata Party (BJP). But the definition does not have the same rigidity with respect to the concept of "holy land" laid down by Savarkar, and stresses on inclusivism and patriotism. BJP leader and the then leader of opposition, Atal Bihari Vajpayee, in 1998, articulated the concept of "holy land" in Hindutva as follows: "Mecca can continue to be holy for the Muslims but India should be holier than the holy for them. You can go to a mosque and offer namaz, you can keep the roza. We have no problem. But if you have to choose between Mecca or Islam and India you must choose India. All the Muslims should have this feeling: we will live and die only for this country."

In a 1995 landmark judgment, the Supreme Court of India observed that "Ordinarily, Hindutva is understood as a way of life or a state of mind and is not to be equated with or understood as religious Hindu fundamentalism. A Hindu may embrace a non-Hindu religion without ceasing to be a Hindu and since the

Hindu is disposed to think synthetically and to regard other forms of worship, strange gods and divergent doctrines as inadequate rather than wrong or objectionable, he tends to believe that the highest divine powers complement each other for the well-being of the world and mankind."

## HINDUISM IN AN AGE OF HINDUTVA

One of the original purposes of the VHP, we have seen, was to consolidate Hindu society, to unite Hindus into the single community that Hindutva proponents postulate. Such an attempt to bring unity to Hinduism is not entirely novel. During the colonial period of the nineteenth and early twentieth centuries, reform organizations like the Brahmo Samaj and the Arya Samaj also envisioned and pursued a more cohesive Hindu faith, with limited success. Based in the Punjab, the Arya Samaj pioneered many of the organizational practices later adapted by the RSS. However, the Hindutva attempt, in its use of new technologies of dissemination and in its proximity to political power, may represent something new and efficacious in the modern period.

The theorist Savarkar attempted to define Hindutva around a shared cultural ethos, and accepted the great variety of existing Hindu religious belief and practice. When it came to religion, Savarkar adopted a laissez faire attitude. The VHP and its relatives have a more ambitious, hegemonizing religious agenda. We have noted the VHP's formation of the Dharma Sansad as a new ecclesiastical order that, it is hoped, will pronounce with religious authority on social and political issues of the day. The VHP and related groups have promoted Rama as the integrating god of Hinduism, and they have launched nationwide campaigns like the Ekatmata Yajna and the Ayodhya mobilization to broadcast their message throughout India. Their activities go still further, with attempts to extend select regional practices throughout India, and to promote upper-caste or brahrnanical rites for all strata of society. Observers such as political scientist Rajni Kothari have charged that this amounts to an attempt to "semiticize" Hinduism: to transform a diverse and pluralistic Hindu religion into a more centrally organized, monotheistic, monolithic faith on the model of the Abrahamic religions of Judaism, Christianity, and Islam.

It is not clear just how successful these Hindutva efforts are, or how far they reach. While much has been written about the political rise of the Sangh groups and about the social upheavals that have accompanied this rise, there has been comparatively little scholarly study of changes in Hindu religious practices instigated by Hindutva. In this concluding section, I will consider two examples described by anthropologists working in Tamilnadu, in the deep south farthest from the main centres of Hindutva organization. One looks at the successful inculcation of a new ritual practice from Maharashtra, and the other describes how the VHP brick campaign entered into the local culture of a Tamil village. When I lived in Tamilnadu in the early 1980s, Hindu nationalism was virtually invisible to me. But during this time, the Sangh brotherhood was beginning to organize a new affiliate, the Hindu Munnani ("Hindu Front"), which would cooperate with the RSS and BJP, and play a role in Tamilnadu similar to that of the VHP elsewhere in India. The group also developed close ties with the Tamilnadu Brahmans Association, which defends the interests of brahrnins in the state.

One of the first activities of the Hindu Munnani was to begin promoting and transforming the Vinayaka Chaturthi, a fall festival devoted to the god Ganesha. Prior to this, most Hindus in Tamilnadu had celebrated quietly with domestic rites or by making special offerings at a local Ganesha temple. In Maharashtra the Vinayaka Chaturthi was an entirely different matter. In the late nineteenth century, the festival was transformed by the anti-colonial activist B. G. Tilak into the primary public festival of the year, with large decorated *mandapas,* public image processions, and dramatic final immersions ofthe images in the sea or other body of water. Another crucial aspect of the Maharashtrian celebrations introduced by Tilak was the dissemination of political messages through public speeches. For Tilak the religious festival was a convenient cover for anti-British agitation, and the political dimension of the festival has continued in Maharashtra in the form of politicized *mandapa* displays.

The Hindu Munnani set out to replicate the Maharashtrian model in Tamilnadu. In 1983 the Munnani initiated the public celebration of Vinayaka Chaturthi in a suburb of Chennai with a procession and an immersion of a Ganesha image in a nearby temple tank. The next year they held several public celebrations around Chennai, and by 1990, the year of the Rath Yatra in northern India, the public celebrations of Vinayaka Chaturthi were expanding to other cities and towns in Tamilnadu. Of course, this spread was never entirely innocent. Also in 1990, a provocative procession of Ganesha past a mosque in downtown Chennai instigated a bloody riot. In the mid-1990s, Chris Fuller reports, the Vinayaka Chaturthi had become a common public festival throughout the state. At the same time, it had lost some of the overt anti-Muslim and anti-Christian rhetoric that was characteristic of the initial celebrations. Other groups beside the Hindu Munnani were organizing their own versions of the festival, so the Munnani no longer enjoyed complete control over the festival. This transplanted regional festival from Maharashtra was now a part of the Tamilnadu religious calendar.

In promoting this ritual innovation, the Hindu Munnani saw Vinayaka Chaturthi as "a means to unite Hindus by overcoming internal divisions among them." They intended the festival for all Hindu castes and classes, including Dalits. It also had the effect of linking Hindu religious practice in Tamilnadu to that of another region, and thereby of promoting the sense of Hinduism's national breadth. As Fuller puts it, "Hindu unity is primarily a political and ideological project to persuade people to become conscious of themselves as Hindus belonging to a single, assertive, majority 'community' on which a strong Hindu nation can be built." The Hindu Munnani's transposing of a new public festival into Tamilnadu offers one example, within the sphere of religious practice, of how that persuasion may be effected. Yet it also suggests how its specific political agenda may recede as new groups adopt their own versions of the festival.

The case of the Vinayaka Chaturthi in Tamilnadu highlights, as I have through this essay, the agency of a Hindutva group in instigating new religious practices that help broadcast the values of Hindu nationalism. However, acceptance of new practices and new values is a matter of choice, of countless decisions that are local and personal. What are the conditions within which a local group chooses to embrace elements of a Hindu nationalist campaign? Diane Mines's anthropological fieldwork in a village in southern Tamilnadu in the late 1980s provides one example.

Yanaimangalam is a small, predominantly Hindu village of about 1700 people. Three caste groups predominate, and among these three the Thevars were attempting to establish dominance in the village during Mines's stay. A group of brahrnins also resided in the village, and they recalled a time when their residential neighborhood was the centre of village activities.

Brahmins formerly owned much of the land, they claimed, and ran elaborate festivals in the now- dilapidated Shiva temple. Once the centre of the dharmic order of the village, the brahmins viewed the village itself as degenerating. So the VHP campaign to liberate that other dharmic centre, Rama's place of birth, must have appealed to them, and the brahmins of Yanaimangalam decided to send a consecrated brick to Ayodhya in October 1989.

The brick had the name ofthe village stamped on one side, and the name of the god Rama on the other. A Brahmin schoolmaster conducted a small ritual to consecrate the brick in his home, and then led a procession of the brahmins and several other members of high-status castes, chanting "Ram!

Ram!" and ringing cymbals. At the border of the village, they gave the brick to a teenage priest, who took it, got on his bicycle, and rode off towards the next village, accompanied by two policemen. The idea was that this brick would join with others, and gradually make its way by train to the district seat Tirunelveli, then to the state capital Chennai, on to the national capital Delhi, and from there to Ayodhya, where it would take its place in the new Rama temple the VHP proposed to build there.

Mines cites the psychoanalyst Sudhir Kakar in observing that it is "a sense of loss that propels people, individually and in groups, to identify with larger cultural and revivalist movements, such as Hindu nationalism."

The loss of a golden age, we have seen, echoes through the rhetoric of Hindutva, just as the brahmins of Yanaimangalam speak of the loss of their own centrality to the village. But so too does a project for the future: building a temple, restoring a remembered way of life, reconstituting a unitary national community of Hindus that (in the Hindutva vision) has always been present.

The participation by the brahrnins of Yanaimangalam in the VHP's brick campaign links them to a national, and even transnational, network of Hindus. Just as important, though, it has to do with the village order. Yanaimangalam's modest brick ceremony was, as Mines puts it, "an effort to redefine and expand this Brahman community's sense of belonging-in-the-world by also finding new ways to define their place in the village."

Other village groups, meanwhile, were pursuing their own agendas. Attempts by the Thevar groups to claim village precedence led to disruptions in the annual festival processions. Members of the Pallar caste, an S.C. or Dalit group, tried to assert their own place in the village pecking order by identifying themselves with Ambedkar, the Maharashtrian Dalit leader of the 1940s who articulated an egalitarian critique of caste privileges.

As with the village brahmins, the Pallars sought to enhance local status through a national marker of identity. All are strategies that, together, remake the village on an ongoing basis. The brahmins' singular act of assertion through brick consecration does not appear to have altered their local situation.

From the perspective of this village, then, the seeming juggernaut of Hindutva appears attenuated. (The English term "juggeranut" derives, appropriately, from the great temple chariot festival at the temple of Jagannatha, in Puri, Orissa.) While the powerful imagery of the VHP's Ayodhya mobilization penetrates even to this distant village, the brick the local brahmins fabricated and sent may never have reached its destination. The new temple, embodying the new order of Ramrajya, remains unbuilt.

## HINDUTVA: THE GREAT NATIONALIST IDEOLOGY

In the history of the world, the Hindu awakening of the late twentieth century will go down as one of the most monumental events in the history of the world. Never before has such demand for change come from so many people. Never before has Bharat, the ancient word for the motherland of Hindus - India, been confronted with such an impulse for change. This movement, Hindutva, is changing the very foundations of Bharat and Hindu society the world over. Hindu society has an unquestionable and proud history of tolerance for other faiths and respect for diversity of spiritual experiences. This is reflected in the many different philosophies, religious sects, and religious leaders. The very foundation of this lies in the great Hindu heritage that is not based on any one book, teacher, or doctrine. In fact the pedestal of Hindu society stems from the great Vedic teachings Ekam Sat Viprah Bahudha Vadanti -- Truth is One, Sages Call it by Many Names, and Vasudhaiva Kutumbakam -- The Whole Universe is one Family. It is this philosophy which allowed the people of Hindusthan (land of the Hindus) to shelter the Jews who faced Roman persecution, the

Zoroastrians who fled the Islamic sword and who are the proud Parsi community today, and the Tibetan Buddhists who today face the communist secularism: persecution of religion.

During the era of Islamic invasions, what Will Durant called the bloodiest period in the history of mankind, many Hindus gallantly resisted, knowing full well that defeat would mean a choice of economic discrimination via the jaziya tax on non- Muslims, forced conversion, or death. It is no wonder that the residents of Chittor, and countless other people over the length and breadth of Bharat, from present-day Afghanistan to present-day Bangladesh, thought it better to die gloriously rather than face cold-blooded slaughter. Hindus never forgot the repeated destruction of the Somnath Temple, the massacre of Buddhists at Nalanda, or the pogroms of the Mughals.

Thus, the seeds of todayUs Hindu Jagriti, awakening, were created the very instance that an invader threatened the fabric of Hindu society which was religious tolerance. The vibrancy of Hindu society was noticeable at all times in that despite such barbarism from the Islamic hordes of central Asia and Turkey, Hindus never played with the same rules that Muslims did. The communist and Muslim intelligentsia, led by Nehruvian ideologists who are never short of distorted history, have been unable to show that any Hindu ruler ever matched the cruelty of even a RmoderateS Muslim ruler.

It is these characteristics of Hindu society and the Muslim psyche that remain today. Hindus never lost their tolerance and willingness to change. However Muslims, led by the Islamic clergy and Islamic societyUs innate unwillingness to change, did not notice the scars that Hindus felt from the Indian past. It is admirable that Hindus never took advantage of the debt Muslims owed Hindus for their tolerance and non-vengefulness.

In modern times, Hindu Jagriti gained momentum when Muslims played the greatest abuse of Hindu tolerance: the demand for a separate state and the partition of India, a nation that had had a common history and culture for countless millenia. Thus, the Muslim minority voted for a separate state and the Hindus were forced to sub-divide their own land.

After partition in Pakistan, Muslim superiority was quickly asserted and the non-Muslim minorities were forced to flee due to the immense discrimination in the political and religious spheres. Again, Hindus did not respond to such an onslaught. Hindu majority India continued the Hindu ideals by remaining secular.

India even gave the Muslim minority gifts such as separate personal laws, special status to the only Muslim majority state -- Kashmir, and other rights that are even unheard of in the bastion of democracy and freedom, the United States of America. Islamic law was given precedence over the national law in instances that came under Muslim personal law. The Constitution was changed when the courts, in the Shah Bano case, ruled that a secular nation must have one law, not separate religious laws. Islamic religious and educational institutions were given a policy of non- interference. The list goes on.

More painful for the Hindus was forced negation of Hindu history and factors that gave pride to Hindus. Hindu customs and traditions were mocked as remnants of a non-modern society, things that would have to go if India was to modernize like the west. The self proclaimed guardians of India, the politicians of the Congress Party who called themselves secularists, forgot that it was the Hindu psyche that believed in secularism, it was the Hindu thought that had inspired the greatest intellectuals of the world such as Thoreau, Emerson, Tolstoy, Einstein, and others, and that it was Hindus, because there was no other land where Hindus were in a significant number to stand up in defence of Hindu society if and when the need arose, who were the most nationalistic people in India.

When Hindus realized that pseudo-secularism had reduced them to the role of an innocent bystander in the game of politics, they demanded a true secularism where every religious group would be treated the same and a government that would not take Hindu sentiments for granted. Hindutva awakened the Hindus to the new world order where nations represented the aspirations of people united in history, culture, philosophy, and heroes. Hindutva successfully took the Indian idol of Israel and made Hindus realize that their India could be just as great and could do the same for them also.

In a new era of global consciousness, Hindus realized that they had something to offer the world. There was something more than tolerance and universal unity. The ancient wisdom of sages through eternity also offered systems of thought, politics, music, language, dance, and education that could benefit the world.

There have been many changes in the thinking of Hindus, spearheaded over the course of a century by innumerable groups and leaders who made their own distinct contribution to Hindu society: Swami Vivekananda, Rabindranath Tagore, Gandhiji, Rashatriya Swayamsevak Sangh, Swami Chinmayananda, Maharishi Mahesh Yogi, International Society for Krishna Consciousness, Muni Susheel Kumarji, Vishwa Hindu Parishad, Bharatiya Janata Party, and others.

Each in their own way increased pride in being a Hindu and simultaneously showed Hindus their greatest strengths and their worst weaknesses. This slowly shook the roots of Hindu society and prompted a rear-guard action by the ingrained interests: the old politicians, the Nehruvian intellectual community, and the appeased Muslim leadership.

The old foundation crumbled in the 1980s and 1990s when Hindus respectfully asked for the return of their most holy religious site, Ayodhya. This demand promptly put the 40-year old apparatus to work, and press releases were chunked out that spew the libelous venom which called those who represented the Hindu aspirations RmilitantS and Rfundamentalist,S stigmas which had heretofore found their proper place in the movements to establish Islamic law.

Hindus were humble enough to ask for the restoration of an ancient temple built on the birthplace of Rama, and destroyed by Babar, a foreign invader. The vested interests were presented with the most secular of propositions: the creation of a monument to a national hero, a legend whose fame and respect stretched out of the borders of India into southeast Asia, and even into Muslim Indonesia.

A hero who existed before there was anyone in India who considered himself separate from Hindu society. The 400-year old structure at one of the holiest sites of India had been worshipped as a temple by Hindus even though the Muslim general Mir Baqi had partially built a non-functioning mosque on it. It was very important that no Muslims, except those who were appeased in Indian politics, had heard of anything called Babri Masjid before the pseudo-secularist apparatus started the next to last campaign against the rising Hindu society. It was also important that no Muslim had offered prayers at the site for over 40 years.

Hindus hid their true anger, that their most important religious site still bore the marks of a cruel slavery that occurred so very recently in the time span of Hindu history. It was naturally expected in 1947 that freedom from the political and economic chains of Great Britain would mean that the systems and symbols that had enslaved India and caused its deterioration and poverty would be obliterated. Forty years after independence, Hindus realized that their freedom was yet to come.

So long as freedom to Jews meant that symbols of the Holocaust in Europe were condemned, so long as freedom to African- Americans meant that the symbols of racial discrimination were wiped out, and so long as freedom from imperialism to all people meant that they would have control of their own destinies, that they would have their own heros, their own stories, and their own culture, then freedom to Hindus meant that they would have to condemn the Holocaust that Muslims reaped on them, the racial discrimination that the white man brought, and the economic imperialism that enriched Britain.

Freedom for Hindus and Indians would have to mean that their heros such as Ram, Krishna, Sivaji, the Cholas, Sankaracharya, and Tulsidas would be respected, that their own stories such as the Ramayana and the Mahabharata would be offered to humanity as examples of the brilliance of Hindu and Indian thinking, and that their own culture which included the Bhagavad Gita, the Vedas, the temples, the gods and goddesses, the art, the music, and the contributions in various fields, would be respected. Freedom meant that as the shackles of imperial dominance were lifted, the newly freed people would not simply absorb foreign ideas, they would share their own as well.

In India, something went wrong. The freedom from Britain was supposed to result in a two-way thinking that meant that non- Indian ideas would be accepted and that Indian ideas would be presented to the world. So long as the part of India giving to the world was suppressed, the freedom was only illusory and the aspirations of the freedom hungry would continue to rise in temperature.

The freedom could have been achieved if a temple to Rama was built and the symbol of foreign rule was moved to another site or demolished. The battle was never really for another temple. Another temple could have been built anywhere in India.

The humble and fair demand for RamaJanmabhoomi could have resulted in a freedom for India, freedom from the intellectual slavery that so dominated India. This freedom would have meant that all Indians regardless of religion, language, caste, sex, or color would openly show respect for the person that from ancient times was considered the greatest hero to people of Hindusthan. For the first time, Hindus had demanded something, and it was justifiable that a reasonable demand from an undemanding people would be realized.

Imagine if the Muslim leadership had agreed to shift the site and build a temple in Ayodhya. How much Hindu- Muslim unity there would have been in India? India could then have used that goodwill to solve the major religious, caste, and economic issues facing the country.

But some of the vested interests in politics and in the Muslim community saw that such a change would mean that their work since 1947 would be overturned and that this new revolution would displace them. Rather than join forces and accept the rising tide, the oligarchy added fuel to the greatest movement in Indian history. One that on December 6, 1992 completely shattered the old and weak roots of Indian society and with it, the old political and intellectual structure.

The destruction by the Kar Sevaks of the dilapidated symbol of foreign dominance was the last straw in a heightening of tensions by the government, and the comittant anger of more and more Hindus to rebuffs of their reasonable demands. The ruthless last-ditch effort of the powers-that-be was the banning and suppression of the leaders of the Hindu Jagriti. The effort of the rulers reminds one of the strategy of all ill-fated rulers. Throughout history, when monumental upheavals have taken place, the threatened interests have resorted to drastic measures, which in-turn have hastened their own death.

Hindus are at last free. They control their destiny now and there is no power that can control them except their own tolerant ethos. India in turn is finally free. Having ignored its history, it has now come face to face with a repressed conscience. The destruction of the structure at Ayodhya was the release of the history that Indians had not fully come to terms with. Thousands of years of anger and shame, so diligently bottled up by these same interests, was released when the first piece of the so-called Babri Masjid was torn down. It is a fundamental concept of Hindu Dharma that has won: righteousness. Truth won when Hindus, realizing that Truth could not be won through political or legal means, took the law into their own hands. Hindus have been divided politically and the laws have not acknowledged the quiet Hindu yearning for Hindu unity which has until recently taken a back seat to economic development and Muslim appeasement. Similarly, the freedom movement represented the supercedence of Indian unity over loyalty to the British Crown.

In comparison to the freedom movement though, Hindutva involves many more people and represents the mental freedom that 1947 did not bring. The future of Bharat is set. Hindutva is here to stay. It is up to the Muslims whether they will be included in the new nationalistic spirit of Bharat. It is up to the government and the Muslim leadership whether they wish to increase Hindu furor or work with the Hindu leadership to show that Muslims and the government will consider Hindu sentiments. The era of one-way compromise of Hindus is over, for from now on, secularism must mean that all parties must compromise.

## POST-INDEPENDENCE MOVEMENTS

### Somnath temple movement

The Somnath temple is an ancient temple at Prabhas Patan in the coastal Indian province of Gujarat, which had been destroyed several times by the Muslim foreign invaders, starting with Mahmud Ghaznavi in 1025 AD. The last of such destructions took place in 1706 AD when Prince Mohammad Azam carried out the orders of Mughal ruler Aurangzeb to destroy the temple of Somnath beyond possible repair. A small mosque was put in its place.

Before Independence, Prabhas Pattan where Somnath is located was part of the Junagadh State, ruled by the Nawab of Junagarh. On the eve of Independence the Nawab announced the accession of Junagarh, which had over 80% Hindu population, to Pakistan. The people of Junagarh rose in revolt and set up a parallel government under Gandhian leader and independence fighter, Shri Samaldas Gandhi. The Nawab, unable to resist the popular pressure, bowed out and escaped to Pakistan. The provincial government under Samaldas Gandhi formally asked Government of India to take over. The Deputy

Prime Minister of India, Sardar Patel came to Junagadh on 12 November 1947 to direct the occupation of the state by the Indian army and at the same time ordered the reconstruction of the Somanath temple.

When Sardar Patel, K. M. Munshi and other leaders of the Congress went to Gandhiji with the proposal of reconstructing the Somnath temple, Gandhiji blessed the move, but suggested that the funds for the construction should be collected from the public and the temple should not be funded by the state. He expressed that he was proud to associate himself to the project of renovation of the temple But soon both Gandhiji and Sardar Patel died and the task of reconstruction of the temple was now continued under the leadership of K. M. Munshi, who was the Minister for Food and Civil, supplies in the Nehru Government.

The ruins were pulled down in October 1950 and the mosque was moved to a different location. In May 1951, Rajendra Prasad, the first President of the Republic of India, invited by K. M. Munshi, performed the installation ceremony for the temple. Rajendra Prasad said in his address, "It is my view that the reconstruction of the Somnath Temple will be complete on that day when not only a magnificent edifice will arise on this foundation, but the mansion of India's prosperity will be really that prosperity of which the ancient temple of Somnath was a symbol." He added "The Somnath temple signifies that the power of reconstruction is always greater than the power of destruction."

This episode created a serious rift between the then prime minister Jawaharlal Nehru, who saw in movement for reconstruction of the temple an attempt at Hindu revivalism and the president Rajendra Prasad and Union Minister K. M. Munshi, saw in its reconstruction, the fruits of independence and the reversal of injustice done to Hindus.

## The emergence of the Sangh Parivar

The Rashtriya Swayamsevak Sangh, which was started in 1925, had grown as a huge organisation by the end of British rule in India. But the assassination of Gandhi and a subsequent ban on the organisation plunged it into distress. The ban was revoked when it was absolved of the charges and it led to the resumption of its activities.

The 1960s saw the volunteers of the RSS join the different social and political movements. Movements that saw a large presence of volunteers included the Bhoodan, a land reform movement led by prominent Gandhian Vinoba Bhave and the Sarvodaya led by another Gandhian Jayaprakash Narayan. RSS supported trade union, the Bharatiya Mazdoor Sangh and political party Bharatiya Jana Sangh also grew into considerable prominence by the end of the decade.

Another prominent development was the formation of the Vishwa Hindu Parishad (VHP), an organisation of Hindu religious leaders, supported by the RSS, with the aim of uniting the various Hindu religious denominations and to usher social reform.

The first VHP meeting at Mumbai was attended among others by all the Shankaracharyas, Jain leaders, Sikh leader Master Tara Singh Malhotra, the Dalai Lama and contemporary Hindu leaders like Swami Chinmayananda.

From its initial years, the VHP led a concerted attack on the social evils of untouchability and casteism while launching social welfare programmes in the areas of education and health care, especially for the Scheduled Castes, backward classes and the tribals.

The organisations started and supported by the RSS volunteers came to be known collectively as the Sangh Parivar. Next few decades saw a steady growth of the influence of the Sangh Parivar in the social and political space of India.

## Ayodhya dispute

The Ayodhya dispute is a political, historical and socio-religious debate in India, centred on a plot of land in the city of Ayodhya, located in Faizabad district, Uttar Pradesh. The main issues revolve around access to a site traditionally regarded as the birthplace of the Hindu deity Rama, the history and location of the Babri Mosque at the site, and whether a previous Hindu temple was demolished or modified to create the mosque.

### Bengali Hindu homeland

Bengali Hindu homeland, commonly referred as Bangabhumi and Bir Bango is a separatist movement to create a Hindu country using southwestern Bangladesh, envisioned by Banga Sena of Bangladesh.

### Panun Kashmir

Panun Kashmir is an organisation of displaced Kashmiri Pandits (Kashmiri Hindus) founded in December 1990 in Jammu, in order to demand that a separate homeland for Kashmir's Hindu population be carved out of the overwhelmingly Muslim Valley of Kashmir. Almost the entire Pandit population was expelled from Kashmir in 1990 by separatist militants for their allegedly pro-India political beliefs.

### Ghar Wapsi

Ghar Wapsi is a series of re-conversion exercises organised by Vishva Hindu Parishad and Rashtriya Swayamsevak Sangh to re-convert non-Hindus to Hinduism. The *Indian Express* reported that Scheduled Caste Manjhi families demanded better facilities along with education and healthcare before they reconverted.

### Bahu Lao, Beti Bachao

Bahu Lao, Beti Bachao is a campaign by Bajrang Dal to encourage young Hindu men to marry non-Hindu girls and to create awareness among Hindu girls about Love Jihad. The movement has been successful in West Bengal.

## THE RISE OF HINDU NATIONALISM

"Nationalism" and "Communalism" are synonymous in an Indian context and are negative concepts. They are identified with the misuse of religion in politics. Worldwide, the first such misuse of religion in politics took place in late 19$^{th}$ century in America when the Conservative Protestants in the face of rationalism and scientific values came up with reassertion of 'fundamentals' of Christianity. Essentially, this was an attempt to re-impose the pre-modern values of birth based hierarchy of gender and class. Later, in Europe, the Nazi and fascist onslaughts used race for similar reasons. In recent times, we have seen the rise of Islamic or communalism in several countries of the middle-east, typified by Ayatullah Kohemini in the Iran of eighties and nineties. Communalism in India made its major appearance, in the pre-Independence era, in 1886, with the formation of two communal streams – the Muslim League (based on Islam) and the Hindu Mahasabha and the Rashtriya Swayamsevak Sangh (based on Hinduism). Over the years, these two streams have constantly tried to fan the communal passions of their followers, be it in the Shah Banoo case or the perennial dispute with regard to the Babri Masjid in Ayodhya. With the emergence of the Hindu right-wing party, the Bharatiya Janata Party (BJP) as a major political force in the country; the proponents of Hindu communalism, better known through its ideology "Hindutva", seem to have gained the upper hand.

## Hindutva

The fundamental goal of the "Hindutva" ideology is the establishment of a Hindu-Nation state exemplified in the fascist doctrine of "one nation, one culture, one language, one religion". It is a very narrow type of "nationalism" which seeks legitimacy through demonizing other religions and faiths, very specially Islam and Christianity. Whilst it is not representative of the Hindu majority of the country, it makes every attempt to appear to champion the concerns of mainstream Hinduism.

These posturings have created a great deal of disharmony in various parts of the country particularly in the last fifteen years when in 1990 one of the main exponents of the "Hindu

Rashtra" namely, Mr. L. K. Advani, (a former Deputy Prime Minister of the country and currently the President of the BJP) went across the country on a "Rath Yatra". This created a great deal of animosity, blood-shed and deepened the divide between the Hindus and Muslims of the country.

In the wake of the demolition of the Babri Masjid on 6$^{th}$ December 1992, India became divided even more, on communal lines. This was followed by several other instances of communal violence which include the bashing up of Christians in Gujarat (Northwest India) in 1998 – 99 and the Gujarat Genocide of 2002 (when more than 2000 Muslims were killed in Gujarat); among the other communal incidents were the horrendous murder of the Australian Missionary Graham Staines and his two sons (in January 1999 in Manoharpur, Orissa) and the attack on the Sisters of Mother Teresa in Kerala in October 2004.

## Comparison between Hindu Rashtra and Secular Democratic India

It is important at this juncture to emphasis that the Constitution of India is a secular one in which all citizens are equal and which guarantees freedom of thought, expression and belief to every single Indian.

India is therefore not a theocratic state and any "nationalism" based on religion or on fundamentalism is bound to create chaos and confusion and ultimately division.

The Hindutva ideology, based on the theory of the nation-state, talks essentially about the "Hindu Rashtra" (nation). This is in total opposition to the Constitution of India which speaks about a sovereign, socialist, secular, democratic republic.

Those of us who have been trying to put a stop to this are convinced that religion should not be used in politics and vice-versa. In fact, religion, if true, has to be used only for the promotion of communal peace, harmony, justice, love and compassion. Any religion worth its salt will not do otherwise.

## HİNDU NATIONALISM OF M. S, GOLWALKAR

The Hindu nationalism of M. S. Golwalkar was dissimilar from that of V. D, Savarkar in the sense that Golwalkar's theory of nationalism was based on Indian spiritualism. Savarkar was a modernist and he did not oppose westernization. But Golwalkar was a supporter of Hindu civilization and opposed the Western method of life. He held that the Indian spiritualism was superior to the Western materialism. He whispered that India was a holy land and it was the divine will that India should lead the world.

### Nation as Motherland

Golwalkar was an exponent of cultural nationalism and he recognized nationalism with love for our motherland. He held that the Hindus measured India as their motherland because, since thousands of years they had been recognized with this holy land. In this holy land only, Hindus registered all their great achievements. Hindus were children of this ancient land as they were nurtured through water flowing from her rivers and food produced through her rich soil. It was wrong to consider that India became a nation in the recent past. In information, she had been existing as a nation since thousands of years. There might be some outward differences, but there lived vital unity in India. All Hindus were bound jointly through similar religion, similar language and similar civilization. The Great Sage Sankara realised this principle and recognized his religious centers at four dissimilar corners of India. He held that all Hindus were permeated through the spirit of unity and solidarity.

While discussing dissimilar elements of Hindu nationality, Golwalkar pointed out that subsistence of contiguous territory was the first element of nationality. The second element of nationality was the features of the people who inhabited that territory. The people should consider this land as a holy land and motherland. They should be united through general civilization, general traditions, and general historical past and general ideals. This commonality brought them jointly and helped them evolve their own method of life. Third element of nationality was general economic interests of the people livelihood in that scrupulous territory. All these elements contributed in creation the national character of our country. Therefore , in Hindu nationalism of M. S. Golwalkar cultural factors played an extremely significant role. Therefore he laid emphasis on developing the right kind of attitude in the minds of the people through giving them proper training and education. He was of the opinion that the Hindu method of imparting right kind of values and practices to the people was useful. It is only through this that the Hindu nation could evolve into national organism pulsating with the spirit of unity and oneness.

## Territorial Nationalism Rejected

We have seen in our previous discussion that M. S. Golwalkar was a supporter of the cultural nationalism and he defined his nationalism in the light of cultural traditions of the Hindus. He rejected the concept of territorial nationalism as humbug. He held that an assortment of people having dissimilar cultures and languages could not become nation basically because they resided in a scrupulous territory. This group of divergent people could not be described nation because it could not function as a coherent whole. It was not permeated through the livelihood spirit of unity and oneness. It lacked the life, blood and the livelihood spring of civilization. Just as Golwalkar, it was the cultural affinity and general historical traditions that bound the people jointly and made them of one mind and one body.

Golwalkar was of the opinion that territorial nationalism was lifeless, unscientific and unnatural If we accepted the principle of territorial nationalism, then the country would get converted into 'Dharmashala'. Anybody could become a member of one nation. But this theory of nationalism was wrong because a nation was normally shaped of the people who had urbanized general cultural affinities and who measured India as their motherland. He was of the opinion that the concept of territorial nationalism was responsible for the partition of the country and disunity in the country. It had sapped our national power and destroyed the life spring of nationalism that nourished the national spirit of the Indian people. Territorial nationalism was unnatural and unscientific because Muslims did not consider themselves as a part of the nation. He maintained that it was this divisive- and anti-national agenda that resulted in the partition of the country. The Partition of India was a standing instance of the failure of the concept of territorial nationalism. As against this, Golwalkar's cultural nationalism was based on five principles: general religion, general race, general language, general civilization and country. These five principles generated the national consciousness in the minds of the people and made them of one mind and of one resolve.

## Hindu Nationalism and Minorities

Golwalkar rejected the concept of the Indian or territorial nationalism as reality. He claimed that due to sure historical and cultural factors, Hindus in India constituted a nation and they measured India as their motherland. But as distant as other religious societies in India were concerned, they did not consider India as their motherland or holy land. They took pride in the information that they were heirs of the invaders of India. They were invaders who waged wars against Hindus to stay them in subjection. They had urbanized extra territorial loyalties. Though mainly of the converted Muslims and Christians were originally Hindus, because of their conversion, they lost their devotion and affection for motherland. They started claiming the foreign racial genealogies as their own. So, Golwalkar was of the opinion that these minorities could not be' measured as a part of the Hindu nation.

Golwalkar was of the opinion that the non-Hindu minorities could also become a part of the Indian nation, if they abandoned their separatist tendencies and accepted all the traditions as their own. He exhorted the Muslims and the Christians to join the mainstream and be a part of the Hindu national custom. He held that these societies should Indianise themselves through accepting and imbibing the Hindu cultural and historical traditions. They should consider themselves as inheritors of the great Hindu heroes described in the epics and take part in the celebration of Hindu festivals. They should imbibe the Hindu method of life. He pointed out that it was not necessary for them to leave their religion. They should practice their religion as they wanted because they had freedom of religion and worship. Also, through accepting the Hindu method of life, they could remain Muslims and Christians. It was high time that they should return back to house and be a part of the great national custom. Golwalkar said that he did not want to do this with the help of coercion or force, but through love and persuasion. He held that the minorities would enjoy all social and political rights but they would not be given any privileges.

Arguing further, Golwalkar pointed out that since extensive, Hindus had urbanized unique method of assimilation and absorption which enabled the foreign elements that entered into society to get integrated into Indian society without losing their identity. The best instance of this assimilation was that of Parsis who came to India from Iran to escape the religious persecution and became a part of the great Indian custom without losing their religion and identity.

Golwalkar was highly critical of the so described progressive and secular Hindus for encouraging the procedure of identity formation in the middle of the minorities and backward castes. They Justified these divisive tendencies on the grounds of secularism and democracy. Instead of promoting the procedure of integration in dissimilar parts of Hindu society, they were encouraging the divisive tendencies to grow. He was of the opinion that these westernised and denationalized Hindus would not be able to forge unity of the Indian nation on the grounds of pluralism and secularism. These procedures were urbanized as a reaction and therefore they would not be in a location to develop a positive content in their behaviors.

## HINDU NATIONALISM OF V. D. SAVARKAR

Savarkar was the first systematic exponent of the Hindu nationalism. He elaborately described his theory of Hindutva in his book 'Hindutva' published in 1924. Through that time, he had abandoned his concept of Indian nationalism that he borrowed from Joseph Mazzini in favor of Hindu nationalism. In the procedure of developing his concept of Hindu nationalism, he rejected some of the arguments of territorial nationalism. He held that the subsistence of a mere territory did not create nation but nation was made through the people who constituted themselves as a political society, bound jointly through cultural affinities and traditions.

### Hindutva as Cultural Nationalism

Savarkar was a supporter of cultural nationalism. He was of the opinion that identity formation was the essence of nationalism. India had received such identity from the Hindu religion. This identity was evolved in excess of an extensive era of time. Despite having outward differences, the Hindus were internally bound jointly through cultural, religious, social, linguistic and historical affinities. These affinities were urbanized through the procedure of assimilation and association of countless centuries. It molded the Hindus into a homogeneous and organic nation and above all induced a will to a general national life. This homogeneity was significant because other sections in the society had divergent cultural traditions.

Savarkar argued that it was cultural, racial and religious unity that counted more in the formation of the nation. While defining nation, Savarkar wrote that nation meant a political society which had occupied a contiguous and adequate territory and urbanized self-governing national identity. This society was internally organized and was bound jointly through cultural and racial affinities. He held that the Hindus had become nation because they possessed all these features.

Savarkar was of the opinion that Hindus constituted nation because they had urbanized secure affinities with the land bound through Himalayas to the Indian Ocean and the Indus River. Hindus measured India as their fatherland and holy land. Savarkar tried to illustrate that those people constituted nation who measured India as fatherland and holy land. In this definition, Savarkar effectively excluded those people who did not consider India as their holy land - because their sacred religious spaces were not situated in India. For him, Hindu nationalism stood for the unity of all Hindus. For him, Hindu society and not Hindu religion came first; Hindus were a nation because they were a self-enclosed society which was internally organized on the foundation of racial, religious and linguistic affinities. The Hindus shared a general historical past Savarkar knew that ultimately, nationalism was a psychological feeling and it was necessary to cultivate national consciousness in the middle of the Hindus. The general affinities should be used to strengthen the national consciousness. He wanted Hindus to cultivate the affinities that encouraged national consciousness and undermine the tendencies that divided the Hindu society.

## Hindu Nation and Indian State

Savarkar wanted the Hindu nation to be strong and powerful so that India could survive as a self-governing strong nation in the ferocious life thrash about that was going on flanked by dissimilar countries of the world. He held that in the modem times, nation had been recognized as the only viable political entity and all the societies of the world had been organized on the foundation of nation. Hence, everybody had to think in relation to the national policies in the context of nation only. There was nothing parochial or sectarian over it.

For Savarkar, Hindus as a society, shaped nation. Hence, he laid stress on the principle of exclusion. He excluded Muslims and Christians from the Indian nation because they did not consider India as a holy land because their sacred religious spaces were situated outside India.

Hence, he laid emphasis on the variation flanked by Hindus and Muslims. So, he wrote that everything that was general in the middle of us weakened our resolve to oppose them; Hindus were constantly fighting against Non-Hindus to save their society. Hence, he launched the Shuddhi movement to reconvert the converted Hindus to Hinduism and to purge Marathi language of Arabic and Persian languages.

The Muslims were not assimilated in India, in information, they tried to absorb Hinduism but they failed in their efforts. The prolonged resistance of the Hindus to Muslim invasions molded them into a strong and resolute nation.

What were the rights and positions of minorities in such a Hindu nation? Savarkar held that nation was a cultural category but state was a political category. All Hindus were the members of the nation. Non-Hindus might not become members at the nation but they were members of the Indian state. He maintained that Hindus did not advance any claims, privileges and rights in excess of and above non-Hindu sections. He wrote, "Let Indian state be purely Indian, and let there be no distinction as distant as franchise, public services, offices and taxation on the ground of religion was concerned. Let all citizens of the Indian state be treated equally just as to their individual worth irrespective of their racial and religious percentage in the common population." He was ready to concede all rights to the minorities but did not think it necessary to concede the demands of special interests advanced through Muslims.

Therefore , Savarkar made a distinction flanked by the Indian state and Hindu nation and measured the Hindu nation as a part of the Indian state.

## Hindu Nationalism of V. D. Savarkar- A Critical Revise

Savarkar was the first Indian thinker who declared that Hindus shaped separate nation in, India. He stood for a strong Hindu nation which would withstand and survive ferocious life thrash about in the middle of the nations. He sought to popularize the Hindu nationalism throughout his life with the help of the Hindu Mahasabha.

There are obvious tensions and logical inconsistencies in the Hindu nationalism of V. D. Savarkar. He could not properly describe the concept of nationalism because Hindus, Muslims and Christians shared general traditions and affinities in India even in the religious field. His advocacy of cause, science and technology was instrumental in the sense that for him they were useful because they helped him forge strong Hindu nation. Cause and science in the West were the culmination of the development of social philosophy which fought against religious prejudices and superstitions. The similar could not be used to strengthen the cause of religious nationalism. From that point of view, the use of the word 'cause' was deplorable because rationally speaking the whole of societies could not be excluded from the definition of the nation on the grounds of loyalty and patriotism because the betrayers of the national interest could come from any society. Also, his distinction flanked by the nation and the state was not convincing because both of them (nation and state) could not be separated and they came jointly as nation state. He conceded all the citizenship rights to non-Hindus except the membership of the nation. This would definitely make distinctions in the middle of the people and destroy national unity. A big part of the society would feel that they were excluded from the national mainstream for no fault of theirs. Savarkar's advocacy of the relativist ethics did not resolve these tensions because cause, science and relativist ethics did not recognize ascriptive loyalties. They had to be applied to all human beings crossways the board.

## RISE OF HINDU NATIONALIST IDEOLOGY

After the failure of Non-cooperation movement, there was growth of communal and separatist thoughts both in the middle of Hindus and Muslims. Both of them claimed that their ideology was not a communal ideology but it was a true nationalist ideology which took into consideration the civilization and religion of the people. After 1922-23, the followers of Lokmanya Tilak started supporting the Hindutva movement. Beside with them the newly educated Hindu middle class also supported it. The Mopala revolt in Kerala created a lot of unrest in the Hindu society.

The main arguments of the Hindutva supporters were as follows:

- In the past, the Hindus suffered several a defeats and lost their independence to the foreign invaders because of lack of unity. They had numbers, velour and possessions at their command but they faced defeat due to lack of unity.
- The Hindus had been losing their numbers due to the aggressive proselitisation through the Christian missionaries and the Muslims. As a result, in an extensive time they would be reduced to a minority in their land of birth. Hence, in order to uphold the stage of Hindu population, the Shuddhi and Samghatana movements should be launched. Shuddhi stands for re-conversion of Hindus.
- There was a need to protect the political interests of Hindus because the British government was hostile to them; the Muslims aggressively pursued their separatist agenda and the Congress under the false notion of secularism was betraying the cause of Hindus.

In India, we could see the emergence of two traditions of Hindutva, the first custom was led through V. D. Savarkar and the second custom was led through M. S. Golwalkar. Though both the traditions professed their allegiance to the ideology of Hindutva, their emphasis and methods differed.

CHAPTER 8

# Hinduism Renaissance and Dharma

## HINDUISM RENAISSANCE

Hindu Dharma has already undergone a remarkable renaissance in the modern age. Less than two hundred years ago Hinduism seemed to be on the verge of complete collapse. It was caught in inertia and under siege by the missionary and colonial forces that had been ruling India for centuries. Yet at that extremity it didn't collapse but renewed itself, going back to its ancient roots to provide for new and expansive growths.

The result was that in the nineteenth century the modern Hindu renaissance began from several angles. Swami Dayananda Sarasvati of the Arya Samaj issued a call to return to the *Vedas*. Swami Vivekananda brought forth a new awakening of Hinduism to Yoga and Vedanta. Many other such leaders arose throughout the country to follow such a vision.

The Hindu renaissance was not limited to India. Vivekananda spread his message throughout the entire world, which rediscovered Hinduism as the deep philosophy of Vedanta and the profound practice of Yoga. With this Hinduism began to go global. It became the main tradition pioneering dialogue and synthesis in religion, promoting a recognition that sages throughout the world have always taught the same message of oneness. After the counterculture movements of the nineteen sixties, many other India-based spiritual groups started in the West.

The twentieth century marked a new and independent India in which Hindus were the majority and no longer had to suffer under the rule of a religion seeking to convert them. This led to a building of many new temples throughout the country. Recent decades witnessed a Diaspora of Hindus throughout the globe, particularly as professionals in new technology fields. With the many new immigrants from India in the last two decades, almost every important sect in Hinduism can be found in the West, with Hindu temples in the main cities of Europe and North America.

## Hinduism under Siege

Yet in spite of this renaissance, Hinduism as a specific religion did not truly flourish in the twentieth century. It remained under siege by colonial and missionary forces that remained active even after colonialism by Christian countries had ended. On top of these, a new leftist and communist thinking arose that attacked it further by allying themselves with residual colonial forces and Islam.

Many countries of Asia like China and Indochina became communist and under its rule tried to destroy their older religious traditions. While India as a whole did not become communist, several states like Kerala and Bengal did, and the communists gained a favored position in the media and universities of the country from which their anti-Hindu message became magnified beyond their political power. Indian intellectuals embraced Marxism as their new religion and few remained to articulate a Hindu point of view to the world.

Free India under Nehru opted for a socialist-communist model that perpetuated the British system of education and a leftist way of thinking that was often unabashedly anti-Hindu and sometimes pro-Islamic and pro-Christian. The economic problems of India, which resulted from the same socialist economies that failed all over the world, were blamed on Hinduism. The social and class problems of the country that were based on medieval customs developed during foreign rule were turned into a permanent stain on Hinduism itself.

At the same time, their Hindu background was downplayed by the very global movements that it spawned. Western Hindu-based groups preferred the names of Yoga, Vedanta or that of their particular guru or sect and sometimes failed to recognize their Hindu connections at all. This was because western Yoga students were so taken in by the anti-Hindu propaganda that they did not want to be associated with such an apparently regressive religion, no matter how great the spiritual teachings they found in it!

The result was that, in spite of the global spread of Hindu teachings and an independent modern India, the world still looked down upon the Hindu religion as primitive or oppressive. Some scholars were reluctant even to recognize Hinduism as a world religion, seeing it rather as a disorganized collection of various cults. The Aryan Invasion theory was used to assert that India had no indigenous culture but was a hodgepodge of various invaders, with the original Hindus being pre-Vedic Dravidians, a very different group from the Vedic sages that the country had always looked to for the origin of its traditions.

## Resurgent Hinduism

This situation has begun to change dramatically during the past few years. Hindus are finally awakening to the many distortions about their religion. They are beginning to assert their rights and insist upon a proper presentation of their tradition in the world forum. More pro-Hindu political movements in India have gained power on both state and national levels, and without the anti-minority pogroms that it was insisted that they intended to do by their opponents. Such Hindu groups are largely responsible for the economic liberalization of the country, as they are the main opponents of the socialist economic policies that modern India under Nehru adopted.

Hindus, both in India and in the West, are becoming affluent through modern jobs in science, medicine and software. In the process, they are realizing that nothing in their religion is out of harmony with progress and success in the modern world. On the contrary, they have seen how Hindu family values have granted Hindu children in the West greater home and emotional stability. They have seen how the traditional Hindu emphasis on learning, including languages and mathematics, has given Hindu children an advantage in schools. In recognizing how Hindu spiritual movements have influenced the world, overseas Hindus are comfortable maintaining their religion in the countries to which they have migrated. They are often better educated, more scientific in outlook and more affluent than their Christian neighbours who would still associate Hinduism with poverty and superstition.

Hindu groups are challenging media distortions both in India and in the West and with success; for example, protesting the use of chants from the *Bhagavad Gita* in erotic scenes in western movies or beef flavoring in so-called vegetarian McDonalds French fries. While such issues may seem minor, it is curious how the world media will respond to such challenges and now considers the importance of not offending Hindus because of these. Such protests help counter the sense of moral offense that westerners like to assert about Hinduism, often because of misinformed stereotypes about the religion. After a few short years, people are aware of Hinduism as a religion and must recognize Hindu activist groups that will no longer tolerate centuries old denigrations or modern stereotypes.

The Ayodhya movement in India, the effort to restore the Ram temple or Ramajanma Bhumi alias Babri Masjid—whatever one may think about it —served to awaken Hindus to their history of oppression by outside groups. It brought about a new examination of what Hinduism is and what it means to be a Hindu. While the term Hindu had long become almost a term of denigration, it is now being rediscovered as a term of pride (Hindu gaurava). Much has been made in the western media of Hindus resisting Christian missionary activities in India, with allegations of Hindu violence against missionaries (though most of these reports were erroneous or exaggerated). Yet, a few excesses aside, it shows that Hindus are more confident of their religion than in previous decades when even devoted Hindus felt a need to invite missionaries in India as if they alone could uplift the country. Missionaries in India no longer have a free reign but must face local Hindu challenges to their attempts at conversion. This is disturbing for them because of the lack of challenge they had in the past from Hindus. In India, Christian groups still have a freedom for their activity not found in any nearby Islamic or communist states.

## TEXTS ON DHARMA AND TEXTS ON THEOLOGY: BIMORPHIC WORLDVIEWS

Classical Hindu texts in the beginning of the Common Era enumerate the goals—or matters of value—of a human being. These are dharma, artha(wealth, power), kama (sensual pleasure), and moksha (liberation from the circle of life and death).

While dharma, wealth, and sensual pleasure are usually seen as this-worldly, moksha is liberation from this world and the repeated rebirths of a soul. There are texts that deal with dharma,wealth, sensual pleasure, and liberation. The multiple Hindu traditions do differ from other world religions in having this variety of goals and the array of texts that accompany them. This means that Hinduism presents adherents with several competing conceptual systems, intersecting but distinct.

The texts that deal with moksha, or liberation, are generally concerned with three issues: the nature of reality, including the supreme being and the human soul; the way to the supreme goal; and the nature of the supreme goal. Generally the nature of reality is called tattva (truth) and corresponds with the term "theology." These texts do not focus much on ethics or righteous behaviour in this world; that is the province of dharma texts.

The theological texts or sections that deal with tattva focus on weaning a human being from the earthly pursuit of happiness to what they consider to be the supreme goal of liberation (moksha) from this life. It is important to keep this taxonomy in mind, because theological doctrines that are oriented to liberation do not necessarily trickle down into dharmic or ethical injunctions; in many Hindu traditions, in fact, there is a disjunction between dharma and moksha.

Thus, a theology that emphasizes the world as a body of God, a pervasive pan-Indian belief that Goddess Earth (Prithvi, Vasundhara, Bhu Devi) is also a consort of Vishnu, or the notion that the Mother Goddess (Amba, Durga) is synonymous with Nature (prakriti) does not necessarily translate to eco-friendly behaviour. Likewise, renunciation, celibacy, and detachment are laudable virtues for one who seeks liberation from the cycle of life and death, but the texts on dharma say that begetting children is necessary for salvation. These bimorphic worldviews have to be kept in mind if we are to see the relevance for the Hindu traditions of Western viewpoints such as deep ecology. On another front, the dissonance between dharma and tattva/moksha texts also accounts in part for the fact that while some Hindu traditions hold the Goddess to be supreme, women may not necessarily hold a high position in society.

It is quite correct to say that some theological/tattva texts speak of certain kinds of "oneness" of the universe and, in some cases, the "oneness" of all creation. Some, though not most, tattva texts speak of the absolute identity between the supreme being and the human soul (atman)—an identity that in fact transcends the concept of equality of many distinct souls. This philosophical system of nonduality is discussed by Western philosophers as an important resource in ecology. Eliot Deutsch writes, "... what does it mean to affirm continuity between man and the rest of life? Vedanta would maintain that this means the recognition that fundamentally all life is one, that in essence everything is reality, and that this oneness finds its natural expression in a reverence for all things." The main thrust of the arguments made by Deutsch, Callicott, and others is to show that Hindu philosophy emphasizes that all creation is ultimately Brahman, or the supreme being, and therefore, if we hurt someone we hurt ourselves.

While the "oneness" doctrine and its ecological implications are underscored by Callicott, Lance Nelson has recently argued that the advaita ("non-dualism") conceptual system does not promote eco-friendly behaviour. Nelson shows how the doctrine developed by the Hindu philosopher Shankara (c. seventh century) actually devalues nature. He concludes that non-dualistic Vedanta philosophy "is not the kind of non-dualism that those searching for ecologically supportive modes of thought might wish it to be." The philosophies of Shankara and Ramanuja are relevant to those who seek liberation, but not to those seeking moral rules to govern everyday behaviour. Hindu communities and customs are established not on the sense of oneness or equality found in moksha, but on many differences and hierarchies based on gender, caste, age, economic class, and so on. With all their limitations and richness, therefore, we have had to deal with the texts, narratives, and traditions of dharma rather than the rule of moksha for actions leading to prosperity of the earth.

What I am urging is a shift in our perspective from the tattva/moksha texts to the resources that have a more direct relevance to worldly be-haviour. These are the popular practices embodied in the dharmic tradition and in the bhakti/devotional rituals. Dharma texts and narratives are in some ways like law codes in other countries: sometimes followed, sometimes flouted, sometimes ignored, sometimes evaded—and so-metimes taken to heart as the right thing to do to maintain social stability. In addition to dharma texts, devotional (bhakti) exercises seem to be the greatest potential resource for ecological activists in India. As we have seen, devotion to Krishna or to Mother Ganga or Yamuna has impelled some people to take action to supply safe drinking water, plant and protect trees, and clean up rivers.

What can we learn from such success stories? Clearly, some Hindu texts, traditions, and rituals can inspire ecofriendly behaviour. Narratives like the story of Shiva and Ganga, Parvati and the saplings seem to have more impact than talking about the universe as the body of God.

The sanctity of rivers as Mother Goddesses has evoked great passion and inspired the cleaning up of the Ganga and Yamuna rivers; other rivers, one hopes, will be taken care of soon. Gurus and teachers can mobilize awareness and organize action, and these teachers may hold the key to avoiding ecological tragedy.

It is when leaders, whether they are from the priestly families like Chaturvedi and Mishra, or gurus, or heads of environmental institutions like Dr. Purohit, team up with temples, scientists, and lawyers that Hindu ecological activists have the greatest potential for success. Stories, gurus and goddesses, hagiographic literature, and dharmic models will all have to be pressed into service before we can make further progress.

Prithvi Devi, or Mother Earth, can protect us if we protect her. If she is abused, she can transform herself from a nourishing mother into a wrathful deity. One of the goals of the Hindu texts is to encourage human beings to seek enlightenment. Vairamuthu, a composer and poet popular in South India, recently wrote a song on the beauty of a tree. In the last line, he urges us to have the right attitude towards the tree. Every tree, he says, is a Bodhi tree. The Buddha was enlightened under the Bodhi tree: now every tree in the world can enlighten us about the burden on Mother Earth.

## SANATANA DHARMA

Sanatana Dharma means the Eternal Religion, the Ancient Law. This is based on the Vedas. This is the oldest of living religions. Hinduism is known by the name Sanatana Dharma. What the Vedas alone declare to be the means of attaining the *summum bonum* or the final emancipation, is the Sanatana Dharma or Hindu Dharma. The foundation of Sanatana Dharma is Sruti; Smritis are the walls; the Itihasas and Purnas are the buttresses or supports. In ancient times, the Srutis were learnt by heart. The teacher sang them to his pupils and the pupils sang them after him. They were not written in book form. All the sects, all the philosophical systems, appeal to the Sruti as the final authority. The Smriti stands next in authority to the Sruti.

Hinduism stands unrivalled in the depth and grandeur of its philosophy. Its ethical teachings are lofty, unique and sublime. It is highly flexible and adapted to every human need. It is a perfect religion by itself. It is not in need of anything from any other religion. No other religion has produced so many great saints, great patriots, great warriors and great Pativratas. The more you know of it, the more you will honour and love it. The more you study it, the more it will enlighten you and satisfy your heart.

## India—The Home of Religions

The religious history of the world tells us that from time immemorial, India has been the home of great sages, seers and Rishis. All the grand religious ideals that have moulded the character of men, the loftiest of ethics and morality that have raised human beings to magnanimous heights of divine splendour and all the sublime truths of spirituality that have made men divine and have moulded the spiritual ideals of nations and saviours of mankind, first arose in India.

The spiritual horizon of India has always been illumined with the glory of the self-effulgent sun of wisdom of the Upanishads. Whenever there was any upheaval in any part of the world, the origin of this could be traced to the wave of spirituality caused by the birth of a great soul—a special manifestation of Divinity—in some part of India.

Hindus have had a culture, civilisation and religion millennia older than those of any other country or people. God did speak to the world through India's Rishis, Yogins, Mahatmas, Alvars, prophets, Acharyas, Sannyasins and saints. Their teachings and Puranas are really inspired. God is the one Light and Truth from whom emanate the teachings of all faiths.

India is the home and abode of religions. It occupies the proud first place in religious devotion and godliness. It is famous for its Yogins and saints. The goal of India is Self-realisation or attainment of God-consciousness, through renunciation. The history of India is a history of religion. Its social code and regulations are founded upon religion. Minus its Yoga, religion and its regulations, India will not be what it has been for millennia. Some Hindus are still not aware of the distinguishing features of Sanatana Dharma. If every Hindu knew and understood what Hinduism is, the Hindus of today would all be gods on this earth. May you all be endowed with the knowledge of Sanatana Dharma! May you all endeavour to protect the Eternal Dharma! May the secrets of Sanatana Dharma be revealed unto you all, like a fruit in the palm of your hand, through the Grace of the Lord! May the blessings of Rishis be upon you all! Glory to the Vedas and Sanatana Dharma! Glory to Brahman, the source for all Vedas and Sanatana Dharma!

### Samanya Dharma

Every religion has a generic form or *Samanya-Rupa* and a specific form or *Visesha-Rupa.* The general form remains eternally the same. It is never changed by any circumstance whatsoever. It is not affected at all by changes of time, place, surroundings and individual differences.

This aspect of religion is called Sanatana or eternal. That which changes according to the change of time, place and surrounding circumstances is the external aspect or ritual, of Dharma.

Samanya Dharma is the general Dharma or law for all men. Varnashrama Dharmas are special Dharmas which are to be practised by particular castes and by men in particular stages of life. The Samanya Dharmas must be practised by all, irrespective of distinctions of Varna and Ashrama, creed or colour. Goodness is not the property of any one class, creed, sect or community. Every man should possess this virtue.

## VARNASHRAMA DHARMA

The principle of Varnashrama Dharma is one of the basic principles of Hinduism. The Varnashrama system is peculiar to Hindus. It is a characteristic feature of Hinduism. It is also prevalent throughout the world according to Guna-Karma (aptitude and conduct), though there is no such distinct denomination of this kind, elsewhere. The duties of the castes are Varna Dharma. The four castes are Brahmana, Kshatriya, Vaishya and Sudra. The duties of the stages in life are Ashrama Dharma. The four Ashramas or orders of life are Brahmacharya, Grihastha, Vanaprastha and Sannyasa.

## The Principle

Human society is like a huge machine. The individuals and communities are like its parts. If the parts are weak and broken, the machine will not work. A machine is nothing without its parts. The human body also can work efficiently if its parts and organs are in sound and strong condition. If there is pain in any part of the body, if there is disease in any organ or part of the body, this human machine will go out of order. It will not perform its usual function or work. So is the case with the human society. Every individual should perform his duties efficiently. The Hindu Rishis and sages formed an ideal scheme of society and an ideal way of individual life, which is known by the name Varnashrama Dharma. Hinduism is built on Varnashrama Dharma. The structure of the Hindu society is based on Varnashrama Dharma. Observance of Varnashrama Dharma helps one's growth and self-evolution. It is very indispensable. If the rules are violated, the society will soon perish.

The aim of Varnashrama Dharma is to promote the development of the universal, eternal Dharma. If you defend Dharma, it will defend you. If you destroy it, it will destroy you. Therefore, never destroy your Dharma. This principle holds true of the individual as much as of the nation. It is Dharma alone which keeps a nation alive. Dharma is the very soul of man. Dharma is the very soul of a nation also. In the West and in the whole world also, there is Varnashrama, though it is not rigidly observed there. Some Western philosophers have made a division of three classes, *viz.*, philosophers, warriors and masses. The philosophers correspond to the Brahmanas, warriors to Kshatriyas and the masses to Vaishyas and Sudras. This system is indispensable to keep the society in a state of perfect harmony and order.

## Hindu Joint Family Structure of Earlier Times and its Strengths

Returning to the Hindu family structure of earlier days,

Karta would normally be the able-bodied able-minded eldest male member of the family. Position of authority and responsibility would be distributed in a hierarchical manner in the sense that elder the member greater the authority coupled with greater responsibility. Younger members would be groomed on the same pattern to learn to assume the authority as well as discharge corresponding responsibility, as they would grow up in the hierarchy.

The respect for the elders would be an unwritten law, and it would be expected of all to observe it without any reservation. With that elders would have the equal amount of responsibility to stay worthy of such respect by their thoughts and actions. This would be the balancing factor for maintaining necessary equilibrium in the family.

Adult male members of the family would have the responsibility of earning for the family to meet its needs, and to provide shelter and protection to the female members and children of the family. Female members would have the responsibility of taking care of the in-house needs of male members of family, and raising the kids in line with the culture and traditions of the family. Elder female members of the family would have the responsibility of grooming up the younger female members of the family in the desired direction. Each new generation would learn the family values from their mothers and grandmothers, and in this manner the female members of the family would play the crucial role through the formative years of growing children. Spirituality would be an essential part of the family values, and women folk would be the custodian and deliverer of these values to each next generation through their growing up process.

Single spouse system and fidelity would be the norm. Exceptions would be found in the context of political marriages where a king would offer his daughter to another king and thus, the two ruling families would unite and not be threat to each other. Such marriages would primarily be conducted for maintaining power balance and political equilibrium. These would be exceptions not rule, and we have references to many kings having only one wife. How Hindu family structure changed so drastically that now we hardly see any evidence of our earlier system. The whole system, however, changed after brutal onslaught of Islam and its direct interference in Hindu way of family life through forced conversions and forced marriages of Hindu girls and Hindu women into Muslim powerful families.

This is when family values started deteriorating substantially though it did preserve a lot of it, as we can see from the testimonies of Sir Thomas Munro as presented below, even after thousand years of inhumane oppression that Max Muller called an inferno and wondered "how any nation could have survived such an inferno without being turned into devils themselves."

If a good system of agriculture, unrivalled manufacturing skill, a capacity to produce whatever can contribute to either convenience or luxury, schools established in every village for teaching, reading, writing, and arithmetic, the general practice of hospitality and charity amongst each other, and above all, a treatment of the female sex full of confidence, respect, and delicacy, are among the signs which denote a civilized people-then the Hindus are not inferior to the nations of Europe, and if civilization is to become an article of trade between England and Bhaarat Varsh, I am convinced that England will gain by the import cargo. Sir Thomas Munro, quoted in Mill's History, vol. i. p. 371, re-quoted by Max Muller, p 57 p 231 The True Culprits have remained unidentified all along. There was so much of beauty left even until early 19th century that the eminent Governor of the then Madras Presidency wrote: If civilization is to become an article of trade between England and Bhaarat Varsh, I am convinced that England will gain by the import cargo. This would mean that real downfall has occurred during past 170 years. All factors remaining constant the only variable has been Christian English education system forcibly imposed on the Hindus by systematic elimination of ancient Hindu education system [documentary evidence in

Hidden face of Christianity]. Hindu Family Values were totally transformed by the Christian English Education system, which was predominantly guided by the values propagated by Jesus Christ in the Christian Bible.

Christian Bible New Testament Luke 12:51 Suppose ye that I am come to give peace on earth? I tell you, Nay; but rather division: 12:52 For from henceforth there shall be five in one house divided, three against two, and two against three. 12:53 The father shall be divided against the son, and the son against the father; the mother against the daughter, and the daughter against the mother; the mother in law against her daughter in law, and the daughter in law against her mother in law. 14:26 If any man come to me, and hate not his father, and mother, and wife, and children, and brethren, and sisters, yea, and his own life also, he cannot be my disciple.

Gospel of Thomas 16 Jesus said: Perhaps men think that I came to cast peace on the world; and they do not know that I came to cast division upon earth, fire, sword, war. For five will be in a house; there will be three against two and two against three, the father against the son and the son against the father. And they will stand because they are single ones. 56 Jesus said: He who will not hate his father and his mother cannot be my disciple. And he who will not hate his brothers and sisters, and carry his cross as I have, will not become worthy of me. To understand Jesus's agenda, as documented in the pages of Christian Bible, you may want to study Christianity in a different Light. Christian missionary educators taught the Hindus for past six generations and media experts created the image in the minds of the Hindus that ancient Hindu Joint Family structure was essentially an evil social structure.

## A NEW ERA OF SPIRITUALITY AND SELF-REALIZATION

Whatever particular calendar we may employ, humanity is undergoing a major change of civilization during this period.

We are moving out of the industrial age into the high tech age. We are moving from nationalist cultures to an international culture. Though western civilization remains the dominant outer force in the world, we must recognize other cultural groups of which Hindu-predominant India is one of the most important.

The problem is that the new global culture is still being defined according to the same old materialistic values or by religious dogma from the Middle Ages. This has created a modern commercial culture of sensation, on one hand, and massive funding for conversion efforts on the other, mainly through petrodollars. While Christianity has declined in the West it has become more assertive in its conversion efforts in the non-Christian world, particularly India, whose traditional tolerance keeps its doors to other religions open. Even in America, the Southern Baptists, the largest Protestant sect in the country, continue a conversion effort against Hindus that labels the Hindu religion as one of the devil, at the same time promoting the Biblical view of creation in schools in America, fighting science as well.

However, longer and more powerful forces are arising than current cultural trends. The destruction of the biosphere and the deforestation of the planet must eventually force us to enter an age of ecological responsibility. This is giving birth to a new ecology philosophy, recognizing the spiritual value of the animal kingdom. Hindu Dharma is being recognized for its importance as a religion of nature. It honours the Divine everywhere in the world around us. It finds holy places on every mountain or where any rivers come together. It honours the Earth as the Divine Mother incarnate. Such a religion that embraces nature as part of ourselves is necessary to save the planet in the years to come.

The global encounter between religions is causing people to recognize that many different religions have their validity and that no single religion, any more than any single race, can claim truth or salvation belongs to it. The old exclusive beliefs of the Middle Ages are falling under the scrutiny of a global reason that must honor all the spiritual aspirations of humanity and can no longer confine itself to the beliefs of one community.

This emerging planetary age provides a much different and more favorable scenario for Hinduism, in which it is bound to spread much further. Hinduism is the world's largest pluralistic religious tradition. It is based upon the view that there is One Truth but many paths. It is not based on any single savior, church or holy book. There are probably more religions inside of Hinduism than outside of it. Within its broad embrace can be found monotheism, polytheism, dualism, monism, pantheism and even atheism. Hindu temples accommodate many names and forms for God, many scriptures and many great sages both ancient and modern. The planetary age is a pluralistic age and must learn to do with the religions of the world what Hinduism has done with the religions of South Asia.

The coming age is one of spirituality and Self-realization, not of formal religion and subservience to God or prophet. It is one of a spiritual culture such as we see in Hindu Dharma that embraces all life and nature. The coming planetary age does not belong to conversion-seeking religions, which divide humanity into the believers and the non-believers, but to the spirituality of consciousness such as revealed in yogic traditions, and sought by great mystics everywhere, which unite humanity into one great family with the entire universe.

Hindus welcome a new era of Self-realization and God-realization beyond the boundaries of dogma and institution, honoring all individuals, all cultures and all spiritual aspiration. Let us honor that Self in all beings regardless of religious affiliation, ethnicity or culture. This will not only lead us to a truly new millennium but also allow us to transcend time and karma altogether, which is the real goal of our eternal striving.

## INDIA AT A CROSSROADS

What is the secret of this great and enduring culture of India? The unique feature of Indian or Bharatiya culture is unity-in-multiplicity or what could be called 'Vedic pluralism.' The oldest Indian text and perhaps the oldest book in the world, the *Rigveda* boldly proclaims: "That which is the One Truth the seers teach in many different ways (*Rigveda* I.164.46)," and "May noble aspirations come to us from every side (*Rigveda* I.89.1)."

The Indic view is that though Truth is One the paths are many. There is no need for any religious exclusivism or cultural uniformity. Many different religions and philosophies must exist relative to the different levels and temperaments of individuals. Even atheism has a place as one possible view of reality for the human mind. A free discussion and representation of all views is necessary to arrive at truth. Even errors and mistakes must be allowed in a free inquiry into truth. Truth can never be destroyed through scrutiny or examination. It is only behind closed doors or in fixed dogma that truth cannot stand.

Vedic pluralism, however, is not mere polytheism or separatism. It is a recognition of a unity that transcends name and form. The Hindu sense of the One is also that of the infinite. Its unity is of the universal, not of one thing as opposed to another, but as the one thing, like a single thread, that links all things together. Such a deep inner unity can embrace a multiple expression, just as the ocean can hold many waves and not get disturbed by them. This bedrock of Indic pluralism gave rise to the many different sects of Hinduism, which remains the most diverse religious tradition in the world with its Vedic, Tantric, Shaivite, Shakta, Vaishnava and other sects both ancient and modern. It also provided the ground for Buddhist, Jain, and Sikh traditions, which themselves have much diversity. It spawned perhaps the greatest diversity of spiritual teachings in the entire world. It respects science and art as part of our spiritual quest, building a great material culture as well as wonderful temples. On its basis people in India could even come to appreciate the spiritual aspects of less tolerant religious groups who invaded them from across the border. Though still largely misunderstood in the West as polytheism or a worship of many Gods, this Bharatiya (Indic) pluralism reflects an open quest for truth and a free flowering of all true human potentials such as the world desperately needs today.

Unfortunately, over the first fifty years since independence India has not discovered its real roots or reclaimed its true soul as a civilization. Its intellectuals have mimicked western trends in thought, particularly Marxism, even after these have been discredited in the West, following them with an almost uncritical Hindu type of devotion. In an excessive pursuit of secularism they found it necessary to denigrate their own pluralistic traditions and favour foreign ideologies of religious or political exclusivism. They have forgotten their great modern sages like Swami Vivekananda and Sri Aurobindo who projected futuristic views of the Indian tradition and instead adulate western thinkers devoid of any spiritual realization. They look at India with jaded eyes and find its salvation in foreign lands. While many westerners come to India seeking spiritual knowledge, Indian intellectuals look to the West with admiration, pursuing materialistic ideologies that have left them unable to understand their own more spiritual traditions. The result is that after fifty years of independence India has not truly awakened; though it may be stirring in its sleep.

We are now entering into a global age in which pluralism must be the foundation of world culture. We can no longer pretend that only one race, one culture or one religion alone is true. The dawning century is no longer a missionary and colonial era in which one group can be allowed hegemony in the world. It is a new age of dialogue and respect in which we learn to honor and cherish all the cultures of the world. This should start with the honoring of tribal cultures that are the custodians of the Earth and the wisdom of nature that we so quickly losing in this artificial age. It must include not just dominant western religions, but the great traditions of the East, like Hinduism and Buddhism, which have a firm foundation in tolerance and synthesis. We must learn to embrace all human beings and their cultures as part of one great family (Vasudhaiva kutumbakam). We can certainly have our differences but should respectfully allow others to be different as well. Let our differences be a cause for admiration and celebration, not for mistrust, hatred and a seeking to eliminate them.

The dharmic traditions of India emphasize an organic pluralism as the model for human development. Just as the human body is one but has different organs that perform various functions for the benefit of the whole, so human society is one in essence but diverse in function, with each person like each cell of the body playing a vital role. This is not a model of democratic uniformity. It recognizes that the male an the female, the young and the old, the artist, thinker, businessman, politician and yogi, with all their differences, all have their special place in society, which is enriched by their diversity.

Yet Bharatiya Pluralism is not a relativism of anything goes. Its foundation lies in universal values like ahimsa, not wishing harm to any other creature and not seeking to interfere with the natural order. It is a pluralism that reflects a respect for the sacred in all things. It is not a pluralism of hedonism or materialism like that of the West that is insensitive of the environment or of other cultures. It is a pluralism of the spirit, not simply of the body; a pluralism of spiritual teachings, not merely of material choices.

It is time for India once more to be a leader and an innovator in world culture, rather than a follower and imitator as at present. To accomplish this, India must discover its own voice and initiate its own action in the global forum. Sri Aurobindo once remarked that India's real role was to be the guru among the nations of the world. At present it can hardly keep order within its own frontiers. The country is crushed by its own bureaucracy, though this grip is gradually loosening. Perhaps because of long foreign rule India developed a sense of apathy and resignation and a tolerance for oppression and inequality. This must go.

A new vitality and creativity is necessary for India that honours the spirit of the country's venerable traditions but does not restrict itself to previous outdated forms. This requires a new generation of thinkers who are global in outlook but grounded in the spirituality of Yoga and Vedanta. Indic thinkers must return to their cultural wellsprings, not to stop there, but to create a new vision of the future. *Out of the old Upanishads they need to envision new Upanishads.* Such a new India would combine science and spirituality in a global perspective, combining the wisdom of ancient rishis with that of modern creative thinkers. It would set forth a new spiritual or yogic science showing us how to realize the consciousness that is the foundation of the entire universe and the basis of universal law. It would develop our material potentials but for the greater glory of the Spirit, the Self of all beings. It would protect the earth which reaching into outer space. It would raise the downtrodden, not to convert people to a belief but to help all people realize their highest potential. Such an awakened India is crucial for world culture, which presently remains trapped between a destructive consumerism on one side and a rigid religious exclusivism on the other.

We can already see how such traditional Indian disciplines as Yoga, Ayurveda and Vedanta are gaining respect worldwide for their global vision. Such an Indic or Dharmic perspective should be added to religion, philosophy, science and medicine all over the world. The new India and the new generation of Indians should take up this task of world-making as their goal. The new world order of the computer and the information revolution gives the country a new chance in the global arena and offers a situation more favorable to its unique talents. But for this to occur India must stand up and speak out according to its real essence—which is as a spiritual superpower—regardless of whether this pleases everyone else in the world.

Today there is only one superpower in the world, the United States. But it is a superpower in the outer world only. Its wealth hides a spiritual poverty and growing psychological and social unrest. No technological superpower can properly guide the world in the planetary age. Only a spiritual superpower can do this. India has the potential to be the world's spiritual superpower, but it requires a great labour to bring it forth. The question is whether the country and its leaders are willing to make the effort. This requires looking back to the inspiration of the great rishis and yogis of the region, not merely following current political and economic compulsions—but looking back only to go forward with a renewed sense of mission and power.

## THE CRISIS IN THE PSYCHE OF INDIA

A defeatist tendency exists in the psyche of modern Indians perhaps unparalleled in any other country today. An inner conflict bordering on a civil war rages in the minds of the country's elite. The main effort of its cultural leaders appears to be to pull the country down or remake it in a foreign image, as if little Indian and certainly nothing Hindu was worthy of preserving or even reforming.

The elite of India suffers from a fundamental alienation from the traditions and culture of the land that would not be less poignant had they been born and raised in a hostile country. The ruling elite appears to be little more than a native incarnation of the old colonial rulers who haughtily lived in their separate cantonments, neither mingling with the people nor seeking to understand their customs. This new English-speaking aristocracy prides itself in being disconnected from the very soil and people that gave it birth.

There is probably no other country in the world where it has become a national pastime among its educated class to denigrate its own culture and history, however great that has been over the many millennia of its existence. When great archaeological discoveries of India's past are found, for example, they are not a subject for national pride but are ridiculed as an exaggeration, if not an invention, as if they represent only the imagination of backward chauvinistic elements within the culture.

There is probably no other country where the majority religion, however enlightened, mystical or spiritual, is ridiculed, while minority religions, however fundamentalist or even militant, are doted upon. The majority religion and its institutions are taxed and regulated while minority religions receive tax benefits and have no regulation or even monitoring. While the majority religion is carefully monitored and limited as to what it can teach, minority religions can teach what they want, even if anti-national or backward in nature. Books are banned that offend minority religious sentiments but praised if they cast insults on majority beliefs.

There is probably no other country where regional, caste and family loyalties are more important than the national interest, even among those who claim to be democratic, socialist or caste reformers. Political parties exist not to promote a national agenda but to sustain one region or group of people in the country at the expense of the whole. Each group wants as big a piece of the national pie as it can get, not realizing that the advantages it gains mean deprivation for other groups. Yet when those who were previously deprived gain power, they too seek the same unequal advantages that causes further inequality and discontent.

India's affirmative action code is by far the most extreme in the world, trying to raise up certain segments of the population regardless of merit, and prevent others from gaining positions however qualified they may be. In the guise of removing caste, a new castism has arisen where one's caste is more important than one's qualifications either in gaining entrance into a school or in finding a job when one graduates. Anti-Brahminism has often become the most virulent form of castist thinking. People view the government not as their own creation but as a welfare state from they should take the maximum personal benefit, regardless of the consequences for the country as a whole. Outside people need not pull Indians down. Indians are already quite busy keeping any of their people and the country as a whole from rising up. They would rather see their neighbours or the nation fail if they are not given the top position. It is only outside of India that Indians succeed, often remarkably well, because their native talents are not stifled by the dominant cultural self-negativity and rabid divisiveness that exists in the country today.

Political parties in India see gaining power as a means of amassing personal wealth and robbing the nation. Political leaders include gangsters, charlatans and buffoons who would stop short at nothing to gain power for themselves and their coteries. Even so-called modern or liberal parties resemble more the courts of kings, where personal loyalty is more important than any democratic participation. Once they gain power politicians routinely do little but cheat the people for their own advantage. Even honest politicians find that they cannot function without some deference to the more numerous corrupt leaders who often have a stranglehold on the bureaucracy.

Politicians divide the country into warring vote banks and place one community against another. They offer favors to communities like bribes to make sure that they are elected or stay in power. They campaign on slogans that appeal to community fears and suspicions rather than create any national consensus or harmony. They hold power based upon blame and hatred rather than on any positive programs for social change. They inflame the uneducated masses with propaganda rather than work to make people aware of real social problems like overpopulation, poor infrastructure or lack of education. Should a decent government come to power, the opposition pursues pulling it down as its main goal, so that they can gain power for themselves. The idea of a constructive or supportive opposition is hard to find. The goal is to gain power for oneself and to not allow anyone else to succeed.

To further their ambitions Indian politicians will manipulate the foreign press to denigrate their opponents, even if it means spreading lies and rumors and making the country an anathema in the eyes of the outside world. Petty conflicts in India are blown out of proportion in the foreign media, not by foreign journalists but by Indians seeking to use the media to score points against their own opponents in the country. The Indians who are responsible for the news of India in the foreign press spread venom and distortion about their own country, perhaps better than any foreigner who dislikes the culture ever could.

The killing of one Christian missionary becomes a national media event of anti-Christian attacks while the murder of hundreds of Hindus is taken casually as without any real importance, as if only the deaths of white-skinned people mattered, not the slaughter of the natives. Missionary aggression is extolled as social upliftment, while Hindu efforts at self-defence against the conversion onslaught are portrayed as rabid fundamentalism. One Indian journalist even lamented that western armies would not come to India to chastise the political groups he was opposed to, as if he was still looking for the colonial powers to save him!

Let us look at the type of leaders that India has had with its Laloo Prasad Yadav, Mulayam Singh Yadav, Jayalalita or Subrahmanya Swamy to mention but a few. Such individuals are little more than warlords who surround themselves with sycophants. Modern Indian politicians appear more like colonial rulers looting their own country, following a divide and rule policy, to keep the people so weak that their power cannot be challenged. Corruption exists almost everywhere and bribery is the main way to do business in nearly all fields. India has an entrenched bureaucracy that resists change and stifles development, just out of sheer obstinacy and not wanting to give up any control. The Congress Party, the oldest in this predominantly Hindu nation, has given its leadership to an Italian Catholic woman simply because as the widow of the last Gandhi prime minister, she carries the family torch, as if family loyalty were still the main basis of political credibility in the country. And such a leader and a party are deemed progressive! The strange thing is that India is not a banana republic of recent vintage but one of the oldest and most venerable civilizations in the world. Its culture is not trumpeting a militant and fundamentalist religion trying to conquer the world for the one true faith but represents a vaster and more cosmic vision. India has given birth to the main religions that have dominated East Asia historically, the Hindu, Buddhist, Jain and Sikh, which are noted for tolerance and spirituality. It has produced Sanskrit, perhaps the world's greatest language. It has given us the incredible spiritual systems of Yoga and its great traditions of meditation and Self-realization. As the world looks forward to a more universal model of spirituality and a world view defined by consciousness rather than by religious dogma these traditions are perhaps the most important legacy to draw upon for creating a future enlightened civilization.

Yet the irony is that rather than embracing its own great traditions, the modern Indian psyche prefers to slavishly imitate worn out trends in western intellectual thought like Marxism or even to write apologetics for Christian and Islamic missionary aggression. Though living in India, in proximity to temples, yogis and great festivals, most modern Indian intellectuals are oblivious to the soul of the land. They might as well be living in England or China for all they know of their own country. They are isolated in their own alien ideas as if in a tower of iron. If they choose to rediscover India it is more likely to occur by reading the books of western travellers visiting the country, than by their own direct experience of the people around them.

The dominant Indian intelligentsia cannot appreciate even the writings of the many great modern Indian sages, like Vivekananda or Aurobindo, who wrote in good English and understood the national psyche and how to revive. It is as if they were so successfully brainwashed against their own culture that they cannot even look at it, even if presented to them clearly in a modern light!

# Bibliography


Berreman, Gerald D.: *Hindus of the Himalayas*, University of California Press, Berkeley, 1963.

Chakravarti, C.: *The Tantras: Studies on their Religion and Literature*, Punthi Pustak, Calcutta, 1963.

Chitkara, M. G.: *Mukherjee and Rashtriya Swayamsevak Sangh: National Upsurge*. APH Publishing. 2004.

Collier, Richard: *The Great Indian Mutiny*, MacMillan, New York, 1963.

Engineer, Asghar Ali: *Babri Masjid Ramjanambhumi Controversy*. Delhi: Ajanta Publications, 1990.

Gellner, E. : *Nations and Nationalism*. Oxford: Blackwell, 1983.

Goel, Sita Ram: *Perversion of India's Political Parlance*. Voice of India, Delhi 1984.

Goetz, Hermann: *The Art of India*, MacMillan, New York, 1964.

Hansen, Thomas: *The saffron wave : democracy and Hindu nationalism in modern India*. Princeton, NJ: Princeton University Press, 2001.

Hassner, Ron E. : *War on Sacred Grounds*. Ithaca: Cornell University Press, 2009.

Hawley, John Stratton: *Songs of the Saints of India*, Oxford University Press, New York, 1988.

Jain, G.: *The Hindu Phenomenon*, UBSPD, Delhi 1994.

Jain, Jyoti Prasad: *Jain Sources of the History of India*, Bhagawati Press, Delhi, 1964.

Jain, Meenakshi: *Rama and Aydhya*. New Delhi: Aryan Books. 2013.

Jha, Krishna; Jha, Dhirendra K.: *Ayodhya: The Dark Night*. HarperCollins India. 2012.

John, B.: *Mantras: Sacred Words of Power*, George Allen and Unwin, London, 1977.

Kapur, Rajiv; *Sikh Separatism: The Politics of Faith*, New Delhi, Vikas, 1987.

Katju, Manjari: *Vishva Hindu Parishad and Indian Politics*. Orient Blackswan. 2013

Kinsley, David R., *Hinduism a Cultural Perspective,* Prentice-Hall, New Jersey, 1993.

Krishna, Ananth V.: *India since Independence: Making Sense of Indian Politics*. Pearson Education India. 20112011.

Kumar, Praveen: *Communal Crimes and National Integration: A Socio-Legal Study*. Readworthy Publications. 2011.

Kunal, Kishore: *Ayodhya Revisited*, Prabhat Prakashan, 2016.

Malik, Yogendra: *Hindu nationalists in India : the rise of the Bharatiya Janata Party*. Boulder: Westview Press, 1994.

Mayer, A. : *Caste in an Indian Village: Change and Continuity 1954-1992*, Delhi, OUP, 1996.

Narain, Harsh: *The Ayodhya Temple Mosque Dispute: Focus on Muslim Sources*. Delhi: Penman Publishers, 1993.

Noorani, A.G. : *Savarkar and Hindutva* : *The Godse Connection*, New Delhi, Leftword Books, 2002.

Partha S. Ghosh: *BJP and the Evolution of Hindu Nationalism : From Periphery to Centre*, Manohar, Delhi, 1999.

Possehl, Gregory L.: *The Harappan Civilization*, London, Aris and Phillips, 1982.

Rajaram, N. S.: *Profiles in Deception: Ayodhya and the Dead Sea Scrolls*. New Delhi: Voice of India, 2000.

Rushbrook, L.F. Williams : *Encyclopaedia of Great Men of India: Savarkar,* Reprint. 1999.

Sharma, Ram Sharan: *Communal History and Rama's Ayodhya*. Delhi: People's Publishing House, 1999.

Sinha, Rakesh: *Dr. Keshav Baliram Hedgewar*. New Delhi: Publication Division, 2003.

Srivastava, Sushil: *Disputed Mosque, A historical inquiry*. New Delhi: Vistaar Publication, 1991.

Thacktson, Wheeler M.: *Baburnama: Memoirs of Babur, Prince and Emperor*. New York and London: Oxford University Press, 1996.

Vable, D.: *The Arya Samaj. Hindu without Hinduism*. Vikas Publ., Delhi, 1983.

Visvantha, K.: *Essentials of Hinduism,* Narosa Pub. House, New Delhi, 1989.

# Index

❑❑❑